# LEE J. COBB

# Lee J. Cobb

## Characters of an Actor

## Donald Dewey

ROWMAN & LITTLEFIELD
Lanham • Boulder • New York • Toronto • Plymouth, UK

Published by Rowman & Littlefield
4501 Forbes Boulevard, Suite 200, Lanham, Maryland 20706
www.rowman.com

10 Thornbury Road, Plymouth PL6 7PP, United Kingdom

British Library Cataloguing in Publication Information Available

**Library of Congress Cataloging-in-Publication Data**
Dewey, Donald, 1940–
  Lee J. Cobb : characters of an actor / Donald Dewey.
    pages cm
  Includes bibliographical references and index.
  ISBN 978-0-8108-8771-8 (cloth : alk. paper) — ISBN 978-0-8108-8772-5 (ebook) 1. Cobb, Lee J., 1911–1976. 2. Actors—United States—Biography. I. Title.
  PN2287.C55D49 2014
  792.02'8092—dc23
  [B]                                                        2013035464

♾️™ The paper used in this publication meets the minimum requirements of American National Standard for Information Sciences—Permanence of Paper for Printed Library Materials, ANSI/NISO Z39.48-1992. Printed in the United States of America

For Joe Mancini

# *Contents*

# Acknowledgments

SCORES OF PEOPLE IN SEVERAL COUNTRIES contributed to the writing of this book. Some were gracious in consenting to interviews about their personal and professional experiences with Lee Cobb; others ferreted through files (okay, most of them pressed a button) for requested documents; and still others fielded relentless phone calls for arranging interviews. There were also a couple of people who weren't very helpful, but why bother with them?

Among those interviewed for their personal and professional experiences were (in alphabetical order) Rene Auberjonois, Norma Barzman, Louis Bershad, Tony Bill, Glen Birchfield, Claire Bloom, Gary Clark, Jimmy Cota, Brian Dennehy, Tony DiNicola, James Drury, Gerald Freedman, Dean Hargrove, Earl Holliman, Stacy Keach, Don Keefer, Jeff Kibbee, Meredith Kibbee, Yaphet Kotto, Donald Kranze, Norman Lear, Mike Livingston, Robert Loggia, Leonard Luizzi, Loring Mandel, Patty McCormack, Christopher Miles, Roger Moore, Franco Nero, Nehemiah Persoff, Gene Reynolds, Mark Rydell, Eva Marie Saint, Amy Saltz, George Segal, William Shatner, Roberta Shore, Robert Stattel, Warren Stevens (since deceased), Daniel J. Travanti, Robert Walden, Eli Wallach, and Gene Wilder.

Because so much time has elapsed since Cobb's death in 1976, many of his important co-players have also passed on, but in numerous instances they had spoken of their work with him with their children, and in this regard I am grateful for the recollections of Stephen Carnovsky, son of Morris Carnovsky; Mark Conte, son of Richard Conte;

Sheila Dehner, daughter of John Dehner; Julie Garfield, daughter of John Garfield; Emily Hubley, daughter of Faith Hubley; John Ireland Jr., son of John Ireland; Laurie Kennedy, daughter of Arthur Kennedy; Karl Kraber, son of Tony Kraber; Cameron Mitchell Jr., son of Cameron Mitchell; Camille Mitchell, daughter of Cameron Mitchell; Danny Opatoshu, son of David Opatoshu; Marina Pratt, daughter of Bud Bohnen; Michael Ward, son of Jane Wyatt; and Martha Wiseman, daughter of Joseph Wiseman.

The remarks attributed to Rod Steiger, Robert Vaughn, and Shelley Winters trace from my previous projects.

The small army of people from libraries, agencies, and institutions who worked in the trenches to dig up documents or set up interviews included Susan Abler from the Department of Information Studies at the UCLA Graduate School; Katie Allen; Ellen Bailey from the Pasadena Playhouse; Mike Bartolic from the California State Archives; Robert Beseda; Charlotte Bonelli; Mark Ekman of the Paley Center for Media; Tammy Fishman from the California State Library; Bonnie Foster; Stewart Gillies from the British Library; Ette Goldwasser from the Jewish Museum; Dennis Goodno; Michael Kinter; Foster Hirsch; Kristine Krueger from the Margaret Herrick Library at the Academy of Motion Picture Arts and Sciences; Judy Milrad; Gareth Owen; Chana Pollack; Jeff Sanderson; David Smith from the New York Public Library; and Morgen Stevens-Gammon from the Museum of the City of New York. Not to be left out are personal friends who came up with solutions to annoying problems or just had to hear about the problems in the first place: Michele Gershman, Rebecca Gribetz, Sidney Gribetz, Grace Kiley, Barbara Mayfield, Odile Pouchol, and Silvana Silvestri. And then there was Bill Baker, who provided all kinds of technical assistance from the start to the end of the project. And sometimes his assistance even paid off.

Despite all the contributions of the aforementioned, even their help would have lacked context without the Cobb family. I am deeply indebted to Julie Cobb for our initial contacts in talking about the project, for her involvement of her brother Vincent, for her suggestions of other people to approach, and for her general encouragement; to Vincent Cobb for his avalanche of family letters, photographs, and DVDs of his father's television appearances, and for the long hours he spent gathering these materials and other items; to Tony Cobb for his photographs, other contact recommendations, and overall geniality when that was more than necessary; and to Jerry Cobb for his recorded conversations with his uncle Norman Jacob. It goes without saying, but we'll say it anyway, that all four of the Cobbs were also incredibly patient and informative when besieged with questions covering everything from their father's professional outings to his doughnut eating at home. I can only hope this book reflects the father they knew.

Unless otherwise noted, photos courtesy of Vincent and Jerry Cobb.

# Chapter 1

─────────○─────────

# The Actor:
# Characters and Actors

THERE IS NO MORE RIDICULED TERM among actors than *character actor*. It bellows a box office system of distinguishing performers billed above the title from those below it; demeans the former with the implication that they are incapable of playing anything but a fixed, pampered persona; suggests the latter can be reduced to mere masters of opportune disguise; and disparages the actor's craft as a whole as structurally dependent on makeup and economic formulas. Craft and range come off as almost incidental to hierarchical appointment. But even those who disdain the term have been exposed to it long enough to cite without hesitation performers who meet the guidelines for this fabled "character actor." The most prominent names don't fall within that "who are those guys?" jokiness that has spawned paperbacks and television shows in recent years, but instead occupy an autograph zone between those who can help fund projects through sheer interest in them and those who report to casting directors for work as members of the jury or the posse. Among those who come readily to mind as character actors from film and theater are Claude Rains, Donald Crisp, Agnes Moorehead, Lionel and Ethel Barrymore, Arthur Kennedy, Thelma Ritter, Jack Warden, Maureen Stapleton, Robert Loggia, Robert Duvall, Judi Dench, James Earl Jones, and everybody who played the chief villain in a James Bond movie. And Lee J. Cobb.

There is more at work here than the notion of "supporting players," those whose roles extend only through a portion of the playing time of a cast's leads or those spurned by celebrity media physical dictates

1

about what leading men and women should look like. At various points in their careers the most noted designated character actors themselves had the leading roles in front of a camera or on the stage, often resoundingly so. Conversely, it is difficult to imagine any producer who ever accepted the likes of an Edward G. Robinson or Dustin Hoffman as a classic physical beauty. But these are satellite considerations for the character actor label habitually stuck on performers who, allegedly unlike "stars," play characters completely divorced from themselves. The presumption of knowing what those true selves are is just the first of the numerous arrogances in such a distinction.

One constant in the careers of performers typified as character actors is their longevity; a comet of the James Dean kind simply doesn't build up enough of a résumé for the broad spectrum of roles earning such an identification. Even before the substantially additional work provided by television series and movies, conspicuous featured cast members working fifty years or more were not that exceptional. In a majority of cases, these performers advanced with the calendar toward the sort of venerable age roles they had probably already been made up to play for some time. Equally constant, the need to play younger rather than older has been rare, the assumption being that these actors, whether in tragedy or comedy, as best friends, worst enemies, or impersonal suits, brought a needed gravitas to the glib worlds of the customarily younger leads.

Another common experience of the designated character actor— one seldom lived by the actor himself and truer of film audiences than of those in the theater—is the palpable stir in the orchestra with his or her first appearance, usually well along into the action. It is the stir of recognition for somebody who even in the dullest or most esoteric work establishes a common ground, and with that a sense of anticipation, with ticket buyers. However briefly, familiarity translates into reassurance, the director gains another few minutes to say what he has to say before the beeline to another theater within the multiplex, the bathroom, or the street door. The familiar face (frequently *more* familiar under the mustaches, beards, or prosthetic devices for the occasion) earns patience. The designated character actor is family.

As one in particular was in mine. I never came close to climbing into the ring as a contender and my brother never ended up hanging from a meat hook in an alley, but the two of us have always identified strongly with *On the Waterfront*. The connection hasn't been the Malloy brothers played by Marlon Brando and Rod Steiger, but their mobster patron in the 1954 film, Lee J. Cobb's "Johnny Friendly." Our uncle Ralph Johnsen might not have controlled the docks, but he was so physically similar to Cobb, down to his heavy jowls, deep bleating eyes, and glistening lips, that we found it easy to imagine him controlling just about everything in Brooklyn that Johnny Friendly didn't. So did other members of the family, and especially one aunt (not his wife) who never tired of addressing him tartly as "Lee J" when she was annoyed with him about something.

Like most males of his generation, Uncle Ralph was a man of hats and cigarettes. You can see him whenever you turn on the Turner Classic Movies channel—black-and-white characters going brim to brim and butt to butt, managing miracles every time they move away from one another without putting out an eye with their everyday weapons. His idea of benevolence, a la Johnny Friendly shoving a few bills into the shirt pocket of Terry Malloy, was what became known as the "money game," as much a part of holidays as Santa Claus was to Christmas and the Easter Rabbit to Easter. The first ingredient of the money game was Ralph's habit of never standing or taking a step without rattling the treasury of coins in his pants pockets. Maybe it was because of the cheap insurance policies he sold for a living, but he never saw a bill that couldn't be broken down into quarters, dimes, and nickels and clumped into easy reach of his musical fingers. The second ingredient was a circle of nagging kids begging him throughout the day to play the game—a chorus of charming innocence that, as the hours went on and Ralph pleaded for four or five more beers first, reached lynch mob timbre. Finally, with the other adults present also entreating him to get it over with, he gathered all the kids in one of the bedrooms and explained the rules. The most important rule was that anyone who threw a punch or gouged an eye would be expelled instantly from the bedroom.

As soon as that was on the record, Uncle Ralph reached into his pockets and came out with enough coins for all the parking meters in Brooklyn. Up they all went into the air, over beds and bureaus and nephews, and the scramble was on. The chaos might not have had the same religious significance as Greeks diving off the Sheepshead Bay piers every year for an Orthodox cross, but the theological principle was the same—be the first to grab and hold on and untold blessings would come your way. And through it all Uncle Johnny Friendly stood with a beatific smile, watching for foul blows but mostly handicapping the winner to himself.

The first time I met the actor rather than the character was when I was doing a weekly interview program for my college radio station. Cobb was in New York for a live TV drama for the DuPont Show of the Month, and the CBS network had no objections to getting a little publicity for it among the supposedly educated. When he opened the door of his Plaza Hotel room, I could hardly guess that my first surprised look at him mirrored one of the bittersweet themes of his career. With one exception in all the movies I had seen him in up to then, he had always had hair; it had never occurred to me that he was bald. Moreover, in the one exception that came to mind, as the dissolute father in *The Brothers Karamazov*, I had pretty much convinced myself that he had been wearing a piece of rubber over his skull to accentuate all that was piggy and lecherous. Uncle Ralph had always had all *his* hair, hadn't he?

The interview consumed a half hour affably, with Cobb touching on a couple of topics that, unknown to me at the time, ran through a good part of his life, and not always happily. One was that baldness, which especially early in his career he had demonized as the major reason he had been barred from getting romantic leads. Another was a definite detachment from the role (a senior doctor in Sidney Kingsley's *Men in White*) he had come from his California home to play; in fact, he said, he was doing the show mainly to qualify for the AFTRA (American Federation of Television and Radio Artists) health insurance, heart problems having complicated his coverage with the policies he had with SAG (Screen Actors Guild) and Equity. The candor was so unexpected that, excitement for college interview scoops aside, it felt faintly gratuitous. When the supposedly educated interviewer suggested that the role must have resonated with him at least a little since *Men in White* had originally been produced by the Group Theatre of which he had been a member (that education kicking in), his reply was a quizzical smile and another puff from the cigar he made sure never went out. Yes, he had been a member of the Group Theatre but only after the Kingsley production, and why go into all that ancient history anyway?

And there matters might have ended if, while packing up my tape recorder, I hadn't told him about Uncle Ralph. In seconds he became a volley of smiles, and with none of the coolness he had shown toward Sidney Kingsley, the Group Theatre, and the Columbia Broadcasting System. He wanted to hear every detail about the money game, at one point releasing a strange yelp of a laugh. How to spoil the moment?

I thought I had found the perfect way when I mentioned that I had written a play in which he would have been ideal for the protagonist. But no, the moment wasn't spoiled. He told me to get it over to his agent Peter Witt and he would take a look at it. If it was a brushoff, it was with a velvet whisk.

Needless to say, the prospect of doing a play with the original Willy Loman from *Death of a Salesman* (not to mention the original Uncle Ralph) occupied more than a few thoughts over ensuing weeks. The high point was when my agent relayed the news from Witt's office that Cobb had found the play "very interesting" and was looking into what were described as "schedule things." The high point next to the high point came when she relayed the news that Luther Adler, another graduate of the Group Theatre, had been sent a copy of the script to ascertain his interest in the second lead. The low point was all the silences in between, plus one phone call. The call was from a woman who, without identifying herself, brusquely fired off questions about my name and whether I had written such-and-such a play. Having needed only seconds to persuade myself that her no-nonsense manner was of somebody inquiring into the rights to the play for the Baltic states, I was dropped savagely back into reality by her announcement that "I just found one of your scripts in the gutter in Midtown on Eighth Avenue." She hadn't found it in a cab or even on a sidewalk, but in the gutter. And it hadn't been the gutter of Fifth Avenue, let alone Park Avenue, but of Eighth Avenue, a scuzzy runway of porn houses, tatty souvenir shops, and street garbage that, apparently, also attracted unproduced plays for ballast. I preferred not to picture the person who had dropped it there. The most probable culprit was an actor or an agent, and who wanted to hate any actors or agents at such a delicate moment?

When the no came, it came not from Cobb, his agent, or my agent, but from his wife, Mary, in a handwritten letter that relayed nice things about his opinion of the play and ugly things about the state of the Cobb family's finances, making any stage venture out of the question. It was shortly after that that Cobb committed to the TV series *The Virginian*, which immediately put Owen Wister on my proscription list.

I didn't see Cobb again for a good decade and not until we were both across the ocean. By then he had added scores of roles in the movies, on television, and, yes, even on the stage to his reputation as that character actor par excellence. With stops at inevitable cop and gangster parts, he had done everything from dressing in drag in the silly *In Like Flint* series to wearing his rages as King Lear. By the standard definition he had run out quite a few non-selves for public consumption. There was no denying that the roles were by and large of the journeyman variety, the middle reliever doing what he did best whatever the score of the game around him. When he was there, the script, the director, or both usually weren't. When the script or the director hinted at large ambitions, the actor kept at his own instinctual pace, occasionally falling back on tics (increased volume was one; an extended accusatory arm shot at a low angle another) that seemed mostly geared for hearing "Cut and print!" For sustained periods there were only glimpses of the power that had radiated from the characters of Willy Loman in *Death of a Salesman*, Johnny Friendly in *On the Waterfront*, and Juror Number Three in *12 Angry Men*. None of this went unobserved, reviewers taking him to task regularly in the tone of having to tow him over to the closet where they had stored so many other disillusions and dreading the avalanche to come when they opened the door to add him to the pile. A couple sounded as if they too had an Uncle Ralph in their backgrounds.

The next and last time I saw Cobb was in Italy, where he spent much of the last chunk of his film career. He was sitting alone in one of Rome's Piazza Navona sidewalk cafes with his ever-present cigar and a tall glass of what looked like iced tea that he totally ignored while studying a team of Somali trinket dealers some yards away. Under all but physical aggression he remembered me, and then opened his eyes altogether at mention of Uncle Ralph. More than once during a lag in the conversation the phrase "money game" escaped his moist lips, never quite moving on to a grunt but with the temptation there. Although he didn't want to talk in any detail about the cops-and-robbers picture he was making, he left little doubt that he was approaching his role seriously. This became clear when he glanced around at the other sidewalk tables, observed that the Piazza Navona was a popular tourist attraction in Rome, and insisted, "But I'm not here to be a tourist, I'm here to work." What lay unsaid was that he would have preferred not having been seen at all in such a place lest someone get the wrong idea about why he was in Italy. There were working actors, and then there were working actors who were actually working instead of watching Somali trinket dealers.

In one sense it was fitting that Cobb spent most of his final filmmaking years in Italy. In the 1970s, especially, the Italian industry was a beacon for American actors generally billed by Hollywood right under the title. In Europe they went above the title as stars, as recognizable international faces, as reasonable insurance that their presence would brand a production as being of respectable caliber and allow it to turn a profit. Although this flight to Italy is routinely invoked for the tale of Clint Eastwood's ascent to stardom, Rome's raids on Hollywood extended far beyond that. Gregory Peck and Paul Newman might not have been lured to Cinecitta, but the Cobbs, Peter Falks, James Whitmores, Eli Wallachs, Martin Balsams, Nehemiah Persoffs, Arthur Kennedys, and George Kennedys (the Italians preferred their own women) were, and, along with dozens of others last seen on Broadway or at the neighborhood movie house, more than once. The money was good, roles were played in the language of the actor (even if that sometimes meant dealing with three different pre-dubbing languages in a given scene), and there was always time for an iced tea at a sidewalk cafe in the Piazza Navona.

There was also some irony to the fashion insofar as the character actors brought over to bolster billboards sometimes appeared in only swiftly executed cameos, making the entire concept of portraying *characters* a very relative proposition under any definition; that is, they were hired more for their billing aura than for their performing abilities. It was the traditional (Hollywood) economic order turned on its head, with the protagonist of the film, more often than not played by a young Italian actor of no particular charisma, billed after the venerable recruits from America. Although this did not change perceptions in the United States about who was a character actor and who wasn't, it did encourage a decades-old European billing practice that has become common today in American movies—the isolation of a prominent featured player after the rest of the cast as a "special guest star" or as somebody "also starring." It wasn't the bank vault, but it was some of the contents of a teller's drawer.

In his book *Slings and Arrows* theater director Robert Lewis passes along a story about character actors attributed to Luther Adler. According to Lewis, Adler, another who was perturbed at not getting romantic leads, once went to a plastic surgeon to have his nose fixed. "Doctor," the actor was quoted as telling the surgeon as he pointed to various areas on his nose, "I want you to cut this off and this and this." "But, Mr. Adler," the physician reputedly said, "if I cut all that off, your face will lose its character." Replied Adler, "Doctor, *wherever* you see character, cut it off."[1]

Lee Cobb would have understood. By the time he was sitting in an outdoors cafe in Rome, he didn't simply epitomize the laziest understanding of the term *character actor*; he had become more representative than most of the in-laws our marriages to the entertainment world have introduced to our living rooms and bedrooms as family. Half relative and half guest, long after his death he sustains images of more than the big money game to which he lent his name for so long. His forty-five-year career on the stage, in motion pictures, and on television has continued to make him ubiquitous even for a recent generation or two trying to place his face next to a credit. He is there in the specialized histories of Method acting, in the contradictory record of ambitious ego and community ideal, and in the demeaning national chronicles of Red Scares. Simply as a ceaselessly energetic personality who prided himself on his knowledge of plumbing as much as of music, who piloted planes and argued with physicists, who intimidated children and fellow actors but who was never above a goofy scene to make them all laugh, who never had a problem knocking directors but had a big one knowing when to knock in gin rummy, he earned an indelibility.

And while Cobb occupies memories just as himself, as the individual who played a personal role in so many major entertainment media events of his time, he also makes one aware of how routinely we give over our television, movie, and streaming hours every day to that odd creature known as the *actor* and to his fictional embroilments. If an alien visiting this planet would have to wonder about a species concerned so much about cops, lawyers, and doctors, not to mention mobsters, it would be even more puzzled by our absorption with people *pretending* so regularly to be cops, lawyers, and doctors, not to mention mobsters (as indeed Cobb played them over and over). Lee Cobb, a man of gargantuan emotions and a demanding intellect that wasn't always on good terms with the emotions, would have said it was a complicated question, then immediately been depressed with the possibility that it wasn't.

## NOTE

1. Robert Lewis, *Slings and Arrows* (New York and London: Applause Books, 1984), p. 27.

# Chapter 2

## Pressrooms
## and Prodigies

ASKED ONCE HOW RELIGIOUS he was, Cobb dodged a direct answer, but laughed that "they say the Jews are the chosen people. But chosen for what?" Nehemiah Persoff, the Jerusalem-born actor who worked with him several times, thought that sardonic reply was an accurate measure of his religiosity. "It was something he seemed to like to keep at arm's length. He observed seders and the big things, but you could also tell he didn't like delving into the subject too deeply. It made him uncomfortable. Lee seemed to think he had his own lines of communication with some things, so why get complicated?"[1]

If Cobb wasn't particularly religious, the reasons began with his father's indifference to Judaism, at least as a faith to be observed. Both his parents were part of the vast migration of Russian and other Eastern European Jews (estimated at some 2.5 million) to the United States between 1880 and 1910. Benjamin (Benzion) Jacob with several siblings and Kate Neilecht with an older sister arrived in New York separately in 1905 as twenty-year-olds, meeting there and marrying shortly afterward. Although some hasty biographies of the actor assert that he grew up in the Lower East Side (and also give his birth name erroneously as Jacoby), it was in fact on Wilkins Avenue (now Louis Nine Boulevard) in the Crotona Park East section of the Bronx, a heavily Jewish area with smatterings of Italians, Germans, and Irish.[2] What the neighborhood did share with the Lower East Side was Yiddish as something of a lingua franca. That was so much so, according to Cobb's oldest son, Vincent, that Yiddish was still his father's

primary language even when he attended elementary school at P.S. 61,
with English and Hebrew battling it out for second place. Although
Cobb wasn't an autodidact, his early language trials remained with
him through a lifelong titillation with high-sounding, relatively unused
words (*chary* instead of *leery*, for instance) and florid phrase making
that sometimes verged on the purple.

It was hardly surprising in such a neighborhood for the father,
Benjamin, to gravitate toward the Hebrew-American Typographical
Union for employment, joining in October 1909 (after a brief stint in
the pressroom of the *New York Times*) and spending the next fifty years
as a compositor for the *Jewish Daily Forward* (*Forverts*), advertised as
the "World's Largest Jewish Daily." What was somewhat surprising,
though, was that Benjamin all but ignored area synagogues, regarding himself as a Jew culturally but not religiously. "Nobody was more
interested in Jewish identity and Jewish history than my father," Lee
Cobb's brother Norman was quoted in the conversations recorded with
his nephew Jerry.

> He would give me books on those subjects all the time. You would've
> thought religion was a natural step. But I never even got Bar Mitz-
> vahed. Whenever we went to the synagogue, and I don't think it
> was more than three or four times when I was a kid, it was because
> of some special event for some friend of my parents'. As far as the
> Jewish religion was concerned, nothing. On Friday evenings we
> might have chicken, but it never had to be kosher chicken. I always
> attributed it to the fact that somewhere back along the line Judaism
> had disillusioned him in some way. My father was disillusioned by
> a lot of things.[3]

Physically, Benjamin was a bullish five foot seven, but with a decidedly intellectual bent. His job as a compositor in the pre-linotype
days encompassed a great deal more than is usually denoted by the
term. Among other things, he wrote more than two hundred short
stories in Yiddish that were published by his newspaper, and he was
also given editorial responsibilities for the annuals and special publi-
cations turned out by the *Forward*. "He was an extremely intellectual
man, always reading books and newspapers," Norman said. "I suppose
my most lasting image of him is of sitting in a chair and reading his
newspaper folded lengthwise."

Benjamin fit in seamlessly with Bronx neighbors who promoted music and other cultural pursuits among their children. His wife, Katie, on the other hand, was described by Norman as "all but illiterate but with an authority that was really the last word in the house. I'm not saying my father was a meek *schlemiel*. But he was what you might call unobtrusive around the house. I guess some people would say he had his head in the clouds." The atmosphere around the house as he was growing up?

> The place where I was born on Wilkins was a tenement, really—small rooms and big furniture, clotheslines out the back window. Every piece of wall space was covered by bookcases for my father's books. One day my mother finally had enough of it and demanded he get rid of some of the bookcases because it had become impossible to walk in the place, it was so congested. There were books even falling out of the closets—in English, Yiddish, Hebrew, Russian, even a few in German and Polish, which he could struggle through. And people—when I was very young, there always seemed to be people in for the evening. Card games were very big, especially poker. But I also remember the impression Dad gave of never really being there even as he was playing. He'd be sitting at the card table, his thoughts elsewhere.

Left-wing politics, especially of the trade union kind, were an assumption of growing up in Jewish communities in New York City at the beginning of the twentieth century, and Jacob's employer, the *Forward*, was a particularly conspicuous hub for them. The Yiddish-language paper was founded in 1897 by dissidents from the Socialist Labor Party who preferred the strain of democratic Socialism then advocated by railroad unionist Eugene V. Debs. Headquartered on the Lower East Side near Seward Park, the daily didn't shy away from descriptions as the "conscience of the ghetto" and, before being outflanked ideologically in later years, as the city's premier defender of union rights. With the growth of New York's Yiddish-speaking population, it reached as many as 275,000 readers a day in the early 1930s.

Benjamin's relations with his employers and even his union had their trying moments. Always a militant on pay and benefits issues, he embarrassed the paper and its vaunted workers-first reputation more than once with public charges that it was slow about meeting payrolls.

The worst conflict came in his twenty-fifth year with the paper when the Depression forced him to file for bankruptcy and the *Forward*'s relatively moderate stances were costing it readers to the *Morning Freiheit* (*Morgen Freiheit*), the largest of nine papers of any language in the country allied with the American Communist Party. Exasperated by his own inability to deal with Benjamin, the paper's general manager B. C. Vladeck appealed to the Hebrew-American Typographical Union to control him. In a nasty letter addressed to the head of Local 83 and dated July 12, 1934, Vladeck asserted in part,

> He has made a habit of borrowing money from members of the chapel and in several other institutions, inducing other members of the chapel to put their endorsements on his obligations and refusing to pay. Some time ago he asked me to write to a bank that we will deduct from his wage a certain amount each week to pay another member of the chapel, from whom he borrowed a considerable amount of money. I refused to do so, not wishing to be embroiled in the personal relations of the members of our shop, but he came again, crying and appealing that he will be ruined unless I consent to this action, and I did, signing my name as manager of the *Forward* on a communication to our cashier, to make these weekly deductions. Now I am being told that he is going thru [sic] bankruptcy and I was served notice by the United States Supreme Court [sic] that these deductions should no longer be made. Because of the fact that many members of our shop have put their signatures to his obligations and because of his bankruptcy, which transfers his obligations to them, the shop is in an uproar, effecting [sic] its morale and efficiency.
>
> I know that such behavior on the part of one of our employees would justify me in discharging him on my own responsibility. For many reasons I do not feel like doing it at present, hoping that your union will consider itself as much interested in the situation as I am myself and will act in accordance with its own interests, rules, and regulations.[4]

Although the union told Vladeck it would look into the matter, there is no record of further action, and Benjamin remained with the paper for another two decades.

The man who would become Lee J. Cobb was born as Leo Jacob on December 8, 1911. If anything distinguished his childhood from that of the thousands of others who attended area schools and were—unlike Norman later on—Bar Mitzvahed at the Congregation

Tipherith Israel on Prospect Avenue, it was music. The first push came from his father, whose love of music prompted budget-straining purchases of phonograph records spanning cantorial hymns, romantic symphonies, and Al Jolson. With the added encouragement of a music teacher neighbor, young Leo took up the violin, and so ably that it became part of his standard biography that he was considered a prodigy on the eve of a recital at Carnegie Hall before he lost muscular control in his wrist following a bad fall. Vincent Cobb said he never heard his father mention any Carnegie Hall performance but recalled impromptu performances years later in California: "In particular there was a nurse who worked for us who played the piano seriously and they played Beethoven duets together."[5] Cobb also made a stab at passing along his prowess with the violin to his son, but Vincent admitted finding the instrument too demanding.

Brother Norman said music was also the occasion for an unexpected incident between the siblings. "We were eleven years apart, so it wasn't like we were always sharing things. But one day he came to me and said I had to hear something even if it meant cutting classes. It was so unlike him, coming to me like that. What it was was a recording of Cesar Franck's Symphony in D, which he had bought a record of and was completely enraptured by it. My father's romanticism hadn't been for nothing."

In addition to the violin, Cobb showed early talent with the harmonica, a more street-wise instrument for a "regular guy" in the eyes of other boys. On at least one occasion he was able to use this skill for the good of others. Months before the actor was born, in March 1911, New York City suffered its greatest plant disaster when 146 women, many of them Polish Jews, were trapped inside the locked doors of the Amalgamated Shirtwaist Factory in Greenwich Village and were killed by either a ferocious fire that consumed the sweatshop or by leaping out of a tenth-floor window in a desperate bid for escape. What became known as the Triangle Shirtwaist Fire left hundreds of children in already-pressed orphanages, a burden that became even heavier as the children grew older. In 1920 several East Coast newspapers sponsored benefit evenings for the relief of the orphanages around harmonica-playing contests. In Baltimore, the daily *Sun* staged a competition in which the winners were the brothers Larry and Jerry Adler. In New York the sponsor was the *Daily News*, and the winner of that contest was the nine-year-old Leo Jacob.

Cobb's harmonica playing generated a claim that his first screen appearance in Hollywood came as a teenager in a short subject at the dawn of the sound era with Borrah Minevitch and His Harmonica Rascals. If so, the short has proved elusive for confirmation. Moreover, Minevitch's son-in-law, the late actor Warren Stevens, denied it outright. "I worked with Lee several times, in the movie *Gorilla at Large* and in several episodes of *The Virginian* TV series. Especially when we did the TV shows, we talked about a lot of things, but never about any short subject with him and Borrah. Plus my wife, who knew all there was to know about her father's career, never mentioned anything like that. I think that's just another Hollywood story that was repeated enough so that it began to sound like the truth."[6]

There were more troubles in the Jacob family during Leo's youth, though, than the missed notes of pursuing a musical career. All told, Katie gave birth to five children—a boy born before Leo who died at three of appendicitis, another boy of five who died in 1922 after being hit by a truck, and a girl who died during childbirth. Norman was born between the street accident and the stillbirth, on December 29, 1922. The deaths of the three children were bad enough, but for Norman they became an obsession when he learned of them only when he was twelve years old. "I was sick in bed and just happened to overhear my mother telling this doctor that she had had five children. I was speechless. I had been living in the house all those years without my father, my mother, or Lee saying anything. They all seemed to think they had to protect me from what everybody else, including the people in the neighborhood, had to know. It was really traumatizing for me. How do you walk down the street and look at people the same way? They've been one up on you all those years."

But, Norman admitted, he went right along with the program. "No, I never brought it up with any of them. Not even with Lee after our parents were gone." Instead, the "trauma" grew into a sullenness of addictive proportions in Norman's later years, and was sometimes sprinkled with an open resentment that his parents favored their first-born over him. "He was a light in their world," Norman acknowledged feeling,

> especially when he became an actor and became something of a man of the world. But even before then he would do things around the house my father and mother couldn't get over. For instance, we had one of those big bulky radios that were really furniture. My father

was crushed when it broke down, but then Lee, who was always great with his hands, fixed it, and my father didn't let anybody forget it for a long time. Plus, my father could share so many cultural and political things with Lee that my mother never had the patience or understanding to be interested in.

Norman had another, if more fleeting, trauma when he witnessed one of his older brother's first stage performances.

> I don't know how old I was, but I couldn't have been that old because I was still in a crib. One night I was crying a lot against all the noise outside in the dining room, and my mother came in and suddenly lowered the railing of the crib and started dressing me. And this at night! She took me down to the basement of the house where all the neighbors were watching a play. And almost as soon as she carries me in, I see Lee up on the stage getting shot! The crying back in the crib was nothing. I started wailing so much I had to be taken right back up to the apartment!

If Norman proved too sensitive for Lee's foray into the arts, it was Lee's insensitivity to Norman's aspirations that added to the distance between the brothers for most of their lives. According to Julie Cobb, her father had, at least in Norman's eyes, helped kill off his dreams of being a concert pianist. "He blamed Dad for that because when they were much younger, Dad had asked the great pianist Jakob Gimpel to evaluate Norman's playing to help him decide if he realistically could have such a career. Gimpel's opinion pretty much led to an estrangement between them for most of their lives."[7] Indeed, for all practical purposes Norman would stay away from the piano for more than fifty years, until shortly before his death.

The Borrah Minevitch story grew out of at least one incontestable fact—that at the age of seventeen, upon graduation from the prestigious Stuyvesant High School in downtown Manhattan, Cobb left home for California with the idea of getting into the movies. The move was nothing if not a contorted compromise between parents and son. Cobb's studies at the science-specializing Stuyvesant had been no accident. Despite his brother's shock at the basement theatrical, Cobb had shown no particular passion for acting as a teenager; where his ardor lay was in aeronautical engineering. But while both Benjamin and Katie raised no immediate objections to pursuing that goal while their son was still in school, they came down strongly against it as graduation neared. Their first reservation was that the field was too dangerous, and no amount of arguing that an engineer was not a pilot could change their minds. Their second objection, according to Norman, was that, based on Benjamin's research into the question, Jews had little opportunity for advancement in the field, that it was very much a white Christian province with decided ideas about "outsiders." What Lee should consider studying in college, they insisted, was accounting. After months of fruitless arguing, Cobb managed a compromise that seemed to come out of left field: he would borrow some money from the family and go to Hollywood for six months to see if he could break into the movies. If that didn't work out, he would return to New York to undertake accounting studies. Benjamin was so relieved by that solution that he gave his son not only the money but a letter of introduction to Paul Muni, an actor whom he had come to know through various *Forward* functions.

Where had the Hollywood option come from? For sure, Cobb had established an ease with audiences through his musical performances. And his neighborhood was never short of community theatricals and the like. "He never came right out and told us why he got into acting, but he grew up in a heavily cultural community where the intellectual, the entertaining, and the political were considered normal life," as Vincent Cobb put it. "It was hardly an outrageous choice." And he wasn't the only one, either. His Crotona Park contemporaries included Jules Dassin, the future director who was as close to Cobb as anyone for more than a quarter century before a bitter breakup. The Jabobs were also acquainted with novelist Joseph Opatoshu, whose son David, six years younger than Cobb, would appear with him in four films.

Even with the letter to Muni, Cobb's stay in California produced little beyond a string of part-time jobs after which he had to ask his parents for fare back home. For a while he attempted to please Benjamin and Katie by taking night courses in accounting at City College while working during the day selling radio tubes. But through people he met on that job plus a burgeoning interest in one of City College's dramatic societies, he was soon showing up at radio stations as well to get small acting jobs. By 1932 it had become evident to everyone that there was going to be no CPA in the family (the actor called his battle with the intricacies of numbers "a standoff"[8]). Benjamin was so resigned to his

son's ambition that he sat down one night with him to work out a stage
name. Norman was present for the birth of Lee J. Cobb. "They were
going through all kinds of names because as usual you had the worry
about sounding too Jewish with a name like Jacob. Dad was sitting at
the dining room table and doodling and Lee was pacing back and forth
behind him. Suddenly, Lee looked over Dad's shoulder to what he had
been scratching and goes, 'That's it! That's it!'" What Benjamin had
doodled owed nothing to either of the most noted Cobbs of the day,
the baseball star Ty and the novelist-screenwriter Irvin S., but rather to
the quick pronunciation of the middle initial and the surname so that
it came out as "Jacob."

In the spring of 1932, Cobb, filled out to the muscular bulk that
would one day have critics mechanically reaching for images of bears,
bulls, and oxen to describe him, made his second trip to Southern
California. ("The truth is, I left New York the second time to avoid
failure."[9]) Once again he struck out with the Hollywood studios, but
this time the grapevine led him to an audition at the Pasadena Playhouse. Being accepted was no small achievement. Long before the
Playhouse became associated with the talents of Lloyd Nolan, Dana
Andrews, Gene Hackman, and Dustin Hoffman (among hundreds of
future Hollywood names), its community identity, fervid local support,
and high-caliber productions were winning praise from no less a figure
than George Bernard Shaw as an "Athens of the West." For eighteen
productions spread over two years, Cobb was a regular member of the
company, not only acting, but also stage managing and even directing.
His professional debut took place on July 26, 1932, when he played
Solveig's father in *Peer Gynt*. Although the twenty-one-year-old could
hardly know it at the time, that very first part established a pattern
that would exasperate him for much of his career even as he exploited
it—portraying characters decades older than he was. Among the other
roles he undertook were Cromwell in *King Henry VIII*, Horatio in
*Hamlet*, the judge in *Volpone*, Herod in *Salome*, Dr. Coutras in *The
Moon and Sixpence*, and Jacob Engstrand in *Ghosts*. He also turned his
hand at directing a piece entitled *Angels and Pitchforks*, of which little
was heard afterward. His last role for the Playhouse, in July 1934, was
the lead of Trampas in a stage adaptation of *The Virginian*, material he
would encounter again thirty years later.

There was also a side benefit to his work at the Playhouse. Hearing that Universal was casting for bit players for a serial called *The

*Vanishing Shadow*, he answered a cattle call and broke his losing streak with the studios by getting hired for a small part as a road foreman in a twelve-episode tale of a son (Onslow Stevens) seeking vengeance on the man who killed his father. The bizarre melodrama involving ray guns and a vest that made its wearer invisible did not require any harmonica playing.

In later years Cobb would call the second trip to California that led him to the Pasadena Playhouse "one of the smartest moves of my life," adding with a grin, "I can't account for it."[10] But for all that he had also remained much closer than three thousand miles to New York. He was very aware that the domestic situation in New York had changed for the worst. After some relatively good years that had allowed the family to move from the Wilkins Avenue tenement to a two-family house on nearby Adee Avenue and then to a Second Avenue apartment building with an elevator just south of Union Square in Manhattan, Depression pressures had forced his father to declare bankruptcy. Even with part-time jobs he could help pay some bills for his parents and eleven-year-old Norman. Then there was another lure: the growth of a new kind of theater in New York City, and not on Broadway. For several years companies had been springing up with a decidedly more political tone in response to the country's chaotic economic state. Moreover, anybody connected to the theater knew of the inroads being made in the East by the teachings of the Moscow Art Theatre actor-director Konstantin Stanislavsky. Their impact would not be felt in California for another decade, mainly through a company in which Cobb was also a member, so if he wanted to know more about them, he had to head back across the country.

## NOTES

1. Interview with author, December 16, 2012. Subsequent quotes from Nehemiah Persoff are taken from this interview.

2. Generations later, during a highly publicized October 1977 visit for underlining the need to combat urban decay, President Jimmy Carter called the district the worst neighborhood in the country.

3. Subsequent quotes from Norman are taken from these recorded conversations.

4. The Center for Jewish History, correspondence collection of the Hebrew Typographical Union, Local 83.

5. Conversation with author. Subsequent quotes from Vincent Cobb are taken from conversations with the author over the course of several years.

6. Interview with author, January 9, 2009.

7. Conversation with author. Unless otherwise indicated, quotes from Julie Cobb are taken from conversations with the author over the course of several years. Since Gimpel migrated to the United States from Europe in 1938, the piano critique would have had to take place when Norman was in his mid-teens.

8. *Los Angeles Times*, September 28, 1958.

9. Ibid.

10. *Los Angeles Times*, June 22, 1947.

# Chapter 3

———————◯———————

# The Actor:
# Stanislavsky in America

THE PUBLIC HAS COME A LONG WAY with actors. It no longer demands they wear masks, as the Greeks did. It no longer assumes they are slaves, as the Romans did. It is willing to accept some of them being women, unlike the Elizabethans. If they want to perform in one place rather than wander the countryside with their pots and pans and acrobatic acts, that's okay. Society even lets them rent rooms ahead of pet owners, Jews, and Irishmen. And what have actors done to show their gratitude for so much progress?

Until the middle of the last century caricatures of American actors depicted a histrionic performer with one hand on his breast and the other extended toward the balcony while he declaimed, "To be or not to be." Then around the 1950s this cartoon image gave way to that of a jittery mumbler in a T-shirt who confided his words to his chest as manically as the earlier thespian had sought to project them miles away from his performance. The image change from a lampooned Edwin Booth to a lampooned Marlon Brando, and the snickering that went with it was a by-product of the established influence of so-called Method acting on both the Broadway stage and in Hollywood movies. And in its own turn, the Method was routinely traced back to the teachings of Russian actor-director Konstantin Stanislavsky at the Moscow Art Theatre at the onset of the century. Everything that the Montgomery Clifts, James Deans, and Paul Newmans muttered and scratched at had started there, we were told.

Well, yes and no. Yes, because decades of acting teachers and theatrical companies in the United States, most conspicuously the Group Theatre in the 1930s and the Actors Studio as of 1947, had indeed been citing Stanislavsky as an inspiration. No, because there was as much misinterpretation of the Russian's ideas on this side of the ocean as there was ostensible devotion to them. And no again, because some of the strongest critics of that misrepresentation were the same Group Theatre and Actors Studio figures held up for mockery by comedians and cartoonists out for an easy laugh. Their criticisms were not always of the polite parlor variety, either. In the name of Stanislavsky, colleagues ruptured relationships, exchanged bitterly worded writings, and set up rival schools in New York, Los Angeles, and elsewhere as the one and only source of theatrical truth. To an outsider, the disagreements might have seemed to be over the most negligible of technical differences, of concern only to the actors and directors most immediately affected by them. But in fact the frictions were instrumental in shaping mass entertainment expectations and viewing habits even for those unaware of them. If actors and their vehicles have come to occupy an inordinate amount of time for most of us over the last century-plus, Stanislavsky has never been far from the steering wheel. And for added spice, those embroiled with his theories in one fashion or another incidentally provided headline names for ugly mid-twentieth-century political events. During the cold war theatrical ideas weren't adjudged as all that harmless or academic when a Russian was in the middle of them.

The usual starting point for measuring Stanislavsky's impact on the performing arts has been in the contention that he was the first to draw a line between centuries of flamboyant posturing and modern psychological realism on the stage, replacing arch melodrama with naturalism. If that sounds simplistic, it is. Long before Stanislavsky there had been an impatience with the kind of theater that equated drama with transparent artifice, dialogue with serial speech making, and company performance with individual bravura. Shakespeare's plays had not been costume theatricals for the playwright's contemporaries, nor had the performers in them been marked only for their elocution. In Russia alone in the nineteenth century several directors had come forward to insist on approaches that could not be confused with putting on an elaborate medicine show. One was Michael Shchepkin, cited by

Stanislavsky as "our great law-giver, our artist."[1] As early as 1848, Shchepkin was warning an actor to "begin with wiping out yourself . . . and become the character the author intends. You must walk, talk, think, feel, cry, laugh, as the author wants." His quest for informing stage action with precise psychological cause knew no national borders. When a touring American company headed by African-American tragedian Ira Aldridge presented *Othello* in Moscow, he couldn't wait to get backstage after the final curtain to take the actor to task for treating the character of Desdemona as a delicate flower. "Othello is a Moor and an army commander who has his men's eyes always on him," Shchepkin was heard to reprimand Aldridge through an interpreter. "Where is the aggressiveness he should have on display at all times, especially with a woman?"[2]

Stanislavsky, who had been immersed in the theater since creating amateur shows at home as a teenager, also acknowledged his debt to Alexander Lensky, regarded as the premier actor of the Russian stage in the nineteenth century. "He was the most talented and attractive actor I had ever seen," he was once quoted, "and I imitated him to the point of disgust." Another who made an early impression was the Italian Ernesto Rossi, whose performance as Romeo during a tour of Russia "drew its inner image to perfection."[3] But as brilliant as he found them, Lensky and Rossi also offered negative models of sorts for Stanislavsky's conviction that the key to dynamic theater was ensemble work, that concentration on a star player often earned applause at the cost of leaving a production at the mercy of that star's whims, health, and ultimatums, not to mention risked suffocating whatever contextual aims the playwright might have had. At the age of thirty-four, Konstantin Sergeyevich Alexeyev (as he was born) found a like-minded thinker in the playwright Vladimir Nemirovich-Danchenko, five years his senior. In what became the most legendary lunch in theater history, the two men took a table at the Slavyanski Bazar at two o'clock on the afternoon of June 22, 1897, and did not part until after breakfast the next morning at Stanislavsky's home, by which time they had outlined the goals and structure of what developed into the Moscow Art Theatre the following year. The original division of labor called for Nemirovich-Danchenko to take on literary matters and company administration and for Stanislavsky to tend to productions.

The initiative got off to a slow start, with stagings of Ibsen and Shakespeare thrilling nobody. But around the same time, and fortuitously for Stanislavsky and Nemirovich-Danchenko, playwright and short story master Anton Chekhov was doing a lot of grumbling about his own theater problems. Two years earlier, Chekhov had entrusted his play *The Seagull* to the Imperial Theatre in St. Petersburg and had come away devastated by the mechanical rendering it had received. "Never will I write another play or attempt to have one produced if I live to be 700 years old," he told those who tried to cheer him up.[4] Whatever Stanislavsky and Nemirovich-Danchenko said to him, though, persuaded him to let them make another pass at *The Seagull* at the Moscow Art Theatre. "Chekhov cannot be presented, he can only be experienced," Stanislavsky intoned. As precious as that might have sounded, it was both recognition of the fact that the playwright's dramas were very much ensemble pieces grounded in psychological nuance—chamber music more than symphony—and a claim that the Art Theatre was the only appropriate venue for them. During rehearsals every member of the company was drilled in what was termed "the law of inner justification"—or probing the deepest feelings of the actors in conjunction with the play's specific dramatic moments, the inward search for the outward form. Stanislavsky did not spare himself and his prominent character of Trigorin during the exercises, and would write frequently in the years to come about his own failures during this or that production to learn from what he was teaching others. When *The Seagull* proved a success, the epitome of the "spiritual realism accessible to all" that the producers had stipulated as their objective, Chekhov committed to more collaborations, leading to presentations of *Uncle Vanya*, *Three Sisters*, and *The Cherry Orchard* at the Art Theatre. For their part, Stanislavsky and Nemirovich-Danchenko felt so indebted to the writer that they hurriedly made him the theater's playwright in residence and the seagull the company logo.

But they did not take their triumph for granted. On the contrary, they were wary that the very praise for the law-of-inner-justification approach in *The Seagull* would overwhelm the longer range aspirations they had for their theater. Stanislavsky could get especially testy about being lumped together with critics who shared his dramatic values but who also appeared content to leave it at that. As he put it, "All that has been written about the theater is only philosophizing, very interesting, very deep, it is true, that speaks beautifully of the results desirable to reach in art, or criticism of the success or failure of results already reached. All these works are valuable and necessary, but not for the actual practical work in the theater, for they are silent on how to reach certain results, on what is necessary to do firstly, secondly, thirdly, and so forth, with a beginner, or what is to be done with an experienced and spoiled actor."[5]

The director's answer to his own question was an articulated system of training the actor for greater control of his physical and sensory faculties, simultaneously urging constant intellectual inquiry into character motives. To intensify a feeling of ensemble discovery, he brought in only actors willing to live communally for the duration of rehearsals and performances, this sometimes running well into a year and even more than that for plays that went into repertory rotation. At the heart of his method (and the source of generations of dispute) were affective memory exercises in which the actor summoned up personal experiences of pain, joy, or some other emotion, then bonding them with parallel character feelings as called for by the play. For Stanislavsky at the time, affective memory was the sine qua non for incarnating a role, the only truthful access to the stage's magical *if*, the essential premise for "the imagined truth which the actor can believe as sincerely and with greater enthusiasm than he believes practical truth."[6] The techniques for crossing from the intimately personal to the theatrically scripted could involve anything from focusing on some prop to humming a familiar tune. Whatever the vehicle, the actor was encouraged to believe in his own freedom for recall in what was actually a very guided situation, a condition not unlike that experienced at the time by Europeans beginning to explore psychotherapy.

Ultimately, Stanislavsky conducted his system of rehearsals for some fifty plays on and off into the late 1930s. At one time or another, his company included the Russian acting elite—his own wife, Maria Petrovna Lilina; Chekhov's wife, Olga Knipper-Chekhova; the playwright's nephew, Michael Chekhov; Ivan Moskvin; Vasily Kachalov; Alla Tarasova; and Vasily Luzhsky, to name a few. Later Hollywood names such as Alla Nazimova and Akim Tamiroff also appeared. When they were not doing original works by Chekhov or Maxim Gorky, they were winning the Art Theatre an international reputation for vibrant adaptations of Shakespeare, Ibsen, Goldoni, and other foreign dramatists. It didn't take long for the company to generate pounds of press coverage from critics and other writers visiting Moscow. For many years, though, even fellow professionals were more interested in the finished plays they saw than in the Stanislavsky process that had produced them.

The company's achievements were all the more remarkable for operating amid incessant turmoil, of both organizational and political kinds. One blow came with Chekhov's death in 1904. When Gorky wasn't named his successor as house dramatist, the embittered author of *The Lower Depths* walked away and took the theater's major financial backer with him. It was only thanks to an acclaimed tour of Germany and Austria in 1906 that the company managed to survive. But internal problems persisted. Stanislavsky had a falling out with Nemirovich-Danchenko over management issues, prompting him to abandon his board role and introducing unwanted tensions around productions. Within this climate some members of the company began protesting the theater's emphasis on naturalistic works. The most vociferous rebels were Yevgeny Vakhtangov and Vsevelod Meyerhold, the former plumping for more spectacular avant-garde productions and the latter for borrowing stylistic approaches from (among others) the Japanese theater and the commedia dell'arte. When their demands fell on deaf ears, they went off to set up their own companies.

The 1917 Revolution brought cries that the Art Theatre be closed as an ornament of the Tsarist age. But the new Soviet regime of Vladimir Lenin not only spurned those calls but funneled government subsidies into the company, at least partly to offset foreign propaganda that the Bolsheviks were an uncultured rabble. By the early 1920s, however, a national economic crisis had dried up those funds, leaving the Art Theatre back to fending for itself. On stage Stanislavsky became skeptical of continuing to produce the sophisticated anguishes of Chekhov's characters amid the grim realities of the Soviet Union and gave more stress to productions that would be typified as Socialist realism. That didn't sit well with some company veterans, who fled abroad. One of them, Richard Boleslavsky, a Pole who had worked with Stanislavsky for more than thirteen years, established the American Laboratory Theatre in New York in 1922, setting the foundations for affective memory's second great arena. The school, arguably the first in America to offer comprehensive training for actors, generated buzz among theater people for its novel teachings but still had only modest success until the following January, when the Art Theatre itself visited the city on an extended stay for, among other things, performances of

*The Cherry Orchard, Three Sisters, The Lower Depths,* and an adaptation of Feodor Dostoyevsky's novel *The Brothers Karamazov.* Not only did Boleslavsky's school profit from the company's critical triumph, but he also talked one of the troupe's leading players, Maria Ouspenskaya, into remaining in the United States as one of his teachers.

One of those captivated by the Art Theatre's performances in New York was Lee Strasberg, then a would-be actor who would become a central player in the onstage and offstage dramas that would grip the Group Theatre and the Actors Studio for the next sixty years. He became even more of a believer after attending classes with Boleslavsky and Ouspenskaya and getting a firsthand education in the method about to gain a capital *M.* And he wasn't the only one. Also taken with the Stanislavsky approach taught by Boleslavsky was Harold Clurman, another fledgling actor who, like the future director and teacher Strasberg, would find a much more expansive role for himself in the theater, first as a producer and director, then as a critic and historian.

Strasberg and Clurman came together in 1925 when they were in rehearsal for a Theatre Guild production.[7] For years afterward, in a protracted version of the 1897 Slavyanski Bazar lunch, they met regularly in cafeterias and luncheonettes to discuss the possibilities for setting up an Art Theatre of their own. On an almost weekly basis they held recruitment evenings during which the more extroverted Clurman held forth in living rooms, hotel rooms, or lofts propounding his views. Actress Stella Adler, who a decade later would marry Clurman after years of living together, said his "very voice . . . expressed a man of overwhelming size. Indeed, it sprang from the universal in himself and in his art. He was eagerly, crazily groping to create a world to match his vision. In comparison to Harold, other theatrical thinkers appeared infantile."[8] Another description said that "one of his most potent weapons was a willingness to make himself ridiculous, to exaggerate wildly, scream and stamp his feet to get his point across—in a ringing Bronx accent somewhat at odds with his almost mystical message."[9] What Clurman would later admit, however, was that his persuasiveness in public was only the top layer of persisting differences with Strasberg on the importance of the actor to theatrical productions. As he put it in *The Fervent Years,* "What I was talking about was literature; what he was interested in was theatre. How much acting is of great quality? I countered: Are we to wait around seeing agreeable mumming in the hope that every once in a while a performance will turn up that will justify so many stupid or negligible plays?"[10]

As their decade-long collaboration demonstrated, they ended up learning from one another. "For my part, I learned to think of theatre not simply in terms of plays performed, but in terms of entities, in which each moment contributes to a total effect that is not to be measured solely by the value of the spoken word. The stage setting, the costumes, the actor's appearance, movement, his silences, gestures, rhythm, his very 'aura,' and the interrelation of all these elements, make the significance of the play."[11] And Strasberg? "[He] began to accept the validity of my insistence on the text, not alone as literary material for its own sake, but, at the very least, as a vehicle of human meaning. It was not alone important, I reiterated, that *Hamlet* is a beautiful piece of writing packed with quotable wisdom, but that it is about something that has meaning for men at all times."[12]

What the two men never differed on was that a new kind of theater necessitated a new kind of actor. In language that would have reminded Stanislavsky of his earliest aims, Clurman observed that "in most theatres the actor is hired to do a part; he was expected to make it live on the stage, but as an individual he stood outside the play or the playwright's vision. His art and the playwright's were presumed to be connected only technically. In our belief, unless the actor in some way shared the playwright's impulse, the result on the stage always remained somewhat mechanical."[13] And even more explicitly: "If man was to be the measure of all things in our theatre, if life was the starting point, and an effect on life the aim of our effort, then one had to have a point of view in relation to it, one had to define an approach that might be common to all members of the group."[14]

Eventually, after a couple of false starts, the Clurman-Strasberg debates and the recruitment gatherings spawned the Group Theatre. For its first couple of years it operated under the auspices of the Theatre Guild, with financial backing for individual productions coming from the likes of Edna Ferber, Eugene O'Neill, and Maxwell Anderson. With Cheryl Crawford along as an occasional director and business reality monitor to fill out a directorial triumvirate, the company showed its wares for the first time at the Martin Beck Theater on September 29, 1931, with a production of Paul Green's *The House of Connolly*. Codirected by Strasberg and Crawford, it was the first of twenty-four plays that would be offered over the next decade. The cast featured future Hollywood leading man Franchot Tone, Stella Adler, and Morris Carnovsky. Others who would be identified with the Group were Stella's brother Luther, Phoebe Brand, Ruth Nelson, Frances Farmer, Sanford Meisner, Jules (John) Garfield, J. Edward (Joe) Bromberg, Art Smith, Roman (Bud) Bohnen, Dorothy Patten, Tony Kraber, William Challee, Harry Morgan, Karl Malden, Leif Erickson, and four future film directors—Elia Kazan, Martin Ritt, Michael Gordon, and Sidney Lumet. And Lee J. Cobb.

The actors drawn to the Group shared the view of their Moscow counterparts that there should be more to their art than the random hits and misses of the commercial theater. Coming together in the politically volatile and economically depressed 1930s, they embraced a social outlook that, while not going as far as some of the smaller radical companies of the period, championed the lower middle-class workingman against business and government exploitations and sought to express that attitude both in the texts of the plays they performed and in their collective organization as such. No surprise, they were all pretty much to the left on the political spectrum at a time when the predominant nonradical theater, saluted though it might have been for being more "realistic" than what had preceded it, still had first-nighter (*the-a-tuh*) connotations. While some members were little more than liberal Democrats or Socialists, others were moved to join the (very legal) American Communist Party—a distinction that was tolerated as much less of one in the Red Scare days after World War II.[15] Another target sewn on their backs for future congressional consideration was that the overwhelming majority of the membership was Jewish, hardly a shock insofar as almost one quarter of New York City's population at the time was Jewish and the young adult generation had been steeped in the entertainment arts, as Cobb had, from an early age.

Despite Strasberg's own infatuation with the avant-garde leanings of Vakhtangov, the trying times and political engagement of Group members made naturalism the preferred dramatic form. Not only were other styles generally eschewed, but except for adaptations of Theodore Dreiser's *An American Tragedy* and Jaroslav Hasek's *The Good Soldier Schweik*, the company's twenty-four productions were original works, usually with a strong urban, second-generation immigrant texture. The most prolific troupe playwright was Clifford Odets (*Waiting for Lefty, Awake and Sing, Golden Boy*), whose knack for having characters express themselves in transliterations of ironic apothegms from other languages ("So life won't be printed on dollar bills") won him widespread admiration for lyrical dialogue in the most kitchen-sink kind of dramatic surroundings. In the case of *Waiting for Lefty*, the realism of the staging so overwhelmed the audience in the play's climactic call for the cab driver characters to declare a strike that the carried away spectators also rose to demand a walkout.

Concerning the Group's overall objectives, Clurman quoted approvingly in *The Fervent Years* from a speech delivered by novelist-historian Waldo Frank to a conference of librarians in April 1932. Frank declared in part,

> The reason why I believe in the Group is because I am primarily interested in what I might call the creating of a new world. . . . There must be a group off conscious people patiently devoted . . . to the ideal. They must be organized to work toward the creating of a new world. The one method whereby the new society may slowly and laboriously be created is a new alliance in place of the alliance of the intellectuals with the money class, an alliance of the men of mind, of vision, the artists, with the People, consciously working toward this creative end.[16]

Some of the Group's organization problems were idiosyncratic, others reminiscent of those that had plagued Stanislavsky in Moscow. Stella Adler, a member of the first family of the Yiddish Theatre and the company's most prominent female player, sardonically acknowledged that collegial playing didn't come easily to her. "You could not put me into an ensemble. I was a princess. My father was a king, my mother was a queen. You couldn't do that to me. I hated it. I hated everybody. It was part of my tradition. I had been treated royally by people who bowed to my father. If they bowed to him, they bowed to me, too. All of a sudden, now, they're my equals?"[17] Odets came to the same conclusion about Adler and her brother Luther, and without her humor, when he told Clurman that "no Adler could ever be made a Group person."[18] But the Adlers were only one of the cracks in the ensemble foundation, and far from being the most collapsible part of the company.

Throughout its decade of existence the company was also in a snit about members who "betrayed" it by running off to Hollywood. The first target of this petulance was Franchot Tone, even though his improved earnings from the movies permitted him to help finance company productions. (Betrayal and gratitude were frequent dance partners with the Group.) When John Garfield made a similar decision, Clurman cited Carnovsky as freezing him out of conversation and Cobb as "lowering his face with wrath."[19] On another level, Strasberg raised hackles by tinkering with the principle of affective memory in favor of what he called emotional memory. According to the company's resident teacher, some members weren't capable of plumbing deep emotional experiences so they were better off just trying to re-create the physical sensations around those experiences. For some the variation decreed by the habitually imperious Strasberg undermined the Group by dividing it into class A and class B talents (anathema for an enterprise that boasted of democratic equality among actors, directors, stagehands, and administrative personnel, to the point that everyone received a salary, whether involved in a given production or not); for others it reeked of condescension toward everyone. It usually fell to Clurman to quell tempests with reminders of Strasberg's unquestioned teaching skills. That did not mean he had to be alerted to the problems created by Strasberg's fractious personality: "With ill-concealed impatience he pointed out that we were the first people to realize this and that, the first to understand that and the other, the first to set forth such and such, and that he, Lee Strasberg, in the realm of theatrical study, had been the first to discover X, Y, and Z. We caused ourselves considerable harm by our appalling lack of grace."[20]

For all the bumpy moments between actors and directors, actors and actors, and directors and directors, though, most of the personality tempests remained pretty much contained and even channeled into richer performances on the stage for the first three years. But then a far more serious crisis erupted in 1934 after Stella Adler met with Stanislavsky in Paris.

Along with Clurman and Strasberg, Adler visited Moscow in 1934 to see the latest productions at the Art Theatre, then fully into the Socialist realism demanded by the Josef Stalin regime. The two men came away convinced they were doing more serious work than their organizational mentor, but that didn't satisfy Adler. When she heard that Stanislavsky, who had been suffering heart problems, was in Paris recovering from his latest illness, she put off her return to the United States and talked Clurman into making a side trip to France. The two spent some days with Stanislavsky, and then Clurman also returned to America, leaving Adler behind for another five weeks during which she exhaustively went over a recent performance she had given, asking Stanislavsky for a critique. The gist of the Russian's response was that she had fallen too much under the spell of affective memory exercises, which he himself had developed more moderate thoughts about because they often paralyzed actors in completing onstage action. He also acknowledged that Meyerhold and Vakhtanov hadn't been totally wrong in calling for more than naturalism, noting that the Art Theatre had produced numerous plays in other styles. (In 1938, weeks before his death, Stanislavsky turned the reins of the Art Theatre over to Meyerhold, calling him its "sole heir.")

When Adler returned to America and conveyed Stanislavsky's observations, Strasberg blew up, going so far as to declare himself a superior director to the Russian and his system more revolutionary than the one devised in Moscow. From that point on, the Group fell into two camps, with Adler's brother Luther, Carnovsky, and Kazan among those subscribing to her calls for change. Strasberg mainly sulked, continuing to teach but gradually withdrawing from directing in what Clurman labeled a mood of "impassivity." Ruth Nelson went much further, saying that Strasberg's response was typical of why there was "no joy" from him then or ever.[21] Over the last five years of the Group's existence he directed only two more plays. His last effort for the company was the 1936 production of *Johnny Johnson*, an antiwar play written by Paul Green but conceived after Strasberg's antagonist Adler had gone to composer Kurt Weill to ask him to compose music for a nonnaturalistic Group undertaking. The resultant work lasted only sixty-eight performances, but its odd mix of antimilitarist speeches, spoken songs, and satirical comedy was as close as Strasberg came to the adventurous style he had claimed to admire in Vakhtangov.

Long before getting to *Johnny Johnson*, however, the Group as an organization had been on a roller coaster of despair, hope, more despair, and one more production. The nadir came in the winter of 1933, after a brutally received staging of Dawn Powell's *Big Night* marked the fourth straight play to raise fundamental questions about the company's artistic coherence and all but wiped out the positive impression made by Green's *The House of Connelly*. The company would pull out of what threatened to be a free fall the following September with its production of Sidney Kingsley's *Men in White*, but over long months before then, Clurman and Strasberg had no choice but to permit their chief actors to go off for work in non-Group productions. Only their determination where the company was concerned prevented any expression of surprise that the actors not only came back, but brought with them necessary new blood like Cobb.

## NOTES

1. Toby Cole and Helen Krich Chinoy (eds.), *Actors on Acting* (New York: Crown Trade Paperbacks, 1949), p. 476.

2. Ibid., p. 476.

3. Ibid., p. 484.

4. Ibid., p. 477.

5. Ibid., p. 477.

6. Ibid., p. 478.

7. Harold Clurman, *The Fervent Years: The Group Theatre & the 30's* (New York: Harcourt Brace Jovanovich, 1975), p. 11.

8. Ibid., p. vi.

9. Wendy Smith, *Real Life Drama: The Group Theatre and America, 1931–1940* (New York: Alfred A. Knopf, 1990), p. 4.

10. Clurman, *Fervent Years*, p. 11.

11. Ibid., p. 12.

12. Ibid., p. 12.

13. Ibid., p. 23.

14. Ibid., p. 34.

15. Ironically, the least political were the company's leadership triumvirate of Clurman, Strasberg, and Crawford.

16. Clurman, *Fervent Years*, pp. 78–79.

17. Barry Paris (ed.), *Stella Adler on America's Master Playwrights—Eugene O'Neill, Clifford Odets, Tennessee Williams, Arthur Miller, Edward Albee, et al.* (New York: Alfred A. Knopf, 2012), p. 372.

18. Clurman, *Fervent Years*, p. 118.

19. Ibid., p. 220.

20. Ibid., p. 49.

21. Helen Krich Chinoy, "Reunion: A Self-Portrait of the Group Theatre," *Educational Theatre Journal* 28, no. 4 (December 1976), p. 528.

# Chapter 4

# Group Experiences

Cobb's SECOND RETURN from California was nowhere near as abject as his first one. His résumé from the Pasadena Playhouse helped him get radio work that, while not paying much, verged on the steady, and there was no more talk of taking up another trade. Further, he found a New York theater scene that had expanded significantly even in his short time on the West Coast. If some companies, including the Group Theatre, had already been active while he had been at City College going through his "standoff" with the principles of accounting, the suppurating Depression and hunger for an animated response to its perceived causes had stimulated many more ensembles in the interim, as often as not with a proletarian thrust. For audiences, simply attending a play could represent a political act, and theater companies aware of that charged minimally for tickets or even nothing at all in some cases. Unless he saw himself as fit only for characters wearing tuxedos and sipping champagne, the average actor was both excited and challenged by the militantly social emphasis on the works being staged mid-decade, and Cobb, for one, was the son of a lifelong trade unionist. In the words of Hallie Flanagan, the future administrator of the Federal Theatre Project,

> There are only two theatres in the country today that are clear as to their aim: one is the commercial theatre which wants to make money; the other is the workers' theatre which wants to make a new social order.

Unlike any art form existing in America today, the workers' theatres intend to shape the life of this country, socially, politically, and
industrially. They intend to remake a social structure without the
help of money—and this ambition alone invests their undertaking
with a certain Marlowesque madness.[1]

In truth, the Group Theatre didn't fall so neatly to one side of the
line or the other, but Flanagan's 1931 observation came before the
company had raised great expectations among nonmembers. What her
confident assertion definitely reflected, though, was how the workers
theater movement had not waited for Black Friday in October 1929 to
be launched, but had in fact been on the rise since the early 1920s,
when labor unions had demanded the raises they had held off asking for during World War I, repeatedly receiving nightstick-swinging
police and government raids on their offices for an answer. Artistic
inspiration for the protest theaters had come from Europe, especially
Germany and the Soviet Union. Michael Gold, a founder of the pioneer New Playwrights' Theatre, couldn't contain his enthusiasm after
attending innovative productions in Moscow: "Acrobatic actors race
up and down a dozen planes of action. The drawing-room play has
been thrown on the junk-pile of history. Things happen—broad, bold,
physical things, as in the workers' lives. There are dangers and the feel
of elementals. . . . Machinery has been made a character in the drama.
City rhythms, the blare of modernism, the iron shouts of industrialism,
these are actors."[2] Even when the plays were more orthodox in their
story telling and had nothing to do overtly with proletarian struggles,
an association with the Soviet Union carried protest weight, leading to
more productions in America of works based on the writings of Chekhov, Gorky, and Dostoyevsky; at the very least such authors had pronounced themselves on the greed and corruptions of the ruling classes.

The overwhelming majority of worker movement companies in
the United States were, at best, at a community or street theater
level in staging agitprop skits in auditoriums off the beaten path, in
workplaces, in union halls, or on picket lines, but they sought to make
up for it in political fervor. Communist Party members invoking the
Bolshevik Revolution propelled some groups, but there were far more
Socialists and non-Communist radicals fed up with the accommodations organized labor had been making with management, especially
in light of the brutal suppression of protests. Some of the theaters had

fallen away by the mid-1920s, but in 1931 there were still so many of them around the country, including German, Hungarian, and Yiddish language groups, that a substantial readership existed for a regular mimeographed newsletter called *Workers Theatre*.[3] Among those decrying the economic and political realities of America in the thirties were Gold's New Playwrights Theatre (begun in 1926), the Workers Drama League (1929), and the Workers Laboratory Theatre (1930). Not the only one, the Workers Laboratory evolved from serving as a mouthpiece for the Communist Party to a combative ensemble that wanted no more to do with imposed party line dramatics ("in the first act we suffer, in the second we pass out leaflets, and in the third we go out on strike"[4]) than it did with the corporate and government villains caricatured in its pieces.

Members of the Group Theatre and worker movement performers based in New York could hardly avoid each other within the ambit of the non-Broadway acting community, but it wasn't until the winter of 1933 that the two sides acknowledged mutual interests of a practical kind. For some time Group members had been edgy about their relative acceptance by mainstream critics who, whether lauding or frowning at specific productions, insinuated that the company remained very much part of the "legitimate theater" in the most conformist sense of the phrase. Typically cutting in this sense was the *New York Times* review of Odets's *Awake and Sing* on February 19, 1935, in which critic Brooks Atkinson described the writer who thought of himself as a political firebrand as a "congenial playwright"—this a month after the opening of the same playwright's audience-rousing *Waiting for Lefty* and even as Group members were conspicuous in an Actors Equity revolt against a politically reactionary leadership. Consciously or not, some members were beginning to believe, critics like Atkinson were out to defang them behind compliments. According to Clurman, "Our actors began to question themselves, their work, their theatre. They seemed to hanker after barricade dramatics, a sense of being in the fight rather than on the sidelines."[5] Although this would persist as a morale issue for much of the Group's existence (Clurman referred to it as a "troubled conscience" spawned by success[6]), the need to step back and rethink the company's future at the beginning of 1933 gave members on hiatus the opportunity to mingle professionally with the worker organizations. Among the consequences of this exposure were incentives for internal changes in the Group's structure.

For their part, ensembles such as the Workers Lab (renamed the Theatre of Action in 1934) and the Theatre Union were only too aware of the performing limitations of in-your-face stagings. This was particularly so of the Theatre Union, a refuge for Cobb that was founded in 1933 with a declaration that it opposed both the commercialism of Broadway and the amateurism of radical theater groups. A manifesto underlining that it was "not agitprop theatre" said it felt an artistic as well as political responsibility to its audience.[7] While remaining critical of the "bourgeois" aesthetic priorities of the Group, both the Lab and the Union invited Odets, Carnovsky, and Strasberg to set up training programs in acting and directing. Kazan benefited the most from the rapprochement, first directing a Lab play (*The Young Go First*) that worked off the paranoid premise that the Civilian Conservation Corps was actually a training ground for American storm troopers and then getting his first taste of film directing on *People of the Cumberland*, a documentary on Tennessee strip miners produced by the Lab's Frontier Films. It was through such cross-fertilization that the Group would recruit new blood, including Cobb, Albert (van) Dekker, Curt Conway, Karl Malden, and Will Lee. Aside from the personal relations formed from the teach-in period, just an association with the worker movement companies soon became a very big plus for those seeking to join the "troubled" Group.

Cobb's bridge to the worker movements after returning from Pasadena was Victor Wolfson, as much of a theatrical Daedalus (actor, director, producer, playwright) as there was in the period. The son of radical Jews who had fled Russian pogroms, Wolfson was barely in his twenties when he was organizing acting classes for striking miners in West Virginia. His special flair was for adapting novels for the stage, and his January 1935 production of Dostoyevsky's *Crime and Punishment* found two small roles for Cobb that marked the actor's New York stage debut. One of the parts, without a line, called for him to hobble out on stage as an old man and simply cross through the set. Cobb was merely twenty-four at the time; it was another investment in the kind of age roles that he would be called on to play for years. It also wouldn't be his last encounter with the works of Dostoyevsky.

The closer ties between the Group Theatre and the Theatre Union enabled Cobb to jump back and forth between the companies for the next couple of years. Only weeks after *Crime and Punishment* ended its fifteenth and final performance, he edged into the Group as an offstage voice in a second production of Odets's *Waiting for Lefty*. When Clurman paired the play on a bill with another Odets piece, *Till the Day I Die*, Cobb took the stage for the first time with the company in the minor role of a police detective. *Till the Day I Die*, churned out by Odets in five days and running 136 performances into the summer of 1935, deals with a German Communist driven to suicide when the Nazis persuade his comrades that he has betrayed them. The play represented one of the earliest explicit denunciations of Nazism in the United States; it also embedded the betrayal theme that would figure so centrally in the personal and professional lives of many Group members, in none more significantly than those of Odets and Cobb.

More indecision by the Group about what to produce next sent Cobb back to Wolfson and the Theatre Union in November 1935. First up was a translation of Bertolt Brecht's adaptation of Gorky's *Mother*, a sentimental exercise in agitprop about a mother's gradual understanding of her son's proletarian goals in pre-revolution Russia. The American production, directed by Wolfson, came with the musical contributions of three composers who would work often in Hollywood—frequent Brecht collaborator Hanns Eisler, Jerome Maross, and Alex North. All the names might have suggested contemporary or future pedigree, but that didn't impress critics at the time, and the play barely made it through thirty-six performances between November and December of 1935. Cobb took on four small parts that occasioned little critical notice. He didn't get much more attention for his next role as a Fascist lawyer in *Bitter Stream*, Wolfson's adaptation of the Italian Ignazio Silone's novel *Fontamara*. Richard Lockridge of the *Times* spoke for most New York critics on March 31 when he said the play was "more apt to inspire respect than affection." That it even inspired respect was a minor achievement given rehearsal conflicts that forced the exit of the original director Jacob Ben-Ami and his replacement by stage manager Charles Friedman. Nevertheless, mainly because of publicity and booking commitments, *Bitter Stream* ran for sixty-one performances into May. For Cobb personally the play assumed importance as his first noteworthy appearance as a heavy. It was also his last role for the Theatre Union, which was soon swallowed up by the Federal Theatre Project.

The Group Theatre to which the actor returned in 1936 as a full-time member had staged fourteen plays over five years, and though most of them had come in for a critical pounding, even a customarily skeptical reviewer like Percy Hammond of the *Herald Tribune* could call the company "the finest acting institution in this if not in any other land."[8] Cobb never stinted on making clear how important the Group's acceptance was to him, and as more than a career move or an opportunity to study Stanislavsky's Method with its chief American proponents. Kazan, with whom the actor would have a frequently tense relationship over his career, put it this way: "A lot of people worked in the Group Theatre solely to work with good people—any political or artistic beliefs or commitments were grafted upon them due to contact or expedience. What I'm saying is that a lot of people were in the Group to get work or to get laid or to get ahead, but Lee understood and supported the idea that the theater could educate and alter people while it was also hoping to be a form of art. He was a fully committed man."[9]

But the Group as an "institution," as Hammond referred to it, had been severely tried since Clurman, Strasberg, and Crawford had formed their partnership. For one thing, the triumvirate had come under attack regularly from members that they had not been given enough say in productions. Although all members got to read scripts that were under consideration for production, the actors argued that their criticisms were routinely ignored if the directors had already made up their minds to go forward with a project. They articulated this charge even more sharply after seeing firsthand how their counterparts in the worker theater movement had involved themselves in administrative details, and the acceptance of aggressive worker theater performers such as Cobb and Dekker didn't lower temperatures. If the stagecraft of the newcomers still needed polishing, their assumptions about the rights of participation didn't. Stormy meetings between the actors and the three directors became something of a routine occurrence, with the survival of the company sometimes rumbling under the procedural disputes. A compromise of sorts was eventually struck with the establishment of the advisory Actors Committee, but that often just concentrated the same gripes in a more structured body.

That there wasn't a final explosion bringing down the Group altogether at any one of several points was due to three main factors: an annual routine of summer camps in upstate New York and various Connecticut locations where members could vent their differences in relatively relaxed circumstances and recharge their enthusiasm for the coming fall season; the underlying belief of all concerned that the Group was special and their commitment to keeping the company going; and, paradoxically, the volatile personalities of the disputants. Among both the directors and the actors, yesterday's bugbears tended to become today's platforms; yesterday's platforms, today's bugbears. At one juncture Strasberg went into rages that entrusting actors with any administrative task was folly; at another, in the passive aggressive mode he had adopted after Stella Adler's criticism of his teaching methods, he declared himself more than ready to surrender administrative obligations he had never wanted ("I am absolutely unwilling to risk my personal sanity in such activity"[10]). When Clurman wasn't saying he was a reasonable man open to any reasonable suggestion or arguing that the triumvirate formula was the best guarantee of the company's survival, he was proposing that he become a sole director. (He was eventually named managing director with the backing of the Actors Committee.) For her part, Crawford hewed to a practiced middle line between her partners (with the slightest of tilts toward Strasberg), her attitude coming off as a grievance that her efforts hadn't been appreciated by the actors (and maybe not even by the other directors).

No surprise given the temperaments involved and the close quarters in which they had to operate, there had been other problems related more to the work than to the organizational structure within which it was presented. One difficulty stemmed from the original decision of Clurman and Strasberg to form a core group of actors before deciding on what plays they wanted to do. This led to shoehorning actors into parts and even more often caused a belabored process of choosing material for precluding the necessity of the shoehorning. Plays with small casts were another source of trouble from those excluded. Everyone in the company might have received a modest salary whether in a production or not, but what about the danger of an actor getting stale in his craft from long layoffs? This dread fostered more criticism of the triumvirate for its selection of scripts and for the extended time periods between shows. Would Clurman consider having roles in a given play performed on a rotation system so that more members could work? No, Clurman would not. Would he consider prescheduled midrun replacements for attaining the same objective? No, he would not. And by the by, producing plays cost money and there was no infinite number of backers out there ready to keep every member happy by keeping him busy.

Tensions were even greater when Clurman or the director of a production went outside the Group for casting. Prior to Cobb's joining there had been only a couple of minor dustups in this regard, but in 1938, with the staging of Robert Ardrey's *Casey Jones*, matters got dicier on several levels. Few members of the Actors Committee or the membership liked the drama about an embittered railroad engineer who, because of his failing eyesight, causes an accident and is shuttled off to a minor post until he retires or dies. But the few who did like the play included Clurman and Kazan, the latter taking it on as his first full-fledged directorial effort for Broadway. With Clurman's approval, Kazan gave the three top roles to outsiders—the Hollywood veteran Charles Bickford, the promising film lead Van Heflin, and the totally untested Katharine Bard. While the company regulars seethed, Kazan, by his own admission,[11] communicated little but trepidation in dealing with the gruff, stubborn Bickford, and Clurman envisioned a catastrophe. His solution for averting the disaster—bringing in Stella Adler as co-director—only made matters worse by compounding Kazan's insecurity of being out of his depth and enabling Bickford to smell more blood in the water. When Adler's sideline attempts to coach the quaking Bard also failed, Broadway veteran Peggy Conklin had to be drafted as a replacement. Later on, Kazan would scold himself for not standing up to Bickford for his bullying and to Clurman and Adler for not defending Bard more ardently, but all the cooks in the kitchen ensured that the play would not last more than twenty-five performances. Only Heflin came out with decent notices.

In many respects Stella Adler was the big gorilla in the room nobody wanted to acknowledge. Not only did she come to the Group with legendary ties to the Yiddish theater through her family, not only had Hollywood been beckoning to her for some time as a leading lady, not only did she have the statuesque looks and talent of a star to go with the dedication and self-awareness that had prompted her meeting with Stanislavsky and clash with Strasberg, but her personal relationship with Clurman seemed to many to make her the most equal of equals. That impression was reinforced by Clurman's public docility before Adler's habit of cornering herself with Meisner and Robert Lewis to exchange gossip or cackle away at rehearsal blunders, the practice earning the trio the reputation of the Weird Sisters among the other actors. If Clurman and Adler fought about such rudeness when they got home, that wouldn't have come as much of a shock, either, since their relationship appeared to thrive as much on screaming arguments about the Group, themselves, or the latest political developments in the Solomon Islands as on romance. The battling became so notorious at times that it was a discussion point at company meetings, this giving Clurman yet another reason to be furious. "It's simply not the Group's business if I've had a fight with Stella," he told the actors on one occasion. "And it's not your business, either, if I want to make up with her."[12]

Stella's brother, Luther, meanwhile, redefined enigma. On the one hand, nobody fired off more bon mots in the middle of company frictions than he did, with the air of somebody out to disprove personally a criticism that Group members might have had a great deal of talent and the noblest of intentions, but lacked a sense of humor. A surface imperturbability was interpreted by others as smugness for regularly drawing the meatiest play roles. His later marriage to Hollywood's Sylvia Sidney also awakened rancor going back to Franchot Tone's "Hollywoodization" through his marriage to Joan Crawford. On the other hand, no one spent more time working on plans for expanding the Group (devoting attention to public relations, proposing a repertory system that would permit more national tours, etc.). It was also Luther who, despite allegations about a leading man smugness, was the first to beg Clurman to give him even a walk-on in productions for which he had not been cast so that the ensemble character of the company would be reaffirmed.

In short, the company that Cobb joined full time after *Bitter Stream*, what he would one day describe as "a place of geniuses and misfits,"[13] was at a constant boil over artistic, organizational, and/or political matters. It would have been hard for him to find a more appropriate incubator for the contradictory impassioned attitudes he would strike in future years, overwhelming some with his humor and generosity, alienating others with his arrogance and nastiness, and perplexing everybody else with his often profound glumness. "He was an emotional man," in the words of screenwriter Alvah Bessie. "A manic depressive type who rarely goes through the manic phase."[14] For brother Norman, Cobb's moods had a simpler explanation: "He was a man who always knew his needs and would do anything to meet them for his art."

What Cobb didn't have to go through to any significant degree was the leeriness that Group veterans, in an us-against-the-world outlook, tended to exhibit toward new recruits (or *apprentices*, as their initial phase of membership was called). To some extent this was due to his gradual transition into the company through offstage and walk-on roles and to the personal relations he had forged through the Theatre Union; the Carnovskys, Adlers, and Meisners didn't have their antennae raised against a would-be usurper of prominent roles. But more important were Cobb's eagerness to plumb Method teachings, whether with a Stanislavsky, Strasberg, or Adler stress, and his exceptional studiousness when it came to stage techniques and the physicalization of roles. Joe Papp, the future producer who worked with Cobb in another company in the forties, was one of many who voiced his admiration for the meticulous preparation Cobb put into even repeat performances of workshop presentations.[15] On a technical level the actor told one interviewer that he studied the mannerisms and dialects of old men (whom he frequently portrayed) "until I built up my own one-man vocal library."[16] He also became a master of the intricacies of makeup. "I had to be," he (sometimes) laughed. "I started losing my hair at 20, so there went one of those fresh-faced romantic leads."[17]

If Cobb was looking for the Group at its most creative and most chaotic, if he wanted exhaustive training in the Stanislavsky Method, and if he wanted to launch a movie career, he couldn't have chosen a better time to join the company full time than in the late spring of 1936. Spurred on by Stella Adler to involve the frequent Brecht collaborator Kurt Weill in a production, Crawford had begun work with the German composer and Paul Green on a stage adaptation of the satirical Czech novel *The Good Soldier Schweik* for fall presentation. By any measure the play shaped up as the most ambitious project ever undertaken by the Group. Cobb was the utility player of the cast, taking on three roles, including that of a doctor and a French military officer. Clurman's plan called for the script to be honed during the company's summer stay at the Pine Brook Club in Nichols, Connecticut, while other members of the company did obligatory shows for local hosts; attended acting classes conducted by Strasberg, Stella Adler, and Carnovsky; and did a lot of dancing and fencing for improving their stage agility. Only with all of those tasks out of the way could they get down to the swimming and picnicking that had always made the summer getaways an important therapeutic break for everyone.

The parts of the plan having to do with the local shows and with the swimming and picnicking worked out. Among the performances staged for the Connecticut residents was a bare-bones but well-received production of Chekhov's *The Cherry Orchard*, with Cobb in the role of Chebutykin and the rest of the cast including both Adlers, Carnovsky, Nelson, Brand, Meisner, and Kazan. The Strasberg, Adler, and Carnovsky classes also set off lively debates with both the veterans and the relative newcomers. More ornery was an additional course conducted by Weill for educating members in his *Sprechstimme* technique of musical theater. "It was a way of talking on the note so it was a kind of musical talking," as Lewis described it—the kind of thing Weill had excelled at in Europe, most notably with *The Threepenny Opera*.[18]

On the surface, the *Sprechtstimme* should have compensated for (or at least disguised) the lack of musical training by most Group members; they weren't being asked to be Placido Domingo, after all. But the novel rhythms demanded by the style (or by Weill's insistence on it as a revolutionary novelty) did not go down easily, giving the actors little command of the script after weeks of drills. What passed for good news was that there wasn't much of a script for them to stumble through in the first place. Endless rewriting by Green and Weill and an aura of self-confidence from Crawford for finally having a project she could come close to calling her own still didn't have the play ready by summer's end. Although he didn't have much more faith in other plays being written for the fall at the same time by Odets and John Howard Lawson, Clurman asked the membership if it wanted to drop the whole idea of *Johnny Johnson*. To his surprise, the members insisted on going ahead. With the clock ticking on such mundane matters as renting a theater in time, he had little choice but to proceed.

Except for its title (coming from Green's discovery that there had been some three thousand American soldiers in World War I with that name), there was nothing simple about *Johnny Johnson*. The play was a sausage of heavy drama, satire, and out-and-out farce tracing the misadventures of the idealistic title character (Russell Collins), who gets drafted into the army, encounters the brutalities of trench warfare, embarrasses his commanders by dosing them with laughing gas so they will sign an armistice, and gets thrown into an asylum where the patients are clearly saner than the head psychiatrist (Carnovsky). Johnny gets out just as the world is preparing for another war, and though he loses his sweetheart to a rival, he intones a Weill curtain melody expressing continued idealism that tomorrow will be better than today. Interspersed throughout the three acts are cowboy tunes, lullabies, military marches, and even "The Marseilles."

The only thing more fractured than the tone of the play was the psychodrama in putting it on. Despite the fact that Crawford had been shepherding it for months and had regained her passion for the Group because of it, Strasberg and Clurman found quick agreement that she didn't have the directorial savvy to handle it for Broadway. A first alternative of appointing Stella Adler and Kazan co-directors sank before the former's even slighter directorial experience and the latter's dislike of his contemplated partner. Clurman, who had expressed everything except enthusiasm for the piece for some time, finally said he would take over the direction—adding a shrug, "What difference does it make who directs it?"[19] That was enough to set off Strasberg, who wondered aloud at a company meeting if Clurman was breaking down under his other responsibilities to be so offhanded about the importance of a director for the company's major production in the fall. Clurman issued a mea culpa, but it was only a question of time (a couple of weeks) before he surrendered the reins to Strasberg. Unfortunately for all concerned, that was time enough to confuse the actors further because of the different approaches of the intellectual Clurman (singling out a play's big idea and then having characters relate to it) and the psychological Strasberg (methodical construction of individual character with the heavy use of emotional memory). Equally disastrous, it was time enough for Clurman to approve sets that doomed *Johnny Johnson* even before it opened.

As rehearsed, the production was geared for a small theater such as the 500-seat Belmont on West Forty-eighth Street where run-throughs were held once the troupe returned from Connecticut. But the set designs of Donald Oenslager were so enormous that only a much larger house could accommodate them. Rattled by a swiftly approaching November deadline and beset by the rival priorities of raising money for the production and introducing some coherence into rehearsals, Clurman, Strasberg, and Crawford all signed off on Oenslager's sets, contending it would take too much time and money for radical changes. That in turn made it necessary to rent the West Forty-fourth Street Theatre, a 1,400-seat arena with a huge stage. The outcome was zanier than anything Green and Weill had written for the lunatic asylum scenes with Carnovsky. Actors began shouting to be heard from one end of the stage to the other, and at that had to consider themselves lucky they didn't take headers from forced expansive movements to cover ground for moving closer to one another.

This would have been bad enough in a Clurman production; through a Strasberg vision it came off close to a lampoon of the emotional memory approach to performing. And several Domingos *were* suddenly indispensable for projecting into the furthest reaches of the orchestra, let alone toward the balcony; in the words of the female lead Phoebe Brand, "It needed opera singers by the time it got on the Forty-fourth Street stage."[20] Writing decades after the fact, Clurman noted that two November previews were so calamitous that only twenty people remained in the audience for the final curtain, calling the evenings "the most distressing experiences I have ever gone through in the theatre."[21]

The previews didn't end the torment. Committed to the play for bad or worse, the company followed up every performance with cutting or rearranging scenes at all-night sessions that brought out a lot of loathing between actors and across-the-board loathing by the actors of Clurman and Strasberg. What kept them going in such a hateful atmosphere was something that could not have been expected from a ragged opening night performance on November 19—the verdict of most critics that *Johnny Johnson* had its virtues if you looked hard enough to find them. The most dismissive critic was John Mason Brown, usually sympathetic toward the company but in this case given to the observation that "most of the actors in the Group Theatre set about the business of being funny with as much self-consciousness as if they were members of an ancient Greek chorus who had wandered onto the stage at Minsky's."[22] (Verdicts of the kind consolidated assumptions about the essential humorlessness of Group actors—an outlook Cobb in particular would have to deal with for most of his career.) Beyond a couple of such snipings, however, words like *charming* and *ambitious* were thrown around liberally. That didn't erase the condescension in the air and certainly fell short of the kind of reviews that would pull passersby along West Forty-fourth Street into the theater, but it provided just enough room, in ferocious circumstances or not, for Strasberg and the cast to shape the play more coherently, so that some reviewers ended up writing follow-up pieces weeks later talking about the improvements that had been made since opening night. It was under these conditions that *Johnny Johnson* survived for nine weeks until after New Year's.

But *Johnny Johnson* took a heavy toll. Clurman sought to cut short persisting anger over how the production had been managed by challenging the Actors Committee (then consisting of Stella Adler,

Carnovsky, Kazan, and Bud Bohnen) to issue a report for the entire membership to discuss. The resultant twenty-nine-page document, handed around in December when the play was still running, was a blistering attack not merely on the handling of the Green-Weill work, but on the Clurman-Strasberg-Crawford management of the company since its founding. Not for the first time, everybody resigned, but with a seeming finality that had not been quite the case previously. For all the barbs aimed at Strasberg and Crawford, Clurman had little doubt that he was the primary culprit in the company's eyes, and he admitted to being "tired—very tired."[23]

In true Group style, however, that was hardly the end of it. Even as the New York theatrical press was pronouncing the death of the Group, Clurman wrote an article for the *New York Times* on January 17, 1937, saying the company would be back after a short hiatus. That would prove to be true, but what he didn't spell out was that he would be taking his break with Stella Adler and Kazan in Hollywood to explore film projects. What he didn't know was that within a matter of weeks he would be followed to California by Luther Adler, Carnovsky, Brand, Bohnen, Ruth Nelson, and several other Group members. One of these was Cobb, for whom the third try with the Hollywood studios would make him more than a vanishing shadow.

## NOTES

1. Hallie Flanagan, "A Theatre Is Born," *Theatre Arts Monthly* 15, no. 11 (November 1931).

2. George A. Knox and Herbert M. Stahl, *Dos Passos and the Revolting Playwrights* (New York: Lund, 1964), p. 21.

3. Smith, *Real Life Drama*, p. 126.

4. Jay Williams, *Stage Left* (New York: Charles Scribner's Sons, 1974), p. 124.

5. Clurman, *Fervent Years*, p. 132.

6. Ibid., p. 129.

7. Morgan Y. Himelstein, *Drama Was a Weapon: The Left-Wing Theatre in New York 1929–1941* (Westport, CT: Greenwood Press, 1976), p. 551.

8. *New York Herald Tribune*, August 2, 1936.

9. Interview with James Grissom, 1993, blogspot.com.

10. Smith, *Real Life Drama*, p. 261.

11. Richard Schickel, *Elia Kazan* (New York: HarperCollins, 2005), pp. 69–71.

12. Smith, *Real Life Drama*, p. 263.

13. *Examiner* (Los Angeles), November 17, 1957.

14. Alvah Bessie, *Inquisition in Eden* (New York: Macmillan, 1965).

15. Kenneth Turan and Joseph Papp, *Free for All: Joe Papp, the Public, and the Greatest Theater Story Ever Told* (New York: Anchor Books, 2009), p. 40.

16. Roy Pickard, "The Self-Preservation Gene," *Films in Review*, November 1977, pp. 525–528.

17. *Los Angeles Times*, June 22, 1947.

18. Smith, *Real Life Drama*, p. 267.

19. Ibid., p. 276.

20. Ibid., p. 282.

21. Clurman, *Fervent Years*, p. 188.

22. *Saturday Review*, November 23, 1936.

23. Clurman, *Fervent Years*, p. 197.

# Chapter 5

———○———

# The Actor:
# How Was School? Fine.

AMID ALL THE FURIES ASSAILING *Johnny Johnson* the play represented rare contact between the Method with its effort to create a self-contained psychologically cogent world and the Brechtian Epic aesthetic that the theatrical experience was important only as a meeting of performers and audience within a patently artificial structure for promoting social and political ends. Although Weill's *Sprechstimme* was less than pure Brecht, it introduced enough didactic detachment from the general narrative to fragment the traditional interior performance arcs inculcated by Strasberg and Method teachers. The results might not have been seamless (and Strasberg spent most of his eleventh-hour direction eliminating songs and scenes inimical to his approach), but they still earned a footnote in the history of American acting—a distinction Group actors ultimately indicated they could have done without. Except for Carnovsky, who seized on the overwhelming sets (think *Metropolis*) to aggrandize his character of the lunatic psychiatrist to farcical levels, none of them waxed poetic afterward about the avenues they had taken into their roles.

The specifics of the *Johnny Johnson* turmoil aside, that has been par for the course for actors for some time. Asking them to reveal the signposts of their route into characters has seldom brought enlightenment, certainly not in modern media profiles that fish for insights into technical methods. At his most defensive the actor will come off as a magician loathe to reveal how he slipped the rabbit into his hat for subsequent extrication; at his most accommodating he will talk vaguely about relating personal experiences to those of the character being portrayed. On occasion the response is hard to distinguish from hostility. Thus Laurence Olivier: "If you buy a diamond ring or any other wonderful bit of jewelry, you don't ask, 'What was your technique in creating this?' If you did, the jeweler might say, 'Why don't you mind your own business? You're not a jeweler.'"[1] The pervasive sense is of a superstition that talking about the craft will dilute it. When all else fails, the pressed actor will land on *listening* as a go-to answer. And why not? Anyone who has ever stepped on a stage or in front of a camera has subscribed to the indispensability of listening (whether or not he actually practices it in performance). Before movie takes James Stewart, for one example, liked going through extra drills in which he and co-players in a scene turned scripted questions into declarations and declarations into questions for honing their engagement in the dialogue and ensuring that once the cameras started shooting everyone would be more keenly attentive to what was being said and would feel more relaxed being so.[2] No other "secrets" were worth hunting.

But that said, the figure of the taciturn actor reluctant to disclose his methods has been pretty recent, flying in the face of centuries of volubility by performers about the nuances of their profession. Without even counting the methodology books aimed at acting students by Strasberg, Stella Adler, Uta Hagen, and others, libraries have long shelves of memoirs and autobiographies from performers around the world recounting their preparations for this or that role and the reasons for their regimens. If there is a common note to these reflections, it is how closely they echo one another, whatever the period and the country, insinuating the suspicion that the main mystery about acting might be why it is a mystery. Inevitably, the similarity of the outlooks on the craft's fundamental commandments has fed into the skepticism of those who have written off Stanislavsky and his heirs as reinventing the wheel. In the early eighteenth century, for instance, the Italian actor Luigi Riccoboni asserted that

> the principal and necessary thing for the actor is . . . to show clearly that he does not depart from the truth, for so he can almost convince his audience that what is feigned is not false, and unless he attains to this he will not please them. The actor, to give a natural effect, should forget not only his four limbs, but perhaps also the fifth, the head; but he must feel . . . love, anger, jealousy; feel like a king or like

Beelzebub, and if he really feels all these emotions, if "with his heart he measures his movements," they will of themselves germinate in him and move him to the right action.[3]

Later on in the eighteenth century the English acting coach Aaron Hill chided actors who merely "indicated" emotions, urging them to burrow deep inside before attempting to render them to an audience: "To act a passion well, the actor must never attempt its imitation, until his fancy has conceived so strong an image, or idea, of it, as to move the same impressive springs within his mind, which form that passion, when it is undesigned, and natural."[4] Early nineteenth-century French actor Francois-Joseph Talma stressed the necessity of craft preparation as a foundation for creative inspiration, warning against actors who were content to memorize lines and get their stage movements down: "By repeated exercises he enters deeply into the emotions, and his speech acquires the accent proper to the situation of the personage he has to represent. This done, he goes to the theatre not only to give theatrical effect to his studies, but also to yield himself to the spontaneous flashes of his sensibility and all the emotions which it involuntarily produces in him."[5]

The most introverted forms of the Method might have been the target of another French actor, Benoit Constant Coquelin, when he told a readership in the late nineteenth century, "The actor ought never to let his part 'run away' with him. It is false and ridiculous to think that it is a proof of the highest art for the actor to forget that he is before the public. If you identify yourself with your part to the point of asking yourself, as you look at the audience, 'What are all those people doing here?'—if you have no more consciousness where you are and what you are doing—you have ceased to be an actor; you are a madman. . . . Art is . . . not identification, but representation."[6] A century later the Italian Marcello Mastroianni also questioned the mentality of Method actors: "[Stanislavsky's teachings] are something far more attuned to the nature and psychology of American actors than to Italians because Americans seem to like to disembowel themselves when they go about things. . . . I can't abide a place like the Actors Studio as an institution. I don't know what its purpose is aside from providing a place where one maniac can meet a whole lot of other maniacs just like him."[7]

But while all these actors had little hesitation in saying what an actor should and should not be doing, they had correspondingly little to say about the tools useful for maintaining (in their eyes anyway) the most effective approach for taking on a stage or motion picture role. That had to await the writings of Stanislavsky and the actor-teachers of more recent times elaborating on him or simply responding to his ideas. But not even that development has eased the battle lines. The very idea that there could be one preferred approach has exasperated those holding to the belief that an actor should take whatever from wherever for sewing together a character. Then there is the contentious subcategory of he "doth protest too much, methinks." The Method-trained Shelley Winters was just one of many who insisted that the hypercritical such as Mastroianni were in fact very much part of what they were railing against: "He was always a Method actor. What he is embarrassed about is any conscious approach that endangers his notions of a private life."[8]

And yet, so what? Clurman wasn't alone in his conclusion that by the mid-1930s debates for and against Stanislavsky's teachings had become academic since, whether or not they deigned to acknowledge it by name, every actor and acting teacher with access to the Method was borrowing from it. Norris Houghton, the long-time director-producer and expert on the Russian theater, could see no controversy in that observation since it followed naturally from what the Riccobonis, Hills, and Coquelins had been saying for generations: "The Stanislavsky system is really only a conscious codification of ideas about acting which have always been the property of most good actors of all countries whether they knew it or not. Its basis is the work of the actor *with himself* in order to master 'technical means for the creation of the creative mood, so that inspiration may appear oftener than is its wont.'"[9]

Down to the present day, however, some prominent people on both sides of the question have objected to the Noughton codification position. For Method adherents this point of view denies the revolutionary nature of Stanislavsky's work; for the skeptics it diminishes alternative systems that have informed conspicuous careers. One formula expression of this persisting antagonism has been in the distinction that some actors work from the outside in and others from the inside out. In the former camp until his death in 1989 was Olivier, who confessed that "to create a character, I first visualize a painting;

the manner, movement, gestures, walk all follow."[10] Symptomatic of how drastically theatrical culture has changed from the days when that might have seemed like standard behavior for an actor, such an approach now invites images of the arch-thespian standing on the table of a western saloon reciting Shakespeare for a shot of red eye or stepping warily before footlight candles to entertain gussied up first nighters. What can be learned going from the outside to the inside except superficiality?

In fact, though, even the most convinced Method actors haven't always been so quick to level that accusation. For the Group Theatre a prime source of hesitation was Michael Chekhov, nephew of the play-wright, one of the original members of the Moscow Art Theatre and an actor-teacher who would spend the last decades of his life in England and the United States offering what he considered refinements on what he had learned from Stanislavsky. The chief refinement was what Chekhov called the Psychological Gesture (PG), a concept not all that dissimilar to the defining "gesture" art teachers tell their students to focus on rather than on particular parts of a model's anatomy. As he explained it in his book *To the Actor,*

> Imagine that you are going to play a character which, according to your first general impression, has a strong and unbending will, is possessed by dominating, despotic desires, and is filled with hatred and disgust.
>
> You look for a suitable overall gesture which can express all this in the character, and perhaps after a few attempts you find it.
>
> It is strong and well shaped. When repeated several times it will tend to strengthen your will. The direction of each limb, the final position of the whole body as well as the inclination of the head are such that they are bound to call up a definite desire for dominating and despotic conduct. The qualities that fill and permeate each muscle of the entire body, will provoke within you feelings of hatred and disgust. Thus, through the gesture, you penetrate and stimulate the depths of your own psychology.[11]

There could be no mistaking the controlling physical place Chekhov gave his PG in the actor's preparation process; as he also empha-sized in his book, its aim was "to influence, stir, mold, and attune [the actor's] whole inner life to its artistic aims and purposes."[12] If his focus on the external as a stepping-off guide smacked of the superficial, however, that didn't bother Stella Adler, Carnovsky, Lewis, Brand, and other Group members in 1935. After attending some of Chekhov's classes on their own, they lobbied Clurman to bring him in as a company teacher. "The actors felt they had achieved some measure of honesty and truth in their work, but Chekhov's gift for combining these with sharply expressive and yet very free color, rhythm, and design was something in which they knew themselves to be deficient, and which they therefore envied."[13]

In the end, Chekhov conducted a few classes but no more. He declined the invitation for full membership, not for any instructional conflicts over the role of PG in molding characters, but because of the political leanings of many Group members. Smith quotes him as telling Carnovsky, "Morris, don't go in for this wickedness of Communism. It encourages the materialistic impulse in our whole society."[14] The loudest sigh of relief came from Strasberg, who had been against inviting Chekhov and what he termed the man's "mysticism" from the start. Clurman sought to pass off the whole episode as "a mirror of the Group's varied and lively state of mind."[15]

Others in the company were not so sure. For Meisner the flirtation with Chekhov mostly reflected how "there wasn't even unanimity in the technical approach" among the Group's players, and not only because of the split between the Strasberg and Stella Adler camps after her Paris meeting with Stanislavsky. According to Meisner, other Group members followed Carnovsky's stress on language and delivery.[16]

There have also been half concessions from the other side of the divide, at least where film acting is concerned. It wasn't Michael Redgrave, England's foremost proponent of Stanislavsky principles in the middle of the last century, but Olivier who admitted that before going in front of a camera, he "build(s) up the role from within, knowing that the camera will expose me if I am not true, if my imagination is askew or only at half-power."[17] His one caveat was, "By all means have Stanislavsky with you in your study or in your limousine or wherever you are three hours before the scene; but don't bring him onto the film set."[18]

On balance, however, the most severe criticism of the Stanislavsky school, at least where the Group Theatre was concerned, came not from the complete naysayers or even from those like Stella Adler who objected to Strasberg's slants, but from Meisner, who himself worked from the Moscow Art Theatre principles in a teaching career that would stretch through six decades. As he told Chinoy, "I think that the way acting was approached in the Group Theatre was extremely introverted. The Group took introverted people and increased their introversion. . . . The result was that many, many young actors in the Group were damaged by the approach. I hate to use the words *healthy* and *objective*, but they do have some place in my meaning. The introverting of the introverted caused a lot of damage." As Meisner saw it, the only actors who survived the process intact were the Adlers and the Carnovskys, those who had already had substantial backgrounds before joining the Group.[19]

Cobb, whose alternately brooding silences and eruptive cheerfulness suggested that some genes could leave Russia more easily than Russia could leave some genes and which had earned him the nickname of "Herr Moody" among his Group colleagues, fell between the two stools.[20] That applied not only to his relationship with the acting techniques of the Method, but also to the collective structure of the Group and the roles he could obtain within it. As he was quoted by Smith, "If I personally thirst for the friendship and understanding of Clifford Odets and haven't got it, I will be unhappy when you're casting me. There's a connection. If Clifford says he likes to write plays for us because he understands us and does, and I can't share in that, then I am not part of that collective. So that when you cast me in the small part, I am unhappy not because of the small part but because it's part of something of which I'm not a part."[21]

Odets himself acknowledged something similar even when it came to studying Stanislavsky's principles with Strasberg: "The only way we could really learn and get the benefit of Strasberg's training was to get a good part. In that way he would work with you solo, he would work with you in pairs. . . . Those actors who had the good parts got the real and best benefits of Strasberg's training; and the others did not; and that's all."[22]

Within all the stated emphasis on ensemble democracy, the realities of Group casting, training, and rehearsing pointed up by Cobb and Odets could only promote a psychic fragility that would manifest itself in various forms in subsequent years. It also provided a different rationale for why being a leading man could be so important, sometimes to the point of obsession, for some actors.

## Notes

1. Laurence Olivier, *On Acting* (New York: Simon & Schuster, 1986), p. 27. But the same Olivier has suggested that "more critics should be encouraged to sit in on rehearsals so that they could see the amount of work, concentration, belief, and love that goes into the construction of a piece, before they take their inky swords to it" (Ibid., p. 363).

2. Donald Dewey, *James Stewart: A Biography* (New York and London: Little, Brown, 1996), p. 494.

3. "Riccoboni's Advice to Actors," Pierre Rames (trans.), *Mask Magazine* 3 (April 1911), p. 175.

4. Cole and Chinoy, *Actors on Acting*, p. 117.

5. Ibid., p. 182.

6. Benoit Constant Coquelin, "Actors and Acting," *Harper's New Monthly Magazine*, May 1887, p. 891.

7. Donald Dewey, *Marcello Mastroianni: His Life and Art* (New York: Birch Lane, 1993), p. 79.

8. Ibid.

9. Norris Houghton, *Moscow Rehearses: The Golden Age of the Soviet Theatre* (New York: Grove Press, 1936), p. 57.

10. Olivier, *On Acting*, p. 153.

11. Michael Chekhov, *To the Actor* (New York: Harper & Row, 1953), p. 63.

12. Ibid., p. 65.

13. Clurman, *Fervent Years*, p. 158.

14. Smith, *Real Life Drama*, p. 220.

15. Clurman, *Fervent Years*, p.158.

16. Chinoy, "Reunion," p. 503.

17. Olivier, *On Acting*, p. 311.

18. Ibid., p. 312.

19. Chinoy, "Reunion," p. 504.

20. Danny Peary (ed.), *Close-Ups: The Movie Star Book* (New York: Workman Publishing, 1978), p. 345.

21. Smith, *Real Life Drama*, p. 370.

22. Chinoy, "Reunion," p. 498.

# Chapter 6

===========================O===========================

# Golden (and Not So Golden) Opportunities

THE GROUP THEATRE'S RELATIONSHIP with Hollywood over its first years was more ambivalent than it liked to admit. On the one hand, the defection to the West Coast of members like Franchot Tone and Joe Bromberg provoked considerable snarling while simultaneously steeling a sense of purpose in those left behind. On the other hand, big studio offers to individuals in the company, especially to Odets and Stella Adler, became routine, posing a constant temptation during the Group's enervating psychodramas. In January of 1937 Odets and Adler were already in Hollywood, and Clurman was on his way to join them. The motive for the moves was professional opportunity, but that lay atop mounds of credulousness, rationalization, and simple exhaustion. For Odets, newly married to the Academy Award winner Luise Rainer, the opportunity was in being contracted to write a screenplay (*Castles in the Air*) championing the cause of the loyalists in the Spanish civil war. If that sounded a little optimistic, if not altogether naïve, in an industry allergic to bloody current events in Europe, Odets trusted in the prospect of working with Lewis Milestone, director of *All Quiet on the Western Front* and a financial contributor to Group productions, including *Johnny Johnson*. Wherever the cause and wherever the effect were to be located, Adler gave up resisting the offers thrown her way behind her fury at the handling of *Johnny Johnson* and her declared certainty that the Group was finished. For Clurman going to California meant ending his separation from Adler, taking advantage of an opening Odets had found for him on the Spanish civil war project, and getting away from the stresses of the Group for a while.

With Strasberg in a new funk over the reception accorded *Johnny Johnson*, it fell to Crawford to keep things together while she went on hoping that Clurman's assurances that the Group wasn't dead were more than bravado. After the closing of *Johnny Johnson*, she couldn't do anything about the scattering of the actors to non-Group productions around the country for keeping food on the table, but she knew that any more siren calls from Hollywood (certain to involve long-term contracts) would put an end to the company for good. Her solution— one that would keep the ensemble going for another nine productions over three years—was to put a collection of actors in a package deal for short-term film commitments while the company restoked its energies. She found the perfect interlocutor in producer Walter Wanger, the overseer of *Castles in the Air* who had taken on Clurman as a consultant.

Wanger had been working in Hollywood since the earliest days of the silents. Moving from one studio to another, he had been associated with everybody from Rudolph Valentino (*The Sheik*) and Greta Garbo (*Queen Christine*) to the Marx Brothers (*The Cocoanuts*). He had also done considerable producing on the East Coast, where he had viewed the Group's acting abilities firsthand. When approached by Crawford, Wanger had recently set himself up as an independent producer and had been reminded that part of the price for his independence was not having access to the bulging rosters of actors MGM, Paramount, and Warner Brothers (three of his former employers) boasted. He also knew he stood little chance of winning a bidding war against the studios for the services of any new discovery on Broadway. It was within this context that Crawford's proposal for the en masse signing of Group members was so appealing. Under the terms of the arrangement, he agreed to pay Luther Adler, Bohnen, Brand, Carnovsky, Cobb, Kazan, Nelson, and Dorothy Patten $150 a week as an advance against their salaries when they were working. If they were working on one of his pictures, they would get $750 a week; if he loaned them out to another producer at a higher price, he and the actors would split the extra money at percentages on a case-by-case basis. Crawford asked that the actors send back 10 percent of their earnings to the Group office in New York to help finance the survival of the company while she and Strasberg were exploring production possibilities. Nobody demurred.

The bad news for Cobb was that he was omitted from the Group players Wanger wanted for Odets's *Castles in the Air*; that was also the good news for him. While Adler, Carnovsky, Kazan, and the others sat around waiting for a picture that would never get made with their participation,[1] Cobb, the newest kid on the block, was loaned out by Wanger for two westerns and a musical comedy. The westerns were both in the popular Hopalong Cassidy (William Boyd) series, shot with grade C programmer speed at Columbia State Historic Park near Sonora. In the first one, *North of the Rio Grande*, Cobb offered a rare glimpse of his natural brown wreath of a hairline as a railroad executive who needs Hopalong's help against outlaws trying to put him out of business; equally rare, he recites his lines woodenly, seemingly as concerned with remembering them as lending them any credibility. In the follow-up, *Rustlers' Valley*, he is more at ease and back to *Bitter Stream* form as the chief villain—a lawyer trying to put his clammy hands on a ranch belonging to a friend of the hero. The musical comedy was an Eddie Cantor fantasy set in old Baghdad in which he did a bit as a generic Arab.

With the exception of Carnovsky, who secured roles in the big-budget *The Life of Emile Zola* (as Anatole France) and in Anton Litvak's *Tovarich*, Cobb was the only one who got as much out of Hollywood as Hollywood got out of him. Most of the others encountered one form of humiliation or another. Patten, who had been ending a long affair with Crawford, had a nervous breakdown before she could get any work and needed sanitarium care. Luther Adler was given a role as a character named Schratt in the spy melodrama *Lancer Spy*, but only after submitting to a nose job. Kazan was advised to change his name to Cezanne; when he objected that this had been the name of a French painter of some renown, he was told not to worry, that once he had a few solid credits, the public would forget about the other guy. Even Stella Adler, whose move west had set off the parade after her, couldn't work under her name for a trifle entitled *Love on Toast*. "Paramount couldn't release it. They said, 'It's not good in the South for a marquee to have the name Adler on it. People might think it's Jewish.' I said it's not mine to change, it was given to me—I can't change it.' The lawyers met, but the studio refused to budge, and I finally had to say, 'Spell it any way you like, but I'm saying it's Adler!'" So *Love on Toast* was released as costarring John Payne and Stella *Ardler*![2]

Already on edge because of the lack of news from Crawford and Strasberg about getting the Group back on its feet, the visitors from the east were only agitated further by such incidents. None of them had ever professed any belief in motion pictures as a serious acting medium, and had certainly never confused Hollywood with a hotbed of progressive politics, and each passing day made them wonder if the industry wasn't getting back at them for thinking of it merely as a cash cow. Patience curdled. Even the normally mild-mannered Bud Bohnen erupted in distaste for his surroundings. "It's truly capitalism gone mad out here," he wrote to his brother Arthur. "Everybody talks salary, pictures, graft, drag, the whole spirit of the place is fake, the acting is fake, the art is synthetic." And (this from somebody with a drinking problem of his own), "You drink yourself to death in the glorious sunlight with oranges dropping in your mouth."[3] It also hadn't escaped scrutiny that because of the need to keep up a social front, Tone and Bromberg hadn't been able to save a penny of the big money they had been expecting to make in leaving the Group.

For all that, there were very practical barriers in the way of getting on a train back to New York. The first was that, aside from Carnovsky, Cobb, and Luther Adler, the tithing Crawford had been counting on from the actors for financial support should not have been counted on. In mid-March she finally had enough of the Group's administrative and creative troubles and announced her resignation. A week later, Strasberg did the same, not failing to accuse the actors, and by name Luther Adler and Bohnen, of being responsible for destroying the company.[4] As fatal for the Group's survival as the resignations might have seemed, however, it was still Clurman the actors were waiting to hear from; or better, waiting to hear from until they heard something they wanted to hear. Repeatedly, he waved off appeals from Kazan and Luther Adler to commit himself to another Group season. What they were supposed to believe was that he was content for the moment living with Stella and consulting for Wanger. When Kazan pointed out that the consulting mostly consisted of lackey jobs like teaching models how to walk in front of a camera, Clurman refused to argue.[5] Kazan, probably the truest believer in Clurman's indispensability for the Group, was about to give up and return to New York on his own. But then Odets provided a deus ex machina.

Still boiling over the aborted *Castles in the Air*,[6] Odets took to his typewriter to work on a drama about a young man who has to choose between careers as a violinist and a professional boxer. The melodramatic *Golden Gloves*, as it was called initially, was a marked departure for Odets in its multiple sets and characters (gangsters, boxing world habitués, Italian Americans), with both the class and ethnicity concerns of his previous work maneuvered into the background of what was essentially a soap opera with a lot of flashy dialogue. Its seed might or might not have been planted by Cobb's teenage years as a violin prodigy; the playwright had certainly known about the would-be musician and the broken wrist. What's more, Odets sometimes went well beyond the innate defensiveness of a writer in talking about the origins of his inspirations; that is to say, he wasn't above lying. He had always denied, for instance, knowing about an actual strike by taxi drivers a year before the premiere of *Waiting for Lefty* although he was seen in the drivers' union hall during protests. Years later, he dismissed the widespread impression that *The Big Knife*, about a once-serious actor who gets chewed up by the Hollywood machine, had more than a little to do with the career of John Garfield. But wherever it had come from, *Golden Gloves* brought excitement back to the Group actors gathered together for a couple of readings of the play in progress. It also shook Clurman out of his doldrums, and plans were made for everyone to return to New York.

In his own description, Clurman was welcomed back at Grand Central Station in August "like a hero returning from exile."[7] There would have been less celebration by some if they had known then and there about the conditions under which he had agreed to join with Kazan, Luther Adler, and Bohnen in a newly formed Actors Council for resuscitating the company. The most significant stipulations were that he was to have a free hand in going outside the Group for casting big names in major roles, that he would be looking for new blood for the company even if that meant shoving aside some of the old reliables, and that, given the even tighter budgets than in the past, those not working on a production would not draw weekly salaries. With the support of Kazan, Adler, and Bohnen, Clurman made good on all three intentions around the casting of the Odets play that had been retitled *Golden Boy*. For the female lead he went to Frances Farmer, then riding a wave of popularity for her role in the Paramount feature *Come and Get It*. As the director was quick to explain, Farmer wasn't just any Hollywood star with box office appeal: she was trained in the Stanislavsky Method and even had a radical political past, having once sold enough copies of a left-wing weekly in her home city of Seattle to win a trip to Moscow. Nevertheless, she was also part of Clurman's new deal for the company. Experienced members such as Russell Collins (the lead in *Johnny Johnson*) and William Challee were ignored for newcomers like Karl Malden and Harry (Morgan) Bratsburg. And those who couldn't be accommodated with backstage jobs (Meisner, for instance, became Clurman's assistant director) were just out, with no guarantees that any play produced after *Golden Boy* would bring them back in.

And there were other causes for resentment. Clurman's casting showed a clear preference for the actors who had been with him in California. These included Cobb, assigned the role of a friend of the violinist-boxer's father (Carnovsky), who was given to such time-capsule Odets observations as "A man hits his wife, and it's the first step to fascism." Then there was the controversy over the leading man. Odets had promised the role to Garfield, but Clurman tapped the thirty-four-year-old Adler, ten years older and nowhere near as physically convincing as a boxer. Garfield was given a smaller role in a not very successful attempt to appease him. According to his daughter Julie, he never really got over the snub. "It was written for Daddy and he was crushed when Luther Adler was given the part. Adler was a good actor, but there was none of that physical magnetism in him that the character (and Daddy) had."[8]

Clurman's explanation? "Garfield was obviously the type, but he had neither the pathos nor the variety, in my opinion, to sustain the role." But why Adler, why not even Cobb who had the physique, not to mention some emotional familiarity with the protagonist's dilemma? "In my view this character was not a fighter—simply a sensitive, virile boy."[9] Without slighting Adler's superior acting abilities, those excluded from the cast had another explanation—that Stella, still in California where she was making more movies, had pressured Clurman to choose her brother and that the director had seen everything to gain by going with a member of the Actors Council that had become so crucial for the continuation of the Group.

Critics were less than dazzled when *Golden Boy* opened at the Belasco on November 4—by the play, anyway. But Clurman was vindicated by his choice of Adler when the strongest praise was directed to the actor's performance as the hapless boxer Joe Bonaparte. General reaction to the writing was summed up by John Anderson of the

*Journal*, who saluted Odets's dialogue but then added, "It has limber, it has the steel tension of girder work, it has the same faultless joining, and it moves the story with smooth precision. . . . It just seems a pity to waste such dialogue and the extraordinarily sharp and persuasive production the Group has given the play."[10] Over and above opinions on the play as such was the question of what its staging said about the evolution of the Group; that is, didn't it make the company as crassly commercial as all those other Broadway producers once regarded as anathema? Even years later, in the writing of *The Fervent Years*, Clurman remained uncomfortable with the question. First, he trivialized its terms as being a glib debate between plays as "entertainment" and plays as "propaganda," then he went on at pointless length about how cast members spent their time away from the Belasco raising funds for the loyalist cause in Spain and doing other volunteer work for left-wing campaigns.[11]

With enticing words like *energetic* and *dynamic* seeping through even mixed reviews, *Golden Boy* became the Group's single biggest success. (It didn't hurt that the whole country, including the Broadway theater crowd, was caught up at the time with the sensational rise of heavyweight Joe Louis.) Not only did the play run in New York until the following June to total 248 performances, but it spawned road companies and was sold to Hollywood for a film adaptation. Although he had a relatively small part in the Broadway production, Cobb owed much of his next couple of years—and beyond—to the play. After receiving commending mentions from New York critics,[12] he was able to take advantage of a touring performance in Los Angeles to make another picture—the minor mystery *Danger on the Air*. In what would soon become a pattern in the roles he was given, he played an Italian immigrant janitor at a radio station who is suspected of being a murderer before he too ends up as a victim. The next time he spoke broken English of the Italian variety would be a lot more significant.

Midway through the spring Clurman received an invitation to travel to London with *Golden Boy*. The move would have added to the Group's prestige, but it came with the proviso that it be for an unlimited run. That was unacceptable to both the director and several actors in the company who, with their stock higher because of the play's box office success, were looking forward to their summer break to once again go after that elusive cash in Hollywood. But then came a second invitation for a two-month limited run that would have internationalized the company's reputation while leaving everyone time to explore West Coast movie offers. Putting up the money for the trip was Lillian Emerson, an actress who had started a somewhat star-crossed Broadway career around the same time as the Group had been introducing itself with *The House of Connelly* a couple of blocks away. It was a distance—and a proximity—she had never gotten over. What Emerson mainly had to show for seven years around Times Square was a secondary role in a 1934–1935 musical comedy *Say When*, which ran for seventy-six performances. Otherwise she had appeared in eleven would-be comedies and suspense-less mysteries that had run for a combined total of 108 evenings. That had been then, however. Not only had she moved to England, but she had done so as an heiress to the Bromo Seltzer fortune who could very easily host the Group.

There was a catch to the invitation, however: Emerson would foot the bill for everything in London only if she were given the leading role played in the Broadway production by Frances Farmer. As a plot turn, it was groaningly trite, but the Group's concession to that demand wasn't majestic drama, either. Depending on whose account was to be believed (and Clurman, Kazan, and Lewis had varying versions), Farmer had been loaned out to the Group only for the New York run, Farmer had a pending lawsuit in California against her agents that made a trip across the ocean out of the question, Farmer had a film obligation she couldn't break, or Farmer had been looking forward to doing the movie because it would have boosted the career of her scheduled costar, her husband Leif Erickson.[13] One way or the other, Farmer was out and Emerson was in as the female lead.

The company invaded England in two waves. Clurman, Odets, and the two Adlers took the faster *Queen Mary* two days after the closing of the play in New York so they could put in more hours rehearsing with Emerson. The rest of the company, which sailed on the *President Harding*, was not exactly a party at sea. Although everyone was aware that appearing at the fabled St. James's Theatre in London's West End could only add to the Group's luster, several resentments were also on board for the six-day crossing. One stemmed from the brusque dumping of Farmer, with even Clurman acknowledging that "one or two people informed me in no uncertain terms that this decision betrayed a thorough-going opportunism on my part."[14] Then there were the bruised feelings over Garfield, who only shortly before had devastated members with the announcement that he had taken screen tests secretly for both MGM and Warner Brothers and had signed a contract to go with the latter. There was little doubt that one of the engines behind his decision was his bitterness at not getting the Joe Bonaparte role promised by Odets. Never at a loss for words, Carnovsky, who had developed a paternal affection for the younger actor, tripled his usual allotment at a company meeting in denouncing the "meretricious, immediate rewards" some people confused with success. Bohnen was so upset that he ran down to Grand Central Station in his stage makeup after a matinee in a final futile attempt to stop Garfield from boarding his train.[15] For his part, Cobb was very much Herr Moody on the crossing to Europe, generally staying away from the photographs company members took of one another incessantly. There was a suspicion that the news about Garfield had struck him in two ways: as a loss of somebody he had begun to grow close to within the company and as another demonstration of how others, specifically those with hair, were likely to hit the ground running as leading men in Hollywood while he couldn't. The disgruntlement emerged more clearly a decade later when he was asked to make a movie with Garfield.

Despite the imposed presence of Emerson and some cuts in the script by the British censors,[16] *Golden Boy* was an even bigger critical hit in London than it had been in New York. The recurrent refrain of the positive reviews was in the group approach to the performance and in the feeling that generated from the stage. The critic for the *Observer* admitted he didn't understand all the American vernacular, and didn't care all that much: "The speakers may sometimes leave one guessing as to the precise significance of what they have said, but never in doubt as to what they feel."[17] The *Times* critic said he had witnessed "a furious energy of acting as though that art had just been invented, totally unlike the English duplication of esteemed successes."[18]

Cobb shared in the glow produced by the reception to *Golden Boy*. Like other cast members, he was also able to use his stay in London for overnight trips to Paris when there was a day off. It was both there and in London that his attention was diverted to another play—or at least to its leading lady.

## NOTES

1. Retitled *Blockade* and rewritten by John Howard Lawson, the picture was released in 1938.

2. Larry Adler, *It Ain't Necessarily So: An Autobiography* (New York: Grove Press, 1984), p. 126.

3. Roman Bohnen Papers, Series II, Personal and Professional Correspondence, Box 2, File 3, Lincoln Center Library for the Performing Arts, New York.

4. Smith, *Real Life Drama*, p. 302.

5. Schickel, *Elia Kazan*, p. 63.

6. One rumor at the time said that Wanger had been told by a couple of studios not to expect a releasing deal for a film that made Italian dictator Benito Mussolini, an ally of the Franco forces against the loyalists, look bad. Prior to World War II, Italy was an important distribution market for Hollywood.

7. Clurman, *Fervent Years*, p. 208.

8. Interview with author, September 27, 2012. Subsequent quotes from Julie Garfield are taken from this interview.

9. Clurman, *Fervent Years*, p. 209.

10. *New York Journal*, November 5, 1937.

11. Clurman, *Fervent Years*, p. 214.

12. *New York Times*, November 5, 1937.

13. An oddity about Cossacks in America, *Ride a Crooked Mile* didn't do much for either of their careers.

14. Clurman, *Fervent Years*, p. 223.

15. Ibid., p. 333.

16. Lines such as "Did you sleep with him?"

17. *Observer* (London), June 22, 1938.

18. *Times* (London), June 26, 1938.

# Chapter 7

———————◯———————

# Married to More
# Than the Mob

GIVEN ALL THE PLACES, people, and pursuits they had had in common, it was a little surprising Cobb had to go to Europe to know Helen Beverley.[1] Also the child of a Yiddish-speaking Russian immigrant father, Beverley was born in Boston on November 9, 1916, to Lou and Anna Smuckler.[2] Her father had been serious enough about becoming a doctor to get as far as premed studies at Harvard before money troubles put an end to that ambition. Even before then, however, Smuckler had been spending his time off campus organizing small Yiddish theater groups. A few years after Helen's birth, the family (there was also a son Edward) moved to the Bronx, where Smuckler wasted little time involving his daughter in his theatrical ventures. Beverley was to recall rehearsing the monologues and stories of Sholem Aleichem with her father on trolleys and trains on their way to performances. Any social gathering at all was an occasion for the preening parent to put his daughter on a table for a recital.

Beverley's direct track to the stage from childhood took all of the family's resources, with Smuckler gradually concentrating on the exhibition side of the theatrical and movie businesses to make a steady living. Her formal education included Hunter College and the American Academy of Dramatic Arts. Indicative of both her talents and her father's zeal for making opportunities for her, her version of dance class included performing with Ted Shawn and Ruth St. Denis, while her acting studies embraced tutoring by Stanislavsky pioneer Maria Ouspenskaya. She was still a teenager when she hooked up with the

Yiddish theater of Maurice Schwartz, then with a roster of some eighty actors to choose from for New York and out-of-town productions. One of the more resonant names of the downtown Second Avenue hub was Jacob Ben-Ami, Cobb's first director in the Theatre Union production of *Bitter Stream*. Before *Bitter Stream*–type quarrels took over, it was Ben-Ami who cast Beverley for the Yiddish film *Grine felder* (*Green Fields*, 1937)—and who, as with Cobb and *Bitter Stream*, saw another director take a production to the finish line. In this case it was Edgar Ulmer, something of a Hollywood itinerant through small studios, whose most conspicuous credit up to then had been *The Black Cat*, the creepiest of horror films with Boris Karloff and Bela Lugosi. As an outsider to Yiddish-language show business, Ulmer didn't presume to override Ben-Ami's choices of Beverley and Michael Goldstein for the film leads.

Based on a twenty-year-old play by Peretz Hirschbein, *Grine felder* had become an instant classic of the American Yiddish stage, so there was no scarcity of potential investors for the film version, most aggressively from the country's three biggest Yiddish dailies. But wary that choosing one of the papers would turn critics of the other two against his project before he started shooting, Ulmer took out a loan from Household Finance and raised other money from individuals, including Beverley's father, Smuckler, and the actor Paul Muni. What they were investing in was an ostensible rustic comedy revolving around the conflicts that ensue when an ascetic student from the city (Goldstein) finds himself among Jewish peasants in a not specified part of the Soviet Union and falls in love with the impish daughter (Beverley) of one of them. But starting with author Hirschbein, few were willing to let the picture go as a Debbie Reynolds comedy in Yiddish. In his detailed history of Yiddish films, for instance, J. Hoberman finds special meaning in the fact that two different characters quote the Talmud's "A man without land is not a man," linking that to a conclusion that what *Grine felder* is really about is a celebration of "an idyllic world of tribal wholeness and innate, stubborn piety, a world where man and nature, work and religion—and even parents and children—can be joyfully reconciled."[3] In other quarters there were more strenuous analyses connecting the picture to the left-wing united front objectives of the 1930s.

*Grine felder* was the first Yiddish picture in America to be shot outdoors instead of in a studio, with New Jersey substituting for

Eastern Europe. And its uniqueness didn't end there. In France it won the equivalent of that country's 1938 Oscar for best foreign film. It proved so popular among American Jews that the Loews theater chain bought subsidiary rights for shortening and captioning it and sending it out as the lower half of a double bill with a Loretta Young comedy. With that kind of success, Ulmer encountered few objections when he teamed up again with Beverley for *Di klyatshe* (*The Light Ahead*, 1939), as tart a Yiddish film as there ever was about the religious and social hypocrisies of shtetl living. Her costar was another Bronx native and frequent future Cobb co-player, David Opatoshu. Although stiffer than *Grine felder*, *Di klyatshe* elicited flattering comparisons to the earlier film, not least because of the performances of its leads. In Hoberman's view, "Beverley and Opatoshu are perhaps the most beautiful couple in the history of Yiddish cinema, and their scenes have a poignant erotic chemistry that helps compensate for the film's overly static *mise-en-scène* and sometimes shrill polemical tone."[4] The pair made public appearances behind their billing as the first "movie stars" of the Yiddish screen.

Between films Beverley also moved to the fore on the Yiddish stage, most notably with Schwartz in an adaptation of Israel Joseph Singer's novel *Di brider Ashkenazi* (*The Brothers Ashkenazi*), about Jewish identity in early twentieth-century Poland. It was while touring with that play in France and England on the eve of World War II and with persecutions of Jews in Germany already well advanced that Beverley met Cobb. After Paris (where she was also celebrated for *Grine felder*), she opened with Schwartz in July at the Phoenix Theatre on Charing Cross Road in the same West End district where Cobb was doing *Golden Boy*. They continued seeing one another back in New York, finally taking a Midtown apartment together at Sixth Avenue and West Fifty-seventh Street. For years, their separations for work triggered torrentially passionate letters back and forth, sometimes on a daily basis. Cobb's were meticulously phrased and grammatically rigorous. The closest he came to a misspelling in more than one hundred missives left after his death was in doubts about the correctness of a Yiddish sentence he sought to include on one occasion. Evidence of his Herr Moody was largely restricted to his repetitively stated anguish at being separated from the woman he referred to as "Dearest" over and over again. On July 1, 1939, while he was on the West Coast for film work, he wrote back to her in New York:

I do see you often, you know. And I talk to you. I would not be able to stand it out here all this time if you weren't with me so much of the time. With every thought of you, another silken strand is woven around us binding us closer together. I've seen those strands grow from strings to strong ropes, until now they're stout, unbreakable chains. And yet this tie between us is just as delicate, just as tender, just as constant as my love itself is for you.

The one doubt he had? "The stark, realistic thought intrudes that we are in a capricious profession—that we must someday be separated again. I don't dwell on that thought, however. When the time comes, I'll have your help next to me to fight it."

Cobb and Beverley were married in a civil ceremony in Philadelphia on February 6, 1940. It made for the third marriage of a Group member in two years. That same year Clurman and Stella Adler formalized their relationship, and while the company had still been in London, Luther Adler had wed Sylvia Sidney in all but secret. Counting Tone and Joan Crawford and Odets and Luise Rainer, the Cobb-Beverley match was the only one that did not have negative professional repercussions for the company.

When the *Golden Boy* troupe returned to America in August 1938, Clurman had four scripts at various stages of readiness to pursue as the company's next production. Even though they involved names like Odets, Irwin Shaw, and William Saroyan, he remained stymied in his attempts to get angels to invest in the Group as a permanent theatrical entity rather than in individual plays. What also remained constant was his determination to go outside the company for casting major roles. In the case of Odets's *Rocket to the Moon*, he once again went back to Hollywood for an actress to play the linchpin other woman in a closet drama about a married dentist's (Carnovsky) love life. This time it wasn't a star of the Frances Farmer caliber, but MGM contract player Eleanor Lynn (Echika Lin, from Brooklyn). Like Farmer, though, Lynn brought arguments Clurman could make to dismayed company members: she had been trained in Stanislavsky, had done shows to raise money for the Loyalist cause in Spain, and had come recommended by Garfield, with whom she had worked. That did little to appease Brand, Nelson, and others who wondered why the outside name option invariably affected the women in the company more than the men. After the favoritism he had been showing Stella over the years, Clurman remained unfazed by the criticism, at most throwing a sop of an understudy role to a protester. He also won vindication on a couple of fronts when Lynn's performance was hailed by critics and Carnovsky, Mister Moral High Ground where many of the company's romantic entanglements had been concerned, fell for his leading lady and almost destroyed his marriage to Brand.

Carnovsky and Luther Adler both appeared in *Rocket to the Moon*, and that was to Cobb's benefit—mostly. Because Clurman wanted the two Group eminences to beef up the new Odets piece, he had to recast a road company tour of *Golden Boy*. Cobb was given a far more prominent role—not as the boxer Joe Bonaparte, however, but as his immigrant fruit vendor father! Cast as the boxer was Kazan, who happened to be two years older than the actor playing Papa Bonaparte. While Cobb kept any complaints to himself and Beverley, Kazan took the opposite tack, declaring that it was a recognition long overdue. As he declared in his seldom-self-effacing autobiography, he had stayed out of the original debate over giving the part of the boxer to Garfield or Adler because he didn't think either one of them had deserved it, that it should have been his from the start. Moreover, he claimed, everything connected to *Golden Boy* had been to his credit.

> *Golden Boy* and the return of the Group would not have happened without me. I knew that. I'd prodded Harold and supported him where he was uncertain. I'd pushed Clifford on, which wasn't always easy. As we'd played handball at the Y, I'd eased Julie Garfield's resentments. I'd given our designer, Max Gorelik, ground plans for the physical production and brought young actors into our cast to replace old Group members who were of no use now. I was the vigilante of the production team. As for my performance [as a gangster in the original Broadway production], everything written about it had been praise of the highest order.[5]

Cobb had his compensations. Following the end of the *Golden Boy* tour, which included a week at the National Theater in Washington, he was cast in the showiest role in the Group's production of Shaw's *The Gentle People: A Brooklyn Fable*. As was becoming habit, Clurman again went after Hollywood names, this time bringing back Tone, reaching into the Adler household for Sidney, and adding Sam Jaffe, then being celebrated for his role in the Ronald Colman fantasy *Lost Horizon*. Since Tone was also putting up money for the show, company gripes were muted, especially when the prospect of so many Hollywood names encouraged unprecedented advance ticket sales. The only thing missing was a good play.

*The Gentle People* tells the bleak tale of an aging Coney Island tailor and a short-order cook (Jaffe and Bohnen) who think about nothing but using their savings for one day retiring and spending their remaining days fishing. Their dreams come to an end when a hood (Tone) comes along to bleed them of their money. When the thug also starts playing around with the daughter (Sidney) of one of the men, however, they kill him, and get away with it. According to Shaw and Clurman, the play could have been read as a battle cry for uniting against the Fascism then sweeping Europe. New York critics failed to read it that way. The ones who didn't laugh at such pretentiousness competed with one another in lamenting (sometimes through crocodile tears) what had happened to the Group. As one paper had already warned as soon as the casting had been announced before the opening, "They prefer not to be compared to organizations which depend more on subscribers for financial returns than on commercial plays. . . . Yes, the Group Theatre is on par with Gilbert Miller, Guthrie McClintic, or Sam H. Harris and just as commercial."[6]

By and large the reviews were brutal. The *Post* was almost lenient in yawning at a "very indifferent play."[7] Like others, Richard Lockridge of the *Sun* opened both barrels: "The Group Theatre seldom gets off on the wrong foot, but when it does it is apt to go up to the knee." According to Lockridge, *The Gentle People* was a "singularly inept" piece of work. With one exception. "Lee J. Cobb provides most of the interest of the evening in the entirely unrelated character of a bankrupt in a Turkish bath."[8] The *Post* agreed with Lockridge: "Lee J. Cobb is a joy. He has the lucky role. Mr. Shaw's longer characterizations are not complete enough to enable the actors to do anything with them." So did Atkinson of the *Times*: "[Shaw] has the greatest difficulty in writing a compact, progressive drama that has steady and coherent life in the theater. Long stretches of *The Gentle People* fritter away their time in a vacuum. . . . Only Mr. Cobb is uproariously plausible."[9] Even with the distance of years Clurman would recall most vividly from the play "a sensationally hilarious scene in a Turkish bath in which Lee Cobb as a bankrupt businessman played with a majestic Rabelasian sweep."[10]

*The Gentle People* turned out to be Cobb's penultimate effort for the Group. But before he got to his swan song there were both ends of Hollywood. To his own surprise, he appeared—without pay—in a

twelve-episode Universal serial entitled *The Phantom Creeps* in which
Bela Lugosi did one of his mad scientist routines. Cobb's role was
actually the recycled scenes he had done for *The Vanishing Shadow*
serial five years earlier, and without residuals. At the other end of the
scale was his first A picture, recreating his road company part of Papa
Bonaparte in *Golden Boy* for Columbia. How he was chosen for the
role rather than the original Papa Bonaparte, Carnovsky, has remained
in dispute. One story said that it was because Carnovsky preferred
working on a projected Group production of Chekhov's *Three Sisters*
and was also tired of having to do the caricatured immigrant accents
the role of the boxer's father called for. Another story said that was just
sour grapes from Carnovsky, that the film's director, Rouben Mamoulian, had seen the road company tour and had simply wanted Cobb.

For sure, Mamoulian (*Dr. Jekyll and Mr. Hyde*, *Love Me Tonight*,
*Queen Christina*) was a big step up from the makers of Hopalong
Cassidy westerns and Bela Lugosi serials. Surrounding Cobb in the
cast were Barbara Stanwyck, Adolph Menjou, and, making his screen
debut in the role of Joe Bonaparte, William Holden. Compared to
Kazan, the very WASPy Holden looked physically (if not ethnically)
plausible as the son of the heavily made-up Cobb, being a whole seven
years younger. But that was the least of the production's problems,
for the first few weeks anyway, when the producers sought to jettison
Holden and had to back down against a threat by Stanwyck to keep
him or watch her take a walk. The conflict did nothing for Mamoulian's customarily refined gloss, already at odds with the subject matter
and mostly evident in the further blunting of the remaining ethnic and
class allusions that had survived from the stage.

*Golden Boy* was given a big opening at New York's Radio City
Music Hall on September 15, 1939. Even if it hadn't been the year
often called Hollywood's greatest and hadn't come up against high
expectations, the lukewarm reviews accurately reflected a lukewarm
picture. Stanwyck and Joseph Calleia, in the gangster role originated
on Broadway by Kazan, emerged with most of the praise. Mamoulian
was scolded for being the wrong director, though the *Times* also asserted that the liveliest parts of the film were the "savagely eloquent"
fight scenes that might not normally have been associated with the
maker of *Love Me Tonight*. There wasn't much enthusiasm, either, for
the decision to drop Odets's original ending of killing off Joe Bonaparte
in a car crash for a Hollywood reconciliation among the Holden, Stan-

wyck, and Cobb characters. Cobb's performance within the stylistic mishmash posed more difficulties for critics insofar as the delivery of his character's aching vulnerability had to come through the strainer of an accent not unfairly lambasted as "a surfeit of Chico Marx."[11]

Cobb was aggrieved that his performance had not brought more benevolent critical insight—a reaction typical of a gradually icy attitude toward critics, especially film reviewers. (As he was to tell the *Los Angeles Times* in 1963, one of many such outbursts over his career: "What are critics? Laymen who get paid for pedestrianism.") When he returned to the Group, it was with a firmer belief that theater acting was the only kind worth pursuing. But he also left behind two mementos in Hollywood: his graduation into A-level pictures and an oddly friendly rapport with Columbia head Harry Cohn, known throughout the industry as a scourge of actors, or for that matter of anyone else not charmed by his crude despotism. Again and again over the years, though, the actor would sign on for a Columbia assignment in a voluntary (noncontractual) way few other actors in Hollywood did and in circumstances suggesting that it was the fruit of a special relationship with Cohn. In a September 22, 1940, letter to Beverley, for example, while working at Paramount, he declared, "I called up to say hello to Harry Cohn and he was extremely warm and friendly." It was a relationship that would come under fire some years later.

The play waiting for Cobb back in New York was *Thunder Rock* by Robert Ardrey, author of the disastrous *Casey Jones* and again teamed with Kazan as the director. There was nothing that promised well about the venture, and the promise was kept. In *The Fervent Years* Clurman makes it clear that he gave the green light to the project only for lack of an alternative and despite almost unanimous hostility to it by the actors at an initial reading.[12] More than anything, the play was meant to get the company back on its feet amid a corroding lassitude prompted by events of both theatrical and political kinds. The theatrical blow had come with the failure—after extensive rehearsals—to get *Three Sisters* on the stage, an enfeebling reminder that the company didn't seem equipped to deal with classic drama. The political trauma had been with the August nonaggression pact between Nazi Germany and the Soviet Union, completely disorienting the Group's Communist members and leaving them teetering between the generic and the apologetic in the ideological positions they took on the scripts submitted to them. The one-two blow had reduced self-confidence to near zero, and it didn't rise any higher with a spate of personal and marital conflicts. Clurman's insistence on doing *Thunder Rock* over all the objections did not extend, however, to taking it on as a director, and thus he handed it off to Kazan. Although he accepted the assignment, Kazan did so without a smile. He devoted a mere paragraph to *Thunder Rock* in his 848-page autobiography, and mainly to acknowledge that not only he but the urban-bred Group as a whole had been the wrong people to tackle what he defined as Ardrey's Midwest sensibility.[13]

The play is set in a Lake Michigan lighthouse where a terminally disenchanted journalist (Adler), a veteran of the Spanish civil war, has isolated himself as the keeper in despair at the state of the world. He ultimately gains more hope for mankind (or Ardrey says he does) after being visited by the ghosts of immigrant passengers who sank aboard a nineteenth-century ship headed for America. In a gray-flecked beard and toupee and exchanging the excitable Italian English of Papa Bonaparte for the Middle European gutturals of an Austrian named Dr. Kurtz, Cobb played the most ambiguous ghost—a scientist who had to flee his homeland after conducting illegal experiments on humans. Kurtz wasn't the only one who wanted to take flight. The female lead Farmer was only too aware that, merely two years younger than Cobb, she had been miscast as his daughter and even more aware of the end of an affair she had been having with Odets, so she took to the bottle as soon as rehearsals began. Adler, who had never liked the play, received the first bad notices of his Group career and blasted Clurman for talking him into taking the leading role. And most critics were impatient with the lugubrious dialogue exchanges that passed for stage action. One reviewer even went after the special effects, saying they "belong in tank-town drama.[14] Despite appeals from literary friends of Ardrey, the play closed after twenty-three performances.

But what was to mark *Thunder Rock* more than anything was the curtain speech by the spiritually revived lighthouse keeper calling for the United States to stay out of the war that had erupted in Europe and to concentrate on improving its democracy at home. For a few months anyway, it was a speech suitable for all sizes—for the isolationists who wanted no part of opposing Nazi Germany on the battlefield, for the Communists who toed the party line after the nonaggression pact, and for the idealists who wanted to believe peace with Hitler could be secured peacefully. But the gossamer nature of that appeal—and its malleability for being rewritten into just the opposite—became increasingly obvious with developments on the war front and the approach of the United States' entrance into the conflict. When the play reached England a short time later, the finale had become a stirring call for human hope and very concrete military action against the Nazis. It was considered such potent propaganda fare by the British that, by moving from one bombed out theater to another, *Thunder Rock* was the only play in London that kept pace with the Blitz until the end of the war.[15]

But by that time, the Group Theatre no longer existed, a successor company was thriving in Los Angeles with Cobb's participation, and he had played all manner of Papa Bonapartes and Dr. Kurtzes. Although he never went into particulars, he would admit more than once over ensuing years that his final months with the Group were unhappy ones. On at least one occasion, fellow members accused him of being more interested in a car he had bought for himself than in company business. Asked about this period by Patricia Bosworth in 1968, he attributed his gradual withdrawal from the company to "a general pattern of acquiescence by members" to whatever Clurman and the other major figures on the administrative committee wanted.[16] As it turned out, Clurman was one of many with whom he would work again outside the confines of the Group.

## Notes

1. According to Julie Cobb, the widespread spelling of her mother's name as *Beverly* is wrong, that her mother always spelled it with the extra *e*.

2. Her mother, Anna Green, was from Poland.

3. J. Hoberman, *Bridge of Light: Yiddish Film between Two Worlds* (New York: The Museum of Modern Art/Schocken Books, 1991), p. 251.

4. Ibid., p. 304.

5. Elia Kazan, *Elia Kazan: A Life* (New York: Alfred A. Knopf, 1988), p. 164.

6. *Journal of Commerce*, December 19, 1938.

7. *Post* (New York), January 6, 1939.

8. *Sun* (New York), January 6, 1939.

9. *New York Times*, January 6, 1939.

10. Clurman, *Fervent Years*, p. 240. Warner Brothers did a film based on the play some years later. Entitled *Out of the Fog* and starring John Garfield and Ida Lupino, it did not let the killers get off at the end.

11. *New York Times*, September 16, 1939.

12. Clurman, *Fervent Years*, p. 299.

13. Kazan, *Elia Kazan*, p. 182.

14. *New York World-Telegram*, November 18, 1939.

15. The British also made a wartime film of the story with Michael Redgrave, James Mason, and Lili Palmer.

16. *New York Times*, November 17, 1968.

# Chapter 8

# The Actor:
# All in the Family

IN AN ARTICLE WRITTEN for the *New York Times* a few days before the New York opening of his *Thunder Rock*, playwright Robert Ardrey confessed to finding himself in an intimidating theatrical situation:

> They give you what amounts to temporary membership in the Group Theatre. You have all the innocence of a bystander on the Maginot Line. If somebody in the company gets a divorce, you discover yourself on the witness stand. If the switchboard girl has a baby, you find yourself in labor pains.
> The light man has a brainstorm. He floods the stage with evil red light. You run shrieking to the director. Go talk to the light man, says he. So you wring the light man's neck, personally. An actor discovers a bad line in his part. Do you find out about it, in nicely tempered tones, from the director? No, in the midst of rehearsal the actor speaks the line, comes to a halt, looks about, "Where's the author? Ardrey, this line stinks." You find yourself with the business manager, worrying about the budget. You find yourself with the publicity man, worrying about the press release. You share [Max] Gorelik's headaches while he works over the model of the set, trying to find room in the base of a lighthouse for half a dozen vital Group actors to express their vitality. And while you're biting your fingernails . . . you're confronted by Morris Carnovsky. For ten minutes, says Morris, I sit over there on the left without anything to say. What am I supposed to be thinking about? So you go to bed at night—if you go to bed at all—worrying not about Carnovsky's lines, but about his thoughts. . . .
> A regular Broadway production finds the author on the outside,

looking in. A Group Theatre production finds the author on the inside, looking cross-eyed.[1]

In those few sentences Ardrey illustrated both the strengths that kept the Group going through twenty-four productions in the 1930s and the constitutional weaknesses that finally caused the company to collapse for good after its December 1940 presentation of Irwin Shaw's *Retreat to Pleasure*. Group relationships were not just theatrical and political, but deeply personal, to a neurotically familial degree. And until it became irreparably disabling, for as long as crisis accelerated clarity, that wasn't all bad. Repeatedly, the dysfunctional triggered as much energy for the company as a whole as it wounded individuals in this or that dispute. Personal grievance was acceptable collateral damage. No matter how bitter a conflict, somebody invariably emerged more persuasive (if not always right), and that meant being able to raise another curtain. The organism described by Ardrey had little to do with the isolated images of the actor as the waitress reciting the day's specials, as the cab driver asking if he should take the bridge or the tunnel, or as the starlet waiting at a drug store counter to be discovered. Even when the jealousies, ambitions, and mediocre plays of the moment reduced it to paper-thin principle, *Group* meant *group*—the single aspiration not only vain without a collective accomplishment, but unworthy for being contemplated. Most of its members might have been thirtyish Jews, but Jews with the consciences of Catholic teenagers alert to falling into sin. Clurman went further. As far as he was concerned, the Group was no mere theatrical organization operating within the Mecca of American theater; it was a universe unto itself:

> The desire for some center around which one might build a complete life was basic, and almost all the people in and around the Group clamored for it ever more insistently. . . .There was something in the Group's attitude that made its members and even many outside its ranks feel it could be, should be, the focus of a world of activity that would make great actors of some, writers of others, directors, designers, teachers, organizers, producers, administrators, or a combination of several of these things of the rest. The Group's inclusive philosophy adumbrated a cosmos; therefore the Group's function, even its duty, was to become a cosmos.[2]

Clurman's "inclusive philosophy" was much flightier than even the "new world" Waldo Frank had foreseen with the Group, and nobody knew that more than he did. That same inclusive philosophy tantalized him to exasperation when he couldn't persuade the company's most reliable financial backers to subsidize the Group as an institution rather than just the play at hand. That thorn pricked throughout the company's existence, drawing even more blood after successes like *Men in White* and *Golden Boy* than after failures; if not now, when? Achievement seemed to usher in only frustration. The actors (and directors and designers and others) needed concrete financial endorsement for the totality of their undertaking, and they needed it from those from whom they wanted to be sealed off so as to be able to define themselves yet more organically.

If that was a contradiction, it was a very material one. With a daily practical resonance. The Group wasn't the Moscow Art Theatre: there were no rules about the actors living collectively while a production was being mounted, no dangers from a revolution in the streets or from a government suppression (that would come later, in official Washington attempts to rewrite history). Aside from instances where members shared an apartment to save on rent, the conditions were lacking for hermetic concentration on theatrical activities. Groceries had to be bought on avenue stores from the small checks doled out. Restaurants were windows to be passed because what was behind them was too expensive. Every corner newsstand in the 1930s was a reminder that there were no artistic insulations but also that for the American actor political commitment had to be very willful, an act of conscience more than an emergency scramble for physical survival. Was the conscience up for it over the long haul? Was criminal world catastrophe the only alternative to daily self-reassurance of being insightful and progressive? Where were the parameters for the noble and the humanitarian but stubbornly remote and abstract?

Rival, even shamelessly mundane, obligations always seemed to press in. For instance from married couples that, according to Clurman, were the source of some of the Group's worst conflicts: "I know of at least four cases where 'Group wives' spoke of the Group as they might of a correspondent in a divorce case. The greater the faith the man had in the Group, the more virulent became the wife's attack on it."[3] Any new cosmos would be very much a mise en abyme part of a dreadfully larger one—hypocritical, commercial, fascistic—already existing.

Accepting that could be scarring. With all the pronouncements of Clurman, Strasberg, Odets, and others about the nature of the Group and with all the criticisms of the Adlers, Carnovskys, Kazans, and the founders themselves about how that nature had been betrayed on given occasions, the company's professional reality was an emotional and intellectual labyrinth of expectations and disillusionments that would mark the entire careers of those who had journeyed through it. In their post-Group work both on the stage and in film, it was the rare Group veteran who didn't gain a reputation as "difficult." No matter how artfully produced, directed, and acted, he would never confuse any of his subsequent projects with a yearned for cosmos. Cobb could tell an interviewer thirty-seven years after the Group that "I've made 58 movies and I hate every one of them. All those films—and I don't remember one with any special fondness or satisfaction."[4] (Of course, being difficult also sometimes meant being difficult with interviewers, especially those who projected contentment with their own lines of work.)

But what about where it mattered most, in the dynamic between performance and audience? Did the Group produce more affecting actors, really generate more of an alerted response in the orchestra and balcony, than other companies on Broadway, in Chicago, or in Dallas? It certainly had more than one testimonial to that effect, especially from critics who, in stark contrast to the potential financial backers Clurman was always hunting, indulged the *idea* of the Group while warning of the deficiencies in its single productions. More generally, to what extent has the Group's impact been romanticized or its polemical history reinforced by the theatrically fabled names at its core and by the political persecutions that followed years after its disbandment?

Of all the hallmarks of a Group performance, whether wet-nursed by Strasberg, Clurman, or Stella Adler, the most characteristic was its meticulous exploration. It was an actor's world, and even Odets, the playwright who brought it its most enduring fame with *Waiting for Lefty*, *Awake and Sing*, *Paradise Lost*, and *Golden Boy*, had started off as an actor for the company. Most obviously, there was the exploration called for by Stanislavsky into character—relating to it psychologically, questioning its development in the script logically, and delivering it physically. But there was also the exploration involved with co-players whose psychological bents, intellectual prejudices, and physical tells became as familiar as one's own, creating the premises for broader instincts. Sometimes that was to the good, sometimes that was to the lazy, but that's also why there were rehearsals so that familiarity didn't breed merely more familiarity. It was also why there was a closed shop mentality in a reluctance to accept newcomers and, most markedly in the second half of the company's existence with the reach for Hollywood figures, why productions impressed despite all their individual ingredients rather than because of them. The fever of a Strasberg to curb outside influences in *Johnny Johnson* was really the flip side of the coin from the already beaten down Clurman and Kazan going through the motions of staging *Thunder Rock* with Adler, Carnovsky, and key performers from better days.

In one sense, the warm reception accorded *Golden Boy* in London was an anomaly, a foreign experience for those with other theater traditions. Much as Americans were startled by the early century visits of the Moscow Art Theatre, the British audiences were stunned by the integration of the smallest bits of business in a deliberately detailed whole, significant moments given due dramatic weight but never to the point of trivializing absolutely anything that took place on the stage. That had been the expectation of American audiences where the Group was concerned for years, down to the democratic casting and alphabetical billing that would have seen an Adler as protagonist in one play and a glorified extra in the next one. The collegiality of the productions was visible to anyone who ever saw more than one of them, and there was no outcry to the heavens for the disrespect shown for the star system then being promoted by Broadway and Hollywood.

At least until a quick fix seemed like the solution for the financial problems that had been afflicting the company since its birth.

The Group might not have realized the cosmos spoken of by Clurman or even animated the kind of world invoked by Frank, but it did create a realm of volatile emotions, intellectual prejudices, and aesthetic tastes that its members would continue to age with professionally, psychologically, and politically for years to come.

## NOTES

1. *New York Times*, November 9, 1939.
2. Clurman, *Fervent Years*, p. 211.
3. Ibid., p. 221. From his other writings, the author appeared to be referring to some combination of the Hollywood Three (Joan Crawford, Luise Rainer, and Sylvia Sidney), John Garfield's wife Roberta, and Molly Thatcher Kazan.
4. Pickard, "The Self-Preservation Gene," p. 525.

# Chapter 9

━━━━━━━━━━━━━━━━━━━━━━━━━━○━━━━━━━━━━━━━━━━━━━━━━━━━━

# Clashes in the East

APART FROM DOROTHY PATTEN, who had recovered from her nervous breakdown in Hollywood, there weren't many familiar names still around when Clurman directed the Group's final production of *Retreat to Pleasure* in December 1940. The only other company play during the calendar year had been back in February, when Carnovsky, Kazan, and Jane Wyatt had appeared in Odets's *Night Music*. In the meantime, the Group's stalwarts had been off looking for work elsewhere, picking up the odd dollar doing radio dramas. Cobb's first big opportunity after the company came with a play that, at first glance anyway, didn't seem so far removed from Group concerns; it also led to some very quick reunions.

Based on an Ernest Hemingway short story, the March 1940 production of *The Fifth Column* was set in Spain during the civil war that had reached its bloody end with the victory of Generalissimo Francisco Franco a few months earlier. Produced by the Theatre Guild, it was directed by Strasberg and starred Tone in the role of a dissolute American war correspondent who describes himself at one juncture as "a second-rate cop pretending to be a third-rate newspaperman." Up to the last minute the cast was also supposed to have included Group veteran Frances Farmer, but she withdrew amid mounting personal problems for Katherine Locke. Cobb's accent this time was of the Teutonic variety, as a German villager named Max who hates the Nazis. One problem with the play, pointed out by several critics, was that it was indeed only *based* on the Hemingway tale. The credited adapter

Benjamin Glazer, a producer-screenwriter whose résumé included the first screen version of Hemingway's *A Farewell to Arms*, decided too much of the original material would be disturbing, if not to audiences or to the Theatre Guild then to him personally. Thus Hemingway's explicit references to loyalist characters as Communists were dropped; instead of comrades, they became amigos. Worse was the treatment of the principal woman in the story, a not-too-veiled representation of future Hemingway wife and fellow correspondent Martha Gellhorn (Locke). Not liking the fact that she was portrayed as sleeping around a lot, Glazer came to the conclusion that she was a nymphomaniac and, in the interests of making her more sympathetic, had the journalist rape her!

Although locked in by a contract that forced him to allow Glazer to proceed, Hemingway made sure that all his drinking companions knew he had disassociated himself from the play. As in the cases of numerous screen adaptations of his work, the novelist ended up counting his money while critics voiced indignation at how he had been abused. The most positive review came from Brooks Atkinson, who called the play "stirring" and lauded Tone, Cobb, and the rest of the cast,[1] but his was a minority opinion. With the names of Hemingway and Tone to help it along, the play nevertheless ran for almost three months and had nurtured plans for a national tour until the leading man bought out his contract and returned to Hollywood.

Cobb's sensitivity to critics judging his work provided a personal footnote to *The Fifth Column* when Alvah Bessie, then a critic for *New Masses* magazine, praised his performance, declaring in part, "With such material into which to get his teeth, and with his own great gifts, young Mr. Cobb was able to achieve a performance that is pure, stunning, dignified, and heartbreaking." To Bessie's astonishment, Cobb wrote to him in response to the review and asked to get together. "[He] said in effect that he would like to meet me because I was the only critic who had ever properly evaluated what he was trying to do. Call it a mutual admiration society if you will, but Lee . . . became one of my latter-day heroes."[2]

Noteworthy about Bessie's complimentary review—and Cobb's response to it—was that it was totally indicative, the writer not proposing *why* the performance might have been "stunning, dignified, and heartbreaking" and not even hinting at what exactly the actor claimed he had been trying to do. That was a line Cobb would make clear in later years he expected critics, professional or otherwise, not to cross. In the meantime, for once Cobb was on the other side of the age differential insofar as Bessie, seven years older, was as much of a disciple as he would ever have—a relationship that would even extend to allowing the future screenwriter to pilot his plane.

While Cobb was doing *The Fifth Column*, Beverley was only a few theaters away as a replacement for Uta Hagen opposite Paul Muni, he of Benjamin's note of introduction, in the final New York performances of Maxwell Anderson's blank verse *Key Largo*. It was her second effort to break out of Yiddish show business and far more successful than her first. That had been the previous year with a grotesque item called *Clean Beds*, about two seedy flophouse keepers attempting to sell her innocent character into white slavery. Ridiculed in and out of the press as "The Lowest Depths," *Clean Beds* claimed the fictitiously named George S. George as its author amid rumors that whoever he was, he had bought a treatment of the script from Mae West. (There was never any concrete evidence that George S. George was in fact West herself.) Directed by sometime-critic, one-time John Barrymore associate, and Russian actor Vadim Uraneff, the play lasted only four performances. With *Key Largo*, on the other hand, Beverley was back to material and with actors well known to her husband. Unlike the heroically romantic Humphrey Bogart–Edward G. Robinson film made some years later, the Anderson play revolves around a cowardly veteran of the Spanish civil war who redeems himself by taking on a band of gangsters, getting himself killed in the process. Others in the cast included Group members Malden and Challee.

After getting her feet wet with the Broadway performances, Beverley did the national tour of *Key Largo* with Muni.[3] But if it was a break for her professionally, it brought strains to her marriage, some of them so severe that her correspondence with Cobb for many weeks flitted around the idea of a divorce. Though there were references to problems with her parents, the main issue appeared to be their separation for her work. At every stop made by the *Key Largo* company, from Chicago and St. Louis out to the West Coast, there was a passionate letter waiting for Beverley from New York. In January 1941, for instance, he wrote her in Los Angeles:

> What kind of poisonous insanity possesses us—what insanity that imposes such a contortion of sobriety and logic in our behavior toward each other? Are we to believe what we are saying to each other?

Do I really want to believe you? Do you really believe that we had better part? Do you get any satisfaction or peace from the pat conclusion "we don't love each other, evidently?" I don't. That phrase is no solution or comfort to me. It doesn't explain matters to me. Who says that is a liar! So please, in the name of truth, of love, of tender goodness, let's stop talking that way. . . . Stripped of all those constricting garments of rationalization and "objectivity," it's impossible to deny or even distort the blinding, shining, beautiful, all-penetrating truth. I love you. I love you. And you love me.

The letters had their effect, and the couple remained married. While in Los Angeles, Beverley received several offers from movie studios but turned them all down with the hope of working on Broadway with her husband. That would come to pass, but only after Cobb had done another play that would haunt him in various ways for years.

The piece was Odets's *Clash by Night*, which the playwright initially extended to the Group with a projected cast of Cobb, Luther Adler, and Sylvia Sidney. But the Group was in no position to produce it as quickly as Odets wanted, and he didn't wait too long to take it to producer Billy Rose. Adler and Sidney fell by the wayside with annoyance at how Clurman had handled the negotiations, but Cobb's own displeasure with the Group in his final months eased his decision to stay with the project. *Clash by Night* was a love triangle melodrama about a Staten Island movie projectionist who carries on an affair with the depressed wife of a carpenter; Clurman saw a political layer to the play that not many others did. Admitting he had only read the script and never actually seen it performed, he pronounced that "Odets's feeling seemed to be weighed down here by the sense of a working class that was basically homeless, racked with inner tension, ignorant, baffled, pathetic, and dangerously close to that breaking point of 'mystic' hysteria and violence that often provides the spiritual soil for the seeds of fascism."[4] That was as close to a political commentary as Odets would instigate with the play.

What he instigated instead was a nightly free-for-all among cast members. After the sore feelings generated with Adler and Sidney, Odets teased further trouble by then offering the lead role of Mae Wilenski to Farmer, whom he had brutally sent packing a couple of years before for fear his still-wife Rainer would find out about their affair; she had been falling deeply into depression and alcoholism ever since. Farmer said no, and not because of the play. He had better luck offering the role of the projectionist Earl, what had been promised to

Adler, to Joseph Schildkraut. As the big-hearted carpenter Jerry Wilenski, Cobb once again found himself directed by Strasberg, even though he would later acknowledge that was not his ideal comfort zone. As his son Vincent recalled, "Dad used to show what he thought of Strasberg by scratching an itch on his ear by throwing his opposite arm over his head to do it. He felt that if there was a more complicated or difficult way to do *anything*, Strasberg would find it."

If Strasberg was less than a comfort zone for the actor, his unquestioned discomfort zone was mapped out by Tallulah Bankhead in the role of Mae. Cobb had seen it coming, too. While fitting in some movie work in California before rehearsals had even begun on *Clash by Night*, he wrote to Beverley in New York on August 28, 1941: "Joseph Schildkraut called me yesterday. He said he got a wire from New York to borrow my script. It seems they're interested in him for Earl! Now that is utterly inconceivable to me. Schildkraut is *so* wrong for the part. He even has an accent. I don't know what the hell they're thinking in New York. What an unfortunate cast—Tallulah Bankhead, Schildkraut, Cobb. Each, individually, o.k. But together in *this* play? For *these* parts? Ruinous!!!"

He didn't have to wait long before being proven right. Not long removed from her Broadway triumph in Lillian Hellman's *The Little Foxes*, the assertive Bankhead had little tolerance for what she deemed Cobb's attempts to dominate the stage by taking his time pulling Odets's dialogue out of his Method introspection; she was given to spitting out "Group Theatre actors!" as a curse requiring no further explanation. When she found him particularly irritating, she made sure to drift upstage center so the audience's eyes would remain with her until he finally disgorged whatever his lines were supposed to be. As flagrant as her tactics were, she wasn't alone in her criticism of Cobb. However unnecessarily contorted Cobb might have found some of Strasberg's direction, it was the director who leveled that accusation against the actor during *Clash by Night*, being quoted as telling him during one out-of-town performance prior to Broadway, "If you're going to make a sandwich, put it together. You put the bread here, and then you put all the ingredients over here and then you put another piece of bread down, but you never put it together. If you're going to do that, do it, don't wait forever. The audience has seen what you're going to eat."[5]

And that was only one front. Another hub of conflict was Bankhead and the second female lead Katherine Locke, with whom Cobb and Strasberg had worked in *The Fifth Column*. A native of Belorussia who had gained Broadway visibility by appearing with John Garfield in the box office success *Having Wonderful Time*, Locke never disguised her feeling that she should have been playing the Bankhead part. Bankhead got the message and made sure Locke didn't look forward to the curtain going up any more than Cobb did. The breaking point came when the star admitted that she dreaded a moment in the play where she was supposed to sing "The Sheik of Araby." Acknowledging how flat she sounded, she took a tip from Locke, who had a musical background, to lower her pitch and not try to be an opera diva.

The remedy proved to be worse than the disease. Bankhead became so confident of her singing that she kept it going several evenings, right through Cobb's cues. Finally, one night he improvised a "Shut up, Mae!" so he could get to what he was supposed to say. Bankhead's furious scolding of the actor as the two of them exited the stage brought Locke back to upbraid her for being so "unprofessional" to Cobb. From that point on it was war between the women on the stage. Bankhead went so far as to ignore rehearsed blocking so she could get closer to Locke and, out of sight of the orchestra, start yanking at the younger woman's hair.[6] To complete the round-robin, she decided her on-stage paramour Schildkraut was a "creep" and a "bore"—the former because he treated his wife as a servant, the latter because he wanted to have the same relationship with Tallulah as he had with Mae.

This farcical run-up to the play's Broadway opening on December 27 portended every kind of disaster, and Bankhead's newspaper columnist friends threw a few logs on that fire by reporting her suffering at the hands of Cobb and Locke. In addition, the angst of the depressed wife of a Staten Island carpenter didn't seem like the most urgent of themes in browned out Times Square with the country's transition to a war footing under way following the Japanese attack on Pearl Harbor. But against all expectations, and probably reflecting at least in part the relief of those who didn't want to have to debate the political ramifications of an Odets work, critics were more positive than negative, give or take a wink at Bankhead cast as a blue-collar housewife. One typical review said, "There isn't a person writing for our stage today who can speak more pungently, with a hard brilliance which conceals tenderness, honest rage, and a cold loathing of the poverty of the world and the maladjustment of wealth which causes it. This is exciting theater, if somewhat overwritten and, as acted by Miss Bankhead, Mr. Schildkraut, and Mr. Cobb, is unquestionably the most interesting play in town, bar none."[7]

John Mason Brown thought a lot of that was due to Cobb's performance: "He is a great ox of a man, this husband that Lee J. Cobb
acts with wonderful skill; a sort of grownup Lennie from *Of Mice and
Men* who has ceased to be a cause of terror to either maids or mice,
and finally won his rabbit farm. It is this dumb brute of a husband who
forces upon his bored wife the acquaintanceship of a friend."[8]

For all that, though, *Clash by Night* could never quite overcome
its box office blues, and closed after forty-nine performances. As soon
as the final curtain came down, both Bankhead and Locke checked
themselves into hospitals for a rest.

A decade later, Cobb would have one more reason not to remember *Clash by Night* fondly. But in 1942 he had at least come away with
his first major stage credit as something other than an ethnic stereotype. He also quickly learned—to his benefit—that *Clash by Night*
wasn't the only Broadway production with problems.

Around the same time that Cobb was telling Bankhead to shut up
her singing, writer-director Samson Raphaelson was looking in vain
for a little music from his leading players in the comedy *Jason*. An
intended satire on the Broadway scene, *Jason* starred the Canadian
Alexander Knox as a theater critic who fears losing his wife (Helen
Walker) to an egocentric playwright (Richard[9] Conte). A glaring draw-
back to the play, aggravated by the fact that reviewers in the audience
were supposed to be watching a representative of their ranks up on
the stage, was the bloodless performance of Knox, leaving little reason
for the wife character *not* to be seduced by the playwright. Buoyed by
the respect shown the comedy in general and by the praise for Conte
and for a ditzy turn by E. G. Marshall, Raphaelson decided to replace
his lead. His first solution was George Macready, but when that didn't
make much of a difference on stage, he turned to Cobb. The change
brought needed air offstage as much as onstage. In contrast to the
reserved Knox and elusive Macready, Cobb was reported by the press
as taking every opportunity to entertain Conte and Marshall (with both
of whom he would work frequently in the future) with his harmonica
playing. If the actor wasn't relieved to be playing a big role without
recourse to his library of accents, he certainly acted as though he was.
More important, some of the critics who had panned the void at the
heart of *Jason* revised their thinking with the substitution. They were
even more enthusiastic after Walker left the play for Hollywood and

was replaced by Beverley. The most radical about-face came from Wilella Waldorf, the only woman critic then working the aisles:

It was evident when the curtain had been up a mere ten minutes . . . that the Cobbs were giving *Jason* a vivid sense of reality and a warm human quality that it lacked at its opening. . . . We were in fact constantly amazed at Mr. Cobb's uncanny ability to rationalize most of the originally exasperating and unbelievable scenes. . . . Where Mr. Knox made the critic a stiffish, cold, effete, often obnoxious prig, Mr. Cobb brings strength, virility, humor, warmth, and an engaging charm to the part. Miss Beverley, playing with sympathy and understanding in the difficult wife's role, manages to resolve most of the irritating deficiencies in the development of this character, and together the Cobbs put a good deal of unspoken feeling into the scenes between the husband and the wife. . . . They do the play the service of making it at once more intelligible and more appealing to theatergoers who do not happen to be profoundly interested either in dramatic critics or eccentric playwrights.[10]

Beverley had to leave *Jason* because of illness in May, and it limped toward the summer before ending its run. But it was to remain the only occasion when she and Cobb worked together on Broadway. When they did costar again, it would be out west in Hollywood, but not for the movies.

## NOTES

1. *New York Times*, March 17, 1940.
2. Bessie, *Inquisition in Eden*, p. 219.
3. In his book *Actor: The Life and Times of Paul Muni* (New York: G.P. Putnam's Sons, 1974, p. 258), Jerome Lawrence said that Uta Hagen and her husband Jose Ferrer worked overtime, even during performances of the play, to make her pregnant so she wouldn't have to do the national tour.
4. Clurman, *Fervent Years*, p. 279.
5. Joel Lobenthal, *Tallulah: The Life and Times of a Leading Lady* (New York: Harper Entertainment, 2008), p. 336.
6. Ibid., pp. 338–339.
7. *Morning Telegraph* (New York), December 28, 1941.
8. *Saturday Review*, December 27, 1941.
9. At the time the future film actor used his birth name of Nicholas.
10. *Post* (New York), March 16, 1942.

# Chapter 10

———————◯———————

# Clashes in the West

ONCE OUT FROM UNDER HIS contractual obligations to Wanger and thanks to the attention he had drawn for his age versatility with *Golden Boy*, Cobb found himself a desirable free agent on the Hollywood market. To take advantage of it, he and Beverley moved to Los Angeles shortly after the closing of *Jason*. But even before then, around *The Fifth Column* and *Clash by Night*, he had made three pictures for three different studios. The first, for Columbia, had him back as an ethnic stereotype called Julio in the Rosalind Russell–Melvyn Douglas comedy *This Thing Called Love*, which mostly caused comment for being condemned by the Catholic Legion of Decency and for being banned outright in Ireland and Australia. The objections came over the picture's premise—the insistence of a new bride that she and her husband remain celibate for three months to demonstrate that there was more to a solid marriage than sex. Cobb's character was a Latin (specified as Peruvian for no particular reason) burdened by a herd of children, not exactly what the Catholic Church had in mind for the sanctity of procreation.

With MGM he then appeared with Spencer Tracy and Mickey Rooney in a let's-put-on-a-reformatory sequel to *Boys Town*, *Men of Boys Town*. Most reviews of his performance as a pawnbroker friend of Father Flanagan stalled at the particular that he was about the only cast member from the original Oscar winner (for Tracy) not to be repeating his role. The best of the three pictures was Universal's *Paris Calling*, the first of several World War II dramas Cobb would make

90

over the next few years. Here he was back to his Teuton accent as a Nazi general trying to uproot the French Underground. The picture's propaganda aims were only mildly thwarted by his getting most of the good reviews for delivering the cast's most complex performance. What *Paris Calling* also underlined was that he was becoming Hollywood's go-to actor for a wide range of foreign characters, caricatures or otherwise. Whereas a J. Carrol Naish would be saved for an Italian stereotype and a John Qualen for one from Scandinavia, Cobb was increasingly deemed right for most of the map of Europe. (He would widen the map to the Middle East and the Far East in the years to come.) As on the stage, the characters that didn't give him distance in age gave it to him in ethnicity.

But there was more to Cobb's sojourn in Hollywood in the early 1940s than movies. Since the disintegration of the Group, there had been a couple of attempts by members to re-form in another company. The most promising try seemed to be the Dollar Top in New York, where Kazan and Lewis collected commitments of scripts from Shaw and old Cobb associate Victor Wolfson for carrying on the Stanislavsky theatrical approach. But they didn't collect funding as easily, and the initiative failed before any production could be mounted. Far more successful was the Actors Laboratory in Los Angeles, launched by Bohnen, Carnovsky, Bromberg, and other Group players who had moved west for film work. Named after the Richard Boleslavsky school in New York, the Lab was both more cautious and more ambitious than the Group as the first important center for spreading the Stanislavsky gospel in California.[1]

The caution was in the decision to start off as a school and a workshop rather than as a producing company. Since it was the actors themselves who were financing things with their earnings from movie jobs, there was no thought of adopting the Group system of issuing weekly checks to members. Unlike the older company, as well, there was far more interest in working on Shakespeare, Chekhov, O'Casey, and other dramatists from the theatrical canon. Yet another departure from the Group, at least in the beginning, was what amounted to a structure of parallel cell companies in which actors seeking to stretch themselves as directors stuck to preferred circles, accounting for the sameness in the casts of, say, Carnovsky or Bromberg projects.

But success eroded this kind of informal organization. With Bohnen emerging as the chief administrative figure and the most

trusted referee between the sometimes-conflicting priorities of other
board members, the Lab expanded in several directions at once during
the war. Even more rapidly than had been the case in New York twenty
years earlier, word of the Stanislavsky Method spread throughout the
company town, and actors began flocking to a loft on Franklin Avenue
to pay $12.50 a month as members to hear more.[2] Screen veterans
such as Charles Laughton and Anthony Quinn volunteered to hold
classes and/or direct workshops, and after a while just about every big
name in Hollywood had dropped by to audit a class or two or to attend
evenings in which a bill of one-acters was presented for invited guests.
Eventually, 20th Century-Fox and Universal International signed
agreements financing the Lab's instruction of such contract players as
Jean Peters and Audie Murphy. It was at that point that the theater,
headed by members who had once scoffed at the very idea, also began
stepping up teaching the specifics of film acting, inviting Garfield and
others (among them, Alexander Knox, whom Cobb had replaced in
*Jason*) with experience in both media to lecture on the differences.
To aid the war effort, Lab companies brought shows to army bases,
military hospitals, and even overseas under the auspices of the USO
(United Service Organizations). This work would make it easier down
the road for the company to be accredited as a legitimate study venue
under the GI Bill for returning servicemen who wanted to get into the
theater in some capacity.

    Theatrically, the Lab had two principal phases, and amid film
assignments and other obligations Cobb figured in both of them, although not as conspicuously as Bohnen and others would have liked.
Invited to become a member of the board of directors, he begged off
with the excuse of having too many outside commitments. The real
reason, he intimated to friends, was that he didn't like the Lab's system of so many parallel workshops, viewing it as the kind of unfocused
activity that would prevent coherent productions from ever being
mounted. But though not a formal member, he did agree to conduct
one teaching class for a few months and to take to the stage. The Lab's
first phase, which lasted more or less through the war, consisted of
the workshop and one-act programs for fellow performers and media
industry people. It was in this setting that Carnovsky, for instance, was
able to delve into the Shakespeare tragedies that would dominate the
latter part of his career. It was also within this format that a playwright
like Tennessee Williams got to air out his stagecraft and that a direc-

tor like Jules Dassin, Cobb's fellow Bronx native, gathered the nucleus of actors he became identified with in the pictures he made after the war. Other names settling in included director Daniel Mann, actor Lloyd Bridges, Cobb's *Clash by Night* costar Schildkraut, and future producer Joe Papp. Then there was the actor couple Betty Garrett and Larry Parks, the latter of whom would have a devastating influence on Cobb's career in the 1950s.

In the Lab's first phase, Cobb's specialty was an Anton Chekhov monologue entitled *The Evils of Tobacco*. Sometimes referred to as one of the Russian writer's "vaudevilles," *The Evils of Tobacco* posits a henpecked husband named Nyukhin lecturing citizens in a town hall about why they should abstain from smoking. But Nyukhin himself smokes whenever his wife isn't around, so he ends up talking more about why she forced him to give the talk than about tobacco. The piece allowed Cobb to run the gamut from the comic to the pathetic to the stentorian, and he performed it more than once to appreciative audiences. One of the only responses to one of his performances found among his papers was an undated letter from Dudley Nichols after a turn as Nyukhin at the Lab. Nichols, long-time collaborator with John Ford and screenwriter of (among others) *The Informer* and *Bringing Up Baby*, asserted in part, "I must confess I never knew what lay inside those lines until you unfolded it last night. Such work is not recreative; it raises the actor to the level of Chekhov himself, as if one heard a Beethoven sonata being composed or watched Cezanne painting a canvas. You raise the hopes and faith of all who love the Theatre and dramatic composition when you create such a magnificent piece of work. I bow to you, sir."

On the same bill as *The Evils of Tobacco*, Cobb had the director's credit for a Sean O'Casey sketch, *A Pound on Demand*, in which Bohnen and Hume Cronyn played tipsy Irishmen trying to get their signature on a postal order so they could finance further drinking. It was due to such one-acters that *Daily Variety* saluted the whole Lab enterprise by declaring, "The Actors Laboratory presentation of one-act plays . . . is the sort of thing that makes the average legit follower rub his hands with glee and run out to tell all his friends they should buy tickets."[3]

The Chekhov monologue also aligned Cobb with Bohnen in the belief that in the right circumstances such a form could be even more effective than the Method in marrying an actor to character. ("The monologues would be based on the character of a play and have a beginning, middle, and end. The actor would set up his own external circumstances and select a place in the monologue where a change of character and emotion occurred. These monologues were . . . of great benefit to the understanding of a character on an organic level."[4]) On the other hand, he locked horns with Bohnen and others at the Lab over the usefulness of improvisation as an exercise, ultimately persuading them to drop it as an instructional tool. As far as he was concerned, improvisation should have been resorted to only for demonstrating its ability to help draw out the subtleties of a given character, not for brandishing as a technique *in se*. This was in keeping with his overall antagonism toward teaching exercises that existed merely as teaching exercises. If this attitude was at least partly conditioned by an actor who was having little trouble finding paid jobs, one for whom too many things that went on in acting classes were academic abstractions for those doing more yearning than acting, it was also a posture he maintained in his leisure activities, where there was no substitute for immediate practical applications, self-taught as many might have been. On occasion he admitted awareness of his skepticism of classroom exercises, such as when some thirty years later hearing that his son had taken a teaching position, he cracked drily to Vincent, "My son . . . in a house of ill repute."

So what would Lee J. Cobb the teacher have been saying to his students? Vincent Cobb: "No doubt Stanislavsky, but in his own way. Dad always felt there was widespread misuse of what Stanislavsky had been trying to do. He felt strongly that the approach was supposed to be 'here, try and do the part, and only if inspiration fails you, draw upon the tools Stanislavsky provided.' And as far as rehearsals were concerned, he always thought they were for trying to do the piece, not for exploration for itself."

When the Lab entered its second phase of full-scale productions in 1945, Cobb had the lead in its very first play. But he had an intense few years before then outside the company. In 1943 alone he made four pictures as three more Europeans and another western heavy; one of the roles had him portraying the father of an actress two years older than he was and a second of an actress four months older. Also in 1943 he volunteered for the Army Air Force after months of private lessons to get a pilot's license. His military service in turn led to his participation in the most extravagant show ever presented on Broadway. And not least, on April 16, 1943, he and Beverley had their first child, Vincent.

The first of the four films, *Tonight We Raid Calais*, had Cobb as a peasant in France helping a British agent (John Sutton) mark off a Nazi factory to make it an easy target for Royal Air Force (RAF) bombers. Complications ensue when his daughter, played by the two-years-older Annabella, informs the Nazis of the intended sabotage because she believes the British were responsible for the death of her brother. Bosley Crowther congratulated Cobb for showing "a fair comprehension of a stolid old French peasant"—a compliment not quite so mild in the context of the critic's lashing of the other Americans playing Frenchmen as "theatrical."[5] It wouldn't be the last time he would be complimented for doing foreign characters while fellow players would be laughed at for it. With *Buckskin Frontier* (or sometimes *Buckskin Empire*) he returned to Hopalong Cassidy territory as a freight wagon owner determined to stop the railroad, and its agent, Richard Dix, at any cost. Once again, though, he has a daughter with contrary ideas—this time the Group-experienced Jane Wyatt, who was born several months before the actor and with whom he would work again in drastically different roles. Most critical attention went to Victor Jory as the villain of villains.

With John Steinbeck's *The Moon Is Down* Cobb moved north to take on the role of a Norwegian doctor in another story of European resistance to Nazi invaders. His character mainly called for him to engage in Socratic exchanges with the mayor (Henry Travers) of an occupied town about the inevitability of a violent uprising by the citizenry and brutal German reprisals. The film was released in the wake of transatlantic polemics about whether Steinbeck's novel was defeatist and counterproductive to the Allied cause. What it mostly was on the screen, according to Crowther of the *New York Times*, was depressing: "This may well be a true picture of Norway and its people. But it fails to strike fire, to generate passion. It leaves one feeling rather proud but also sad."[6]

Cobb remained in the medical profession for *The Song of Bernadette*, up to that time the most ballyhooed picture he had been involved with. Based on a best-selling novel by Franz Werfel about the Virgin Mary's appearance to a peasant girl in the village of Lourdes, numerous critics echoed Crowther that the film was all but critic proof (in the mainstream press, anyway) because of its religious subject matter in the middle of the war.[7] That proved to be the case when star Jennifer Jones walked off with one of its several Oscars. Cobb's character of a worldly doctor amused (but not too amused) by the conniptions of church and secular authorities over having to deal with the innocent Bernadette more or less personified the disclaimer at the start of the picture: "To those who believe in God no explanation is necessary. To those who do not believe in God no explanation is possible." The production became almost as noted for the scramblings behind the scenes as for what ended up on the screen. Although she was "introduced" as a new actress for the picture for maximum publicity gain, Jones had in fact appeared in several other productions previously under her real name of Phyllis Isley. The original score was supposed to have been written by Igor Stravinsky, but when he showed up with something he had already written for another film and refused to change it, he was fired. And most notoriously, Werfel demanded that his name be taken off the picture when he heard that Linda Darnell had been cast as the Virgin. According to the novelist, that was the worst possible choice because Darnell had a reputation for her serial affairs. He was talked out of his protest, and Darnell ended up doing the Virgin scenes—despite being pregnant.

The passion and meticulousness that Cobb put into his acting carried over to his pastimes. Whether or not it had distracted him from company business, the testiness directed at him by other Group members for his absorption with a new car had been plausible. Indeed, automobiles would remain an obsession with him throughout his life, and he was known to travel at Indianapolis raceway speeds when nobody in a uniform was hovering. Always on the lookout for greater zing, according to his children, he went from Packards to Rovers to Volvos to Ferraris to Jaguars to BMWs. But cars had a serious rival in airplanes. In 1942, revisiting his aeronautical engineering studies at Stuyvesant and confirming his parents' old fears, he spent three months in Tyrone, Pennsylvania, taking a government course to qualify for his pilot's license with instrument, multiengine, and instructor's ratings, and soon afterward owned his own Waco biplane. In the 1940s and 1950s he thought nothing of flying cross-country for engagements, and that habit helped secure the biggest role of his life. But during the war his more immediate aim was to have all his credentials in order for enlisting in the Army Air Force and being sent to Europe as a fighter pilot.

He went one-for-two. He joined the Army Air Force, but instead of being put in a cockpit was given the tasks of teaching the ins and outs of radio transmissions to recruits in California and doing voice-overs for a series of military documentaries and training pictures, some of them produced by friend Norman Corwin. He never ceased being baffled by that duty, but if nothing else it made him available for the Broadway spectacular known as *Winged Victory*.

The play had several midwives, including War Department generals and the talent agent Irving (Swifty) Lazar, but it was principally the creation of playwright Moss Hart. The idea was to create a drama that would depict the various aspects of air force life in the interests of bolstering morale at home and building up the coffers of the Army Emergency Relief Fund. After visiting Army Air Force bases around the country for material, Hart presided over a cattle call of just about everyone in uniform with any theatrical or performing experience. From more than one thousand candidates he culled a cast of three hundred, including numerous actors who were already or who would soon be familiar to theater- and moviegoers. Among them were Red Buttons, Edmond O'Brien, Karl Malden, Mario Lanza, John Forsythe, Brad Dexter, Kevin McCarthy, Gary Merrill, Alfred Ryder, and Barry Nelson. Being in the service, they were listed in *Playbill* by their Army Air Force rank; that is, "Private Lee J. Cobb." But even his uniform couldn't spare Cobb one of his Hollywood-type roles. Lacking a part for another aged, outlandish ethnic, he played yet again an avuncular physician.

With music added for choral interludes, *Winged Victory* first won raves during a Boston tryout, then on November 20, 1943, moved into the Forty-fourth Street Theatre in New York, the venue for the *Johnny Johnson* debacle. There was no problem with the dimensions this time, and the show ran for more than two hundred performances to packed houses. Cobb came in for mention only as one of the handful of performers with prior theatrical experience. If there was any carping about the production, it was over the assignment of the three hundred cast members to the Broadway stage instead of to normal military duties. Repeatedly during the Broadway run, both the Army Air Force and the producers had to point out that only one cast member had won his wings and even he had been disabled from further air duty. It was, however, an odd situation, and Cobb was the first to acknowledge it in letters to Beverley during the play. The normal routine called for the cast to participate in military drills for a couple of hours every morning in Central Park, after which they were free to return to their personal quarters (Cobb's was at the King Edward Hotel on West Forty-fourth Street, from his description only a step above a fleabag) or show up for scheduled rehearsals and/or performances. As the cast member with arguably the biggest professional credits, he also found himself getting somewhat special treatment from Hart in having what he termed "a bit" expanded into something resembling a monologue. Hart's attitude, he told Beverley, was "both flattering and embarrassing," since he was trying to slip into the company as anonymously as possible.

He also made it clear in his letters to Beverley that he didn't take his uniform lightly, and had little but contempt for those who did. Writing to her in October 1943, for example, he recounted a meeting with an acquaintance proud of the fact that he had bamboozled the draft board into excusing him from military service and suggested Cobb do the same.

> I thanked him for his unsolicited advice and assured him. . . . I was at least as convincing an actor as he was and could probably fool the Army Authorities into believing I was a psychiatric case, but that under the circumstances staying here and doing whatever I could was the very least I could do. . . . I didn't make it sound as noble and lofty as it does on paper, but I conveyed to him—ever so mildly—my thorough disgust for what he did and for his colossal stupidity in boasting of it to others! . . . I'm sorry I saw him. I never again want to see anybody looking and sounding so slimy. I was inwardly sick, revolted!

A month after his letter about the slacker, he wrote another in some purple ink confessing to unprecedented self-doubt about where a thirty-two-year-old husband and father of an infant saw himself in life:

> I've been experiencing a sense of fear—a vague special fear—for some time. The meaning of this has now finally come to me. When I was a little boy, snugly sheltered under the protective eyes of my parents, I was sad, happy, aware (I suppose as much as most little boys) of the risks and rewards growing out of the circumstances of my young life. When I grew to young manhood and I left home, I felt I was strong, intelligent, handsome, talented, etc., and out of all this I developed an attitude of independence; I felt I was chosen; I could succeed at whatever I attempted. I could never lose! I led a charmed life. Fear as such retreated into some hidden recess of my subconscious. And why not? I had what it takes! And by and by I saw results. My self-confidence was justified!
>
> And now we come to the present time. I've reached the estate of mature manhood. Though most of those virtues and capabilities are

still with me, I feel they have been somewhat modified, at least by the sober reflection of adult thinking and circumspection. Where, then, does fear enter into this? Especially the ambiguous fear of—I don't know what!

I do know now, and I'm grateful! I should be only partly alive if I never knew this fear. I have you, my love, and Vincent. You both have become such a living part of my life—so precious, so indispensable—that the thought, however foolish or groundless, of ever having to live without you panics me to distraction! That is, very simply, the basis for this phobia of mine. You might get sick or hurt, or Vincent might. My mind simply can't cope with that hypothesis. I'm no longer that invulnerable, carefree young knight. I'm not a love warrior. I love you. I love and need you so very much. Hence, my fear of losing you!

Subsequent letters took up the theme, if a little less intensely. But as always in his relationship with Beverley especially but also with others, some of his stiff wording was very secondary to his openness to undertaking any wording at all. Few people encountered by Cobb in his lifetime ever had to guess what he was thinking.

Meanwhile, *Winged Victory* might have attracted Broadway crowds indefinitely except for a commitment to 20th Century-Fox to start production on a film version. Under terms of the agreement the entire stage cast was drafted for the picture, directed by George Cukor and with the additions of actresses Judy Holliday and Jeanne Crain. No surprise, it proved to be even more critic proof than *The Song of Bernadette*, and along with another morale booster, *Hollywood Canteen*, it was one of the highest grossing films of 1944. Records of the play and film's music also sold well.

With her new son to take care of, Beverley put her career largely on hold during Cobb's military service. Her one exception was a Charlie Chan quickie for Monogram in 1944, initially entitled *Black Magic* and subsequently either *Meeting at Midnight* or *Charlie Chan in Meeting at Midnight*.[8] In March 1945, however, with Cobb back home, she appeared with him in the first full-scale Actors Lab production, Andre Obey's *Noah*. Directed by Robert Lewis, the fabled story of Noah and the ark on its way to Ararat received a much better reception in Los Angeles than it had during a brief run in New York a decade earlier. Much of this was attributed to Cobb's performance as a simple Noah, neither the stern patriarch nor the passive slave to God frequently portrayed in other works. Particularly noted was the delivery of his final cry to the heavens after hitting land "Are you satisfied?"—in the Obey-Lewis context not a question about the safe delivery of the transported animals and handful of humans, but a bitter wonder over the signs that human foibles are about to begin all over again. The subtlety and thoroughness of Lewis's production under less than expansive financial conditions deepened a love affair between the Lab and the local press for proving that Los Angeles could do more than produce movies. In the estimation of one critic, "the Lab refutes beyond all argument the myth that good theater is impossible in the stultifying atmosphere of Hollywood. Its record of excellence is unbeatable."[9]

For a while, anyway. For *Noah* the answer to "Are you satisfied?" was a curtain-dropping rainbow in the sky. There were different answers for both the Lab and Cobb.

## NOTES

1. Boleslavsky and Ouspenskaya themselves were in Hollywood at the time for movie work and conducted classes, but on a relatively modest level and with none of the publicity the Lab would attract.

2. As Delia Nora Salvi points out in her unrivaled study of the Lab ("The History of the Actors Laboratory, Inc. 1941–1950," unpublished PhD dissertation, University of California, Los Angeles, 1969, p. 30), there was no clear distinction between students and members, with even organization records remaining ambiguous, at least until 1945.

3. *Daily Variety*, August 4, 1944.

4. Salvi, "History," p. 91.

5. *New York Times*, April 15, 1943.

6. *New York Times*, March 27, 1943.

7. *New York Times*, January 27, 1944.

8. The change was dictated by a later, bigger-budgeted film called *Black Magic* in which Orson Welles played Cagliostro.

9. *Los Angeles Daily News*, June 25, 1946.

The two-year-old Cobb with
his parents (1913).

At camp at the age
of fourteen (1925).

As Horatio in a Pasadena Playhouse production of *Hamlet* (1932).

Helen Beverley in the Yiddish hit *Green Fields* (1937).

As Papa Bonaparte
in the film version of
*Golden Boy* (1939).

The group theater production of *Thunder Rock* (1939) with (left to right) Frances Farmer, Cobb, Luther Adler, and Morris Carnovsky.

Beverley with Paul Muni in *Key Largo* (1940).

Beverley in *Jason* (1942), the only time she appeared on Broadway with Cobb.

Cobb and Beverley in 1942.

Cobb and Beverley with their first-born, Vincent, in 1944.

Grandmother Kate (1945).

Grandfather Benjamin
still at work (1945).

Getting fitted for *Anna and the King of Siam* (1946).

One of his many Latin guises, this time for *Captain from Castile* (1947).

Showing Vincent the ropes in his woodworking shop (1949).

At the beach with Beverley, Vincent, and Julie (1949).

In front of the bonanza aircraft that he flew to New York to get the part of Willy Loman in *Death of a Salesman* (1949).

With Mildred Dunnock in *Salesman* (1949).

Arthur Kennedy and Cameron Mitchell trying to get through in *Salesman*.

Richard Conte seeking vengeance from Cobb in *Thieves' Highway* (1950).

With Humphrey Bogart in *Sirocco* (1951).

The climactic fight scene with Marlon Brando in *On the Waterfront* (1954).

# Chapter 11

———————◯———————

# The Actor: The
# Thought That Counts

MORE FREQUENTLY THAN NOT, the entertainment media have been slow learners. It took time for the phonograph to record more than what was played from a stage, for motion pictures to overcome the framing confines of photographs, and for television to accept that it could be more than radio with pictures. Sometimes many years had to pass for a medium to wean itself off what had gone before and realize its own innovative character. Nor was it an instant discovery that film acting was not the same thing as theater acting, that a camera lens and vacationers seated in a summer stock barn had different criteria for fulfillment. The culprit usually fingered for the belatedness of this awareness is the army of Broadway actors hurriedly pressed into service in Hollywood with the advent of sound: Since they could deliver newly required dialogue without the squeaks and lisps of some silent movie stars, patience with theatrical recital was deemed a small price to pay for exploiting to the maximum what technicians had worked up in their labs. And eventually it did get better, didn't it?

As half stories go, this one has aged comfortably, having survived the best part of a century. But it also continues to rest on a subsidiary suggestion that there was nothing so at odds at the beginning of the twentieth century as actors practicing their craft before the cameras and those plying it on the stage. But in fact, no matter how demonstrative most of them were, silent film performances weren't really very much more flamboyant than what was customarily being enacted in East Coast theaters. Whether the actor was playing "big" above rapidly edited visuals in film or playing "big" above elaborately embroidered speech on the stage, thespian subtlety was not in great demand for any kind of performance before, during, or after World War I. There was a reason why the chamber music dramatics of a Chekhov made such an impact, as there was a reason why so many Strasbergs were affected by their exposure to the Moscow Art Theatre and the Stanislavsky system. In itself the technical breakthrough signaled by *The Jazz Singer* might have caused excitement as the latest mass entertainment toy but it was not all that convulsive for audience expectations of the fictional diversion being served up. Except for the extreme cases such as John Gilbert, where a high-pitched voice had made an unfortunate marriage with a dated style, the silent movie actor did not suddenly get sent to the wrecking yard to make room for a revolutionary model singularly gifted for making speeches; he himself had delivered those speeches for years, only silently.

What the sound film did introduce to acting was a muted complexity of performance that the spectator could share to a degree not known previously in any kind of theater, with or without a screen draped over the stage. Rather than the captioned sentiments conveyed by silent film, the dialogue of the sound film (including deliberately wordless moments) sewn into such media techniques as close-ups and isolated reaction shots imposed a more layered challenge for the actor through a relentless succession of emotions, assertions that contradicted the emotions, and regrets that he had opened his mouth at all. Thanks to dialogue and the camera's intimate access for interpreting it, the actor had gained a new level for his character to be believed—or not believed. It was not his responsibility to know which specific feelings would preoccupy the spectator at this or that moment (that was the job of the director and the editor), but it was his new task to navigate decisively through a range of possibilities in a way that the distance of a theatrical stage from the audience could not provide.

There were numerous aspects to this change, running from the purely mechanical to the murkily psychological, and all of them conditioning the timbre of a performance and the way it was received. At first, physical movement became constricted because of rudimentary audio systems: the lopsided tables of seedy tenements had to bloom into botanical gardens so a microphone could be hidden among the flowers in a centerpiece vase; the roughhouse tenants in the tenement had to demand their supper slop with fine Gielgud-like articulation and had to have it thrown in front of them without knocking over the vase. The gradual sophistication of sound equipment allowed for more naturalistic movement on the screen, but speech's halftones, no matter how appropriate and even necessary for a character's actions, lagged behind; the ideal was still the enunciation to be heard at a finishing school for oratory. Occasionally, the technical improvements themselves created idiosyncrasies, including some of a cultural nature. Michael Caine has pointed out one difference between British and American approaches to sound: "In British films, the sound technician tries to get rid of any extraneous noises on the sound track—for example, the noise of cutlery on a plate. He puts bits of putty under the plates and all that. The Americans just live with the clatter. That's because the British make talking pictures; Americans make moving pictures. We British filmmakers have a theatre tradition, whereas Hollywood was about 3,000 miles away from America's theatre center." In America, Caine observed, "you can help yourself by not putting the knife down just when you say, 'I love you, darling.'"[1]

Once physical movement became less of a stress, framing became more of one. The studios had too much invested in their stars to accept endless long shots; that didn't make for the provocative, outsized glamour that entranced orchestras and prompted magazine covers. But hypnotic close-ups of faces and their over-the-shoulder-shot cousins, easy enough in the silent era, necessitated more intercutting on dialogue. For the actor this meant having to regather his energies for conversational exchanges, often for numerous takes and with the unseen participants in the scene standing next to the camera, maybe with script in hand. In the worst cases, when the unseen player was more prima donna than actor and had stalked off to his dressing room as soon as he wasn't needed by the cameraman, the on-scene actor still working had to direct his regrouped energies to a script assistant or the director. This could be so potentially distracting that some performers, Orson Welles was one, preferred to deliver their close-up dialogue (with pauses injected for the imagined responses of a co-player) to nobody at all rather than to some crew substitute. One way or another, the actor was tested sharply at such moments to remain in character and not fall back on solipsisms extraneous to the script.

Given these kinds of demands, the Group Theatre veterans reassembled in the Lab with their background of ensemble performing might have had acute reasons for being antagonistic to everything about movies except the checks, but they weren't the only ones skeptical about the actor's status within the medium. Motives for their suspicions abounded, aesthetically as much as from any technical or business point of view. One striking example was the famous pre-sound experiment conducted by Russian director Lev Kuleshov with the actor Ivan Mozhukhin and written about at length by V. I. Pudovkin in his seminal *Film Technique and Film Acting*. What Kuleshov did was to shoot Mozhukhin in close-up with the actor having a totally neutral expression. Then he shot three more scenes without Mozhukhin and combined them. As Pudovkin explained,

> In the first combination the close-up of Mozhukhin was immediately followed by a shot of a plate of soup standing on a table. It was obvious and certain that Mozhukhin was looking at this soup. In the second combination the face of Mozhukhin was joined to shots showing a coffin in which lay a dead woman. In the third the close-up was followed by a shot of a little girl playing with a funny toy bear. When we showed the three combinations to an audience which had not been let in on the secret the result was terrific. The public raved about the acting of the artist. They pointed out the heavy pensiveness of his mood over the forgotten soup, were touched and moved by the deep sorrow with which he looked at the dead woman, and admitted the light, happy smile with which he surveyed the girl at play. But we knew that in all three cases the face was exactly the same.[2]

For Kuleshov the responses to this and similar experiments were sufficient for his conclusion that "while the theatre is unthinkable without actors, the cinema does not need actors . . . has no use for actors."[3] The Russian might have been one of the few to come right out and say it, but his attitude wasn't foreign in Hollywood, either, especially among those captivated by the possibilities in animation. An insecure actor might have begun thinking that his chief professional value lay not in his performing abilities on the screen but in the publicity he generated from them for his employer, actual talent and its execution secondary to physical virtues and other potential profit centers.

None of this did much for the actor's self-confidence. Nor did the common practice of shooting scripted scenes out of order for location or budgetary reasons, compelling the actor to enter cold into a character phase that he had not journeyed to reach. Congratulated once backstage in a New York theater for having also become a movie star,

Paul Muni was quoted as replying, "I don't know what that means. Here at the Plymouth, I walk through the stage door, I put on my makeup, and I do a performance. Back there, I'm a lot of little pieces of film glued together. In November, they'll ship me back here in a couple of cans."[4] Teaching the acting process of "little pieces of film glued together" was no small step for the Actors Lab, even if Fox and Universal were supplying needed cash for the classes and other studios were showing their goodwill by lending props for the company's stage productions. And indeed there were continual squabbles among the board members over how far they should take their gratitude toward the studios, with Dassin usually the most in favor of broadening the Lab's reach, Bromberg and Carnovsky most likely to insist on first theatrical principles, and Bohnen, though tilting slightly toward Bromberg and Carnovsky, doing most of the mediating between the two sides. Garfield was hardly betraying secrets when, as an invited lecturer, he told one class that "many people have not been able to adjust to movies from the Group."[5]

And they had a great deal to adjust to. It wasn't just the implications for the actor of camera setups or location schedules. It wasn't even only to the Kuleshov kind of verdict that the actor was superfluous to the moviemaking process. The contradictions and disorientations for the Group veterans went still deeper. As actors of tested theater experience the Lab instructors were also only too aware of being called on to proselytize for a medium that, beyond the intellectual fantasy offered by the stage, proposed a very physical fantasy as well. In sequence or out of sequence, a film scene undertaken by the actor remained attached to the gossamer, and that was without worrying about the possibility that his effort would be thrown out by the director in the editing room a month later anyway. Except for master shots in which the actor could establish some sense of rhythm with co-players, clouds volunteered more stability. The actor did not have to be a film historian, for instance, to sense that the next director to shoot a persuasive dream sequence, whether in a surreal or leadenly literal key, would be the first one. Spun-off fantasies could not distinguish themselves effectively from the film medium's central reality as a fantasy any more than a home run hitter in baseball could get away with rounding the bases twice in order to double his runs batted in.

So where was the point of contact for the Bohnens and Carnovskys with such a medium? How could professional performers who had spent years debunking the seriousness of screen acting suddenly arrogate to themselves an instructional role in it? And conversely, how could a motion picture studio entrust its young and inexperienced contract players to these instructors who, when examined with any objectivity, had put together fairly modest motion picture careers? By the end of the war, Cobb had more conspicuous screen credits than any Group-into-Lab members, but aside from the one class he ran for a few weeks, he wasn't one of the staff teachers. The bridge—explicitly for the Lab people and with a taste for try-anything-new-to-see-if-it-works on the part of the Darryl Zanucks and other studio executives—was Stanislavsky.

In his book *Acting in Film,* Caine contended that "the modern film actor knows that real people in real life struggle *not* to show their emotions."[6] According to the actor, this insight followed generations of motion picture performers who had done just the opposite—sobbing or roaring because some predecessor had been acclaimed for doing so. What that reflected, he asserted, had been more concern with the superficialities of theater and film tradition than with authentic human behavior. Long before the particulars of film acting had become a topic of study, Stanislavsky had made a similar observation and integrated it into his teachings. As he and his successors in Europe and America noted, the actor portraying a drunk was merely copying other unconvincing actors if he staggered across the stage instead of, as was more likely the case in real life, laboring to walk soberly. Equally, the actor playing an enraged character increased dramatic tension not by shouting or screaming but by doing the very opposite, deepening his quiet to cold menace until it finally shattered. It was these ostensibly counterintuitive approaches, playing the piano's black keys instead of the white ones, that intensified a performance—lessons second nature to the Group actors. Whether they preferred Strasberg to Stella Adler or vice versa, they had all learned that less was more.

On the stage the less-was-more approach was more apt to tell over an entire performance than in single moments. Motion pictures didn't have that patience, not with the constant magnifications of character revelations. There the eyes, and the thoughts informing them every moment, ruled as film's most emphatic contribution to a performance. Caine, and he wasn't the only one, went so far as to insist that this was the true test of a film actor, of his mastery of character, because the camera couldn't lie, that it ruthlessly searched out every drop of sincerity in a portrayal. That has not been a unanimous opinion. Richard Brestoff, another actor with considerable experience as a teacher, has warned against taking such claims religiously: "The truth is, you *can* lie to the camera. It is not some kind of foolproof lie detector. If it were, politicians would avoid it like the plague, instead of seeking it out."[7] But Brestoff agreed more generally about the eyes as the focus of a screen performance, displaying as they did the true embrace by the actor of a character as opposed to, say, a newsreel presentation of a man on the street. "Can the camera see into your soul? It can. But you hold the key. Will the camera believe a lie? It will. If it is a believable lie. And a good thing, too. If it didn't, actors would never be able to do their job; which is to create the reality of fiction."[8]

Creating that reality of fiction on film proved to be a lot easier in the postwar years for the Lab and many of its members than dealing with the steady intrusion of fiction into reality.

## NOTES

1. Michael Caine, *Acting in Film: An Actor's Take on Movie Making* (New York: Applause Theatre Book Publishers, 1990), p. 79.

2. V. I. Pudovkin, *Film Technique and Film Acting* (New York: Grove Press, 1976), p. 44.

3. Quoted by Richard Brestoff in *The Camera Smart Actor* (Lyme, NH: Smith and Kraus, 1994), p. 9.

4. Lawrence, *Actor*, p. 180.

5. *Drama Review* 28, no. 4 (Winter 1984).

6. Caine, *Acting in Film*, p. 6.

7. Brestoff, *Camera Smart Actor*, p. 5.

8. Ibid., p. 7.

# Chapter 12

─────────────○─────────────

# Trotting with Fox

TWENTIETH CENTURY-FOX'S TIES to the Actors Lab were not just at a company level. Studio chief Darryl Zanuck's compulsion to be ahead of every curve when it came to trends or fashions that might be translated into bigger audiences for his pictures included the Stanislavsky Method, so company producers kept Lab regulars close by giving them pretty steady work. Cobb went one step further after being discharged from the Army Air Force by extending an earlier nonexclusive multipicture contract with the studio. The pact remained in force for several years, through good pictures and bad pictures, until the threat of another bad picture laced with propaganda led to a blowup with the front office. By then the actor had become one of the most recognizable faces on the American screen, usually in first support of James Stewart, Tyrone Power, and other established stars and always with a simmering ambition to be the leading man himself. When he finally realized that goal, it was not at all in circumstances he had anticipated.

Fox wasn't the worst place for him to harbor starring role ambitions since Zanuck had never shown reluctance to cast otherwise below-the-title players of ambiguous age as the protagonists of major features; in the war years alone, Monty Woolley in *The Pied Piper* and Alexander Knox in *Wilson* had secured Best Actor Oscar nominations for company productions. Nevertheless, Cobb's commitment to the long-term deal initially baffled some since by his own pronouncements he had never given up on his stage priorities in New York—an intention given more credence by his work at the Lab with *Noah*. But he had also become more security-minded where his family was concerned, especially after his move from an apartment near the Lab to a Spanish-style home in Beverly Hills and the birth of his second child, daughter Julie, on May 29, 1947. Moreover, in addition to his taste for high-end automobiles and private planes, he had developed other pastimes that required some spending. One was woodworking and a zeal for fitting out his home with his own workshop furniture. An older one, dating back to his teenage years in the Bronx when he had even put together his own darkroom, was photography. Most conspicuously, there was his passion for gin rummy and other kinds of gambling that would eventually cause serious worry among friends and make him too familiar to loan sharks. But that was still in the future. Professionally, the guaranteed salary from Fox looked even better when the closest he came to returning to Broadway immediately after the war, an elaborate production of Bertolt Brecht's *Galileo*, foundered on his misgivings at having to second Charles Laughton in the title role. Aside from not being enthusiastic about sharing a stage with the omnivorous Laughton, he was put off by the older actor's conversion to the Brechtian principle that "no psychology" would be the directorial approach for depicting the characters. He was in no mood to repeat the experience of the Group's production of *Johnny Johnson*.

Cobb's first three pictures after the war were with directors who would figure prominently in the anti-Communist witch hunts that overwhelmed Hollywood in the late 1940s and through the 1950s; two of them were with Fox, the third an exercise of his contractual right to work for other studios. His work with John Cromwell, old friend Elia Kazan, and Robert Rossen would not go unnoticed by the congressional and state politicians bent on clearing Southern California of leftists, Communist or not. The first feature, Cromwell's *Anna and the King of Siam*, had the actor back in heavy makeup, this time as a Siamese prime minister. Adapted from an account by a nineteenth-century English woman of her relations with the royal Siamese household during her stay in Bangkok as a teacher of the king's children and itself the basis for the popular musical *The King and I* some years later, *Anna* won more acceptance than excitement from critics for emotions that were worn on Irene Dunne's hoop skirts. One (familiar) negative consensus was around the opinion that most of the white actors playing Asians were hackneyed Hollywood creations, exceptions made for star Rex Harrison as the monarch and Cobb. In the middle of tittering at some of the other performances, for example, Crowther of the *Times* allowed as how Cobb was "quietly commanding."[1]

The smoothest of the Fox pictures was the next one, Kazan's *Boomerang*. Like *Anna*, it was based on approximately real events, but there the similarities ended. A strong example of the black-and-white documentary-type storytelling Fox specialized in during the postwar years, many of them with the stentorian Reed Hadley doing a newsreel-type voice-over, *Boomerang* was inspired by the killing of a Connecticut minister and the political machinations set in motion around prosecuting an innocent man (Arthur Kennedy) for the murder. Cobb had the strongest film role of his career up to that point as a stubborn police chief who first blocks out all the bloodlust around him for condemning the suspect, then becomes convinced enough of the man's guilt to turn belligerent toward a prosecutor (Dana Andrews) who systematically undercuts the police case. The press had nothing but praise for Kazan's direction and the performances of the cast ("Lee Cobb broods in dark and towering silence as the badgered chief of police"[2]) but questioned the jiggering of facts from the actual murder in the interests of presenting a better story. As Crowther put it, "As a piece of melodrama with human and social overtones there is nothing theatrically faulty. . . . It is only in its implications that it reenacts an actual case . . . that violence is done to propriety. By making this circumstantial claim, *Boomerang* is as guilty of presumption as the evidence-rigging villains in the piece."[3]

As would be the case with his best films to follow, Cobb's performance in *Boomerang* benefited greatly from the ensemble cast feel that had been palpable at the height of the Group's success. *Boomerang* wasn't the blue-collar Group, and it was a movie and not a play, but he found himself within a family of fellow professionals for whom traditional motion picture glamour was a dalliance and who would mark or had already marked significant steps in his career. Kazan and Karl Malden as another cop had been Group members. Jane Wyatt in the role of the prosecutor's wife had not only been with the Group, but had played his daughter in *Buckskin Empire* and would costar with him again as illicit lovers in another film. Sam Levene as an investigative reporter was a board member of the Actors Lab and had been in the film version of *Golden Boy*. Ed Begley as the slimiest of the politicians would appear with him on television and in *12 Angry Men*. And most important after Kazan, Kennedy, an apprentice with the Group, would not only work with him on television but costar in a landmark stage performance a few years later. The film's black-and-white faintly begrudging reportorial style within such familiar surroundings—the truth even if it hurts us all—brought out subtleties in his performance that weren't always to be seen in glossy features alongside actors with whom he had had little previous working experience. On the contrary, the more Technicolor on the screen, the more he seemed to take it upon himself, if not urged to do so by his director, to go very, very garish—and not always appropriately.

Which should have made his next outing, Rossen's *Johnny O'Clock* for Columbia, another promising opportunity. If it wasn't a documentary-like fiction shot on location in the Fox style, it had aspirations to being a film noir like other successful pictures of the kind made in the period by star Dick Powell. But the noir wasn't nearly noir enough, involving Powell's slick casino operator character with too many femmes fatales and a mystery about the bad guy (Thomas Gomez) that wasn't all that mysterious. More than one of Cobb's scenes as a police detective keeping his eye on Powell's title character amounted to being responsible for the exposition of a turgid plot. (According to Bessie, he only agreed to do the picture because the producers agreed to pay him with a new Bonanza aircraft.) In evaluations of the picture the two male leads and Evelyn Keyes came out better than the tepid drama. For *Variety* they gave "ace performances,"[4] for the *Times* they "went through their paces ably."[5]

The actor might have generated more enthusiasm for another role if he hadn't let his persisting vanity about his hairline get in the way. Around the same time that he was getting ready for *Johnny O'Clock*, he was approached by director Abe Polonsky to costar with Group colleague Garfield in *Force of Evil*, the kind of noir the Powell picture aspired to be and then some. A fatalistic tale of state lottery frauds with a narrative voice midway between that of a racing tout and Jean-Paul Sartre, *Force of Evil* would have cast Cobb as the head of a penny-ante numbers operation who was relatively more honest than his self-delusional slick lawyer of a brother played by Garfield. As forceful as the role promised to be, however, it was also a reminder that Garfield, the Group colleague who had skipped off to Warner Brothers instead of going to London with *Golden Boy*, was merely two years younger than this older brother portrayed by the script as practically a generation older in his world weariness. "I'll do it, but I want to wear a hair piece," Cobb was quoted as telling Polonsky. "You're not losing that much hair," the director was said to have (lied) replied. "Why a hair piece?" "Because I'm thinking of becoming a leading man" was the terse answer. When the actor refused to budge from his position, Polonsky and Garfield gave the role to Gomez in what turned out to be Garfield's most haunting film.[6]

Instead of with *Force of Evil*, Cobb followed up *Johnny O'Clock* with another of his European types, as a Spanish adventurer in the schizophrenic Fox spectacle of *Captain from Castile*. A Henry King production about Cortez's conquest of the Aztecs, the big money spent on the picture went mainly for what were supposed to be lush backdrops shot on location in Mexico, for one cast-of-thousands marching scene after another, and for a triumphal Alfred Newman musical score to match. The trouble with the lush backdrops was that they didn't look all that lush, and Cobb complained to Beverley more than once that King could have obtained the same visual effect remaining at the Fox studio. Moreover, the picture made strenuous efforts to keep off camera the two major historical events sparking all the action—the Inquisition cruelties that motivated the lust for revenge by the characters played by Tyrone Power and Cobb against the chief villain (John Sutton) and, even more glaringly, the slaughters perpetrated by Cortez (Cesar Romero) against the Aztecs. Since these events had been set out graphically in the novel upon which the picture was based, Zanuck was seen as being wary of alienating the Catholic Church and its Legion of Decency mouthpiece with too explicit a history lesson. (Already that same year the Legion had condemned the studio's *Forever Amber* and had even attacked the Christmas caramel *Miracle on 34th Street* because the divorced mother character played by Maureen O'Hara had been treated sympathetically.) In place of the religious tortures in Spain and the genocide in Mexico, *Captain from Castile* doted on honor-first speeches by Romero to Power and forgiveness-first bromides by a friar (Gomez yet again) whose every utterance began with "My son." The verdict by the *Times* that the whole enterprise was "windy" and oddly static for an epic was shared by most critics.[7] With its skittishness about offending the Catholic Church, it also reflected the growing fear of studios when it came to forces helping to propel the Red Scare after the war.

Cobb's extended location work in Mexico's Guayangareo Valley, first in Morelia and then further west in Uruapan, occasioned a steady

stream of letters back to Beverley in Los Angeles, and in a kaleido-
scope of moods. For starters, he had to assure her more than once that
a fall he had taken from a horse because of a badly cinched saddle had
left him with some shoulder and head bruises but nothing beyond that.
His onscreen enemy, the Briton Sutton with whom he had already
worked in *Tonight We Raid Calais,* was his biggest pal away from the
camera because he played gin—the pastime Cobb increasingly (and
often detrimentally) made his chief leisure activity on location shoots.
He and Power also organized baseball games, charging admission to
the crew so proceeds could go to Mexican charities. ("I had four hits
in four at bats, but my fielding was lousy.")

But what he looked forward to more than anything were the flights
that he and Power, also a pilot, managed to sneak in over the Mexican
wilds when they weren't needed for work. "I've just returned after
spending 45 glorious minutes in the air over this singularly beautiful
country," he wrote in one of his almost daily chronicles to Beverley.
"I wish you were here with me to see the sun setting from the air. It
almost made me weep. . . . When I found myself in the air again pilot-
ing a ship, it was as though an old real friend of my choice paid me a
visit." And on another day: "There's an active volcano in the vicinity.
The name of it is Paracutin. Ty and I flew around it several times. It
is one of the most spectacular and awe-inspiring sights I have ever
seen. It is belching rocks, lava, and black smoke. . . . At the foot of the
mountain one can see the upper half of a church—all that remains of
a town that was buried under the lava when the volcano became active
a few years ago."

As the weeks dragged on to months, however, awe ceded before
impatience and a marked fury at the director King. On January 13,
1947, Cobb told Beverley, "The morale of the company is pretty low.
People are pretty much disgusted. It seems the studio hasn't missed
an opportunity to betray its cheapness and smallness, and the people
are simply fed up. Some are sick, others drink very heavily, still others
are despondent." Three days later, it was, "The work is so uninspired
and boring. This is mainly due to the fact that King is not only devoid
of a single creative fibre, but he's an insufferable crank. He's petty and
unreasonable, like an aged invalid. Everybody hates and resents him.
I don't say this because I have had trouble with him. On the contrary,
he likes to pick on the little fellow, someone who is holding down some
menial job and is afraid of losing it."

As Cobb had predicted in one of his earliest letters, Zanuck was so appalled by the rushes sent back to Los Angeles that he sent a second cameraman to Mexico for extensive reshooting aimed at assuring audiences that the picture had indeed been filmed in Mexico. For supplementary material, there was always . . . the studio's back lot and some potted plants!

Cobb's next venture was nowhere near as arduous. With *Call Northside 777*, however, he found himself overshadowed in his scenes for one of the few times in his career thanks to his own underwritten role as a newspaper editor and the aggressively sarcastic character of an investigative reporter played by James Stewart. Like *Boomerang*, *Northside 777* traced back to a real criminal case—the false imprisonment of a man (Richard Conte) for eleven years for the killing of a Chicago cop. Overcoming his own acid doubts about the prisoner's innocence, the Stewart reporter gradually finds evidence of a police cover-up, and with the help of pedantic lectures by nonactors about how lie detectors and printing machines work, the jail doors are opened. Both Cobb and Conte were lost in the critical focus on the embittered Stewart character that reminded nobody of *Mister Smith Goes to Washington*. Some liked the change, others didn't. While the *New York Times* found the star's performance "winning,"[8] the industry's trade press sounded offended that Stewart had made a move toward changing his image without its permission. Typical was the weekly *Variety*, which declared that "among the film's principal drawbacks was Jimmy Stewart's jarring and unpersuasive performance. . . . He shuffles between phony cynicism and sob-sister sentimentalism without ever jelling the portrait into a recognizable newspaperman."[9]

There were no allusions to factual events for *The Miracle of the Bells* and *The Luck of the Irish*; what there was instead was a restless Cobb having second thoughts about his Fox contract. If any picture had driven home the difference between leading man and featured player, it had been *Call Northside 777*. As a gifted actor as well as star, Stewart had been a reassurance that one status didn't have to be traded away in exchange for the other. It also couldn't have escaped Cobb's attention that Stewart was as much a customer of hairpieces as he was. But none of this had much weight in his talks with Zanuck for a leading role, especially after one script the actor had been eying, a screen version of Odets's *Clash by Night*, had been grabbed by another studio before Cobb could mount his case for repeating his stage role. Take it or leave it, what there was at Fox was *The Miracle of the Bells* and *The Luck of the Irish* and an actor who was learning about the lows as well as the highs of being continually in demand.

Since Zanuck didn't consider it wholly complimentary to have such hard-edged black-and-white dramas as *Boomerang, Kiss of Death,* and *Cry of the City* compared to the Cagney-Robinson-Bogart gangster film era at Warner Brothers in the 1930s, he sought to offset that image of his studio with family-oriented fare that was as likely as not to include clergy as characters. With *The Miracle of the Bells,* he also envisioned a repeat of the critical and financial success of *The Song of Bernadette.* He didn't get it. Written by the personification of Hollywood jadedness, Ben Hecht, *Bells* follows the manipulations of a public relations man (Fred MacMurray) to get publicity for the funeral of an actress (Alida Valli) who completed a movie role as Joan of Arc before her death. Most of the story is told in flashback from the woman's coal mining home-town in Pennsylvania with the PR man recalling how he had champi-oned her before a skeptical producer (Cobb) and had fallen in love with her. If the first 98 percent of the picture didn't satisfy by veering between the insipid and the predictable, the last 2 percent of it atoned with an earthquake under the church where the funeral is being held, forcing the statues to turn on their pedestals toward the coffin with presumably blessed thoughts about the dead actress. This brings on a mixture of exclamations that a miracle has occurred, knowing sneers that only an earthquake has, and another *Bernadette* kind of reminder from Fox that for those who believed in God no explanation was neces-sary and for those who didn't none was possible. The *Times* called the sequence "distasteful" for everyone but "the ultra-devout."[10] Despite ef-forts to take the picture relatively more seriously, the *New York Herald Tribune* had to conclude that "only when Lee J. Cobb, in an excellent performance, snaps out and throws away a remark about God not being interested in the movie business do these words seem to come alive."[11]

Wandering around in the middle of everything was Frank Sinatra as a local priest whose cassock weighed more than he did. As it turned out, this was the most fortuitous development in the picture for Cobb, who a decade later would have life-and-death reasons for being grate-ful for having worked with the singer-actor.

With *The Luck of the Irish,* sanctimoniousness gave way to the cutes when a reporter played by Power has a leprechaun to thank for straightening out his life before he gets into a loveless marriage with the scheming daughter of a politically ambitious magazine tycoon (Cobb). For Cobb himself the picture—written off by one critic as being funny only when characters relished at pronouncing the name "Higginbottom"[12]—was the biggest of red flags for straightening out his career. Then, at the height of the Red Scare, he received an extra incentive when he was asked to appear in *The Iron Curtain*, a blatantly anti-Communist propaganda feature about a defecting code clerk at the Soviet embassy in Canada that had been "recommended" to the studio by representatives of the House Un-American Activities Committee (HUAC). When Cobb refused to do the picture, he was placed on suspension, though the studio made the announcement without going into specific details lest it look overly responsive to production suggestions from Washington. Finally, the two sides had a meeting. As Alvah Bessie told it, "When he was called into the office of the studio's executive producer, [Lee] told him why he would not play the role and suggested that they cancel his contract on the spot. 'I could no more play such a role [a brutish and sadistic Soviet Army officer] than I could be an anti-Semite,' said Lee, 'and I'm a Jew. What's more, I consider the script un-American, fascistic, and dangerous to the peace and well-being of my fellow Americans.'"[13] However pompous the last part, and whether from Cobb or Bessie, an accord was reached with Zanuck for making one more Fox picture to liquidate the actor's obligations to the studio. That picture, *Thieves' Highway*, turned out to be the most provocative made under the contract.

Before *Thieves' Highway*, though, Cobb teamed with the Golden Boy Holden again at Columbia for *The Dark Past*, a remake of the 1933 melodrama *Blind Alley* as attuned to Psychiatry 101 as to psychological tensions. Both actors won praise for the story of a gun-crazy hood (Holden) and his confederates who burst into the home of a psychiatrist (Cobb) during a dinner party, but largely in a tone of relief that critics could talk about acting instead of having to sound knowledgeable about the dark arts. Most of the action is centered on the shrink's probing of the reasons for the gunman's hostility toward society, with terms like *subconscious* and *Oedipus complex* tossed around as the golden keys to a treasure box. Overall, the film was regarded as a serviceable programmer without much directorial flair from Rudolph Maté.[14] Cobb would play another psychiatrist to much greater notice a few years later.

Since his screen appearances were generally part of big studio confections that received attention for good or bad upon release and were then consigned to film history and TV reruns, Cobb's career has never had underground connotations and has seldom been associated with a picture that gained cult-like respect only after reexamination years later. However adventurous, even innovative, his stage résumé might have been with the Theatre Union, the Group Theatre, and the Actors Lab, when it came to motion pictures, he stuck to the industry's main streets and could sound less than ironic about being recognized by fans in the street. In her book *The Red and the Blacklist*, screenwriter-novelist Norma Barzman recalled a vacation in Mexico City that she and her husband took with the Cobbs in the late 1940s: "At the thieves market Lee noticed with satisfaction that a man was staring at him. Lee strutted like a peacock. 'How nice it is,' he said, all puffed up, 'to be recognized. Even in Mexico I'm a star.' As the man approached, Lee murmured 'I guess he wants my autograph.'"

Not quite. "The man gazed at Lee appraisingly. *'Bist a Yid?'* he asked. 'Are you a Jew? Even from a distance,' the man continued in Yiddish, 'I could see you were.' He looked around, then leaned confidentially toward Lee. 'Mexicans!' he whispered. 'A *vilde volk*! A primitive people! How long since you had a morsel of good Jewish food in your mouth?' He held out a card. 'Here. Let me give you the address of my restaurant.'"[15]

The closest Cobb came to entering controversial neighborhoods with film projects was with Jules Dassin's *Thieves' Highway*, which after decades of neglect acquired a reputation as one of the director's best films, if not *the* best, during his years in Hollywood. Even this case, however, would be stretching the definition of unrecognized classic since the picture was praised almost unanimously upon original release, opened in New York in the showcase Roxy theater, and was paired with a stage show headed by no less than Ed Sullivan as master of ceremonies. In short, it had to work to gain the obscurity into which it fell for most of the last half of the twentieth century.

*Highway*'s plot is sparked by the return from the war of a long-haul truck driver (Conte) who embodies all the optimism of postwar youth but who is quickly disabused of that attitude when he discovers that his father has been left robbed and crippled by a produce market thug (Cobb) and his henchmen. The vet undertakes a long-haul drive from Fresno to the fruit market in San Francisco with the twin purpose of selling the apples he is carrying and exacting vengeance on the thug. Instead, he loses the apples to the mobster and the life of his best friend to a road accident and becomes as hardened a cynic as the market boss he has gone after. The only one who is capable of reminding him of his humanity is a prostitute (Valentina Cortese[16]) with whom he shacks up. ("You need a friend, strong man, and I'm friendly.")

In the version of the picture released by Fox, the Conte character ultimately gets money for his apples, turns Cobb over to the police after a roadside diner brawl, and drives off with the hooker. But that happy ending was pure Zanuck after Dassin had left the premises. For the director there could be no illusions about the triumph of fabled American get-up-and-go against organized crime or, by extension, that of the single blue-collar worker against organized capitalism. Although other postwar films questioned through the characters of returning veterans what exactly had been won on the battlefields of Europe and the Pacific, *Thieves' Highway* did so from within very specific, restive ethnic ambiances, identifying the hero and his family in detail as Greek and the villains as Italians; that is, there was nothing abstract about the conflict on view, least of all to second-generation immigrants hooked on the American dream. What wasn't simply concrete was startlingly sensual, most markedly in the scenes between the Conte and Cortese characters. Years after the Bronx boy Dassin had resettled in Europe and had made a second reputation for himself as the maker of *Rififi*, *He Who Must Die*, and *Never on Sunday*, he would be called "European" in sensibility or even be identified as French or Greek by writers who should have known better for such *Highway* moments as Cortese and Conte playing tic-tac-toe on his bare chest.

In spite of Zanuck's jiggery-pokery in the editing room, *Thieves' Highway* and its stars won some of the best reviews of the year in 1949. For Crowther, Dassin "got the look and feel of people and places in the produce world. You can almost sense the strain of trucking and smell the crated fruit. . . . *Thieves' Highway* is a first-class melodrama which just misses—yes, just misses—being great." As for the actors, the mobster character was described as "a beauty—and as played by Lee J. Cobb, he grows on the screen to the full dimensions of a believable rascal of the business world."[17] Even dailies normally happiest with *The Luck of the Irish* kind of features from Fox called the picture "dynamic." Kate Cameron of the *Daily News* was particularly struck by

Cobb's performance, saying he made the market boss (a run-up to his role as Johnny Friendly in *On the Waterfront*) "as tough a scoundrel as the screen has seen in many a day."[18]

The Zanuck-decreed ending to *Thieves' Highway* and the silence from Dassin at the time contributed to reports that the director was preoccupied with fleeing the United States before he was subpoenaed by the HUAC and that the studio chief was only too glad to see him go. What actually happened was more complicated. At Dassin's challenge, Zanuck agreed to hire blacklisted writer Albert Maltz to adapt his novel *The Journey of Simon McKeever* for a Fox picture that would be directed by John Huston and star Huston's father, Walter; Zanuck's only condition was that Maltz not say anything about it until shooting had gotten under way so that the Fox board would have long second thoughts about calling off a project it had already spent money on. Although Dassin conveyed this condition to Maltz, the latter wasted little time in declaring to the industry press that the blacklist was over thanks to Zanuck and Dassin. The executive immediately denied any knowledge of Maltz's claims. Then, even as the HUAC investigators had another reason to zero in on Dassin, Zanuck made a late-night call on the director and urged him to get out of the country before he had to testify. As an incentive, he gave him a Fox project, *Night and the City* with Richard Widmark, that was to be shot in London with some of the frozen funds the company couldn't get out of England because of postwar restrictions. This time it was Dassin who was told to shoot as many scenes as quickly and as secretly as possible before the Fox board heard about the project—a strategy that ultimately worked. It was this potentially embarrassing (to Zanuck) story as much as anything else that ensured that *Thieves' Highway* didn't go into significant rerelease for many years.[19]

At the time of Dassin's hurried departure for Europe, where he would remain for the rest of his life except for occasional visits back across the Atlantic, Cobb had merely lost one of his oldest friends in Hollywood. Within a few years he would shiver before the thought of seeing the director again. In the meantime, though, he was visited by a genie who granted his three career wishes all in one project—he got to stop making the first movie that came along for supporting his expanding living style, he got back to Broadway, and he got to be a leading man.

## NOTES

1. *New York Times*, June 21, 1946.
2. *New York Times*, March 6, 1947.
3. Ibid.
4. *Variety*, January 23, 1947.
5. *New York Times*, March 27, 1947.
6. Robert Nott, *He Ran All the Way: The Life of John Garfield* (New York: Limelight Editions, 2003), pp. 230–231.
7. *New York Times*, December 26, 1947.
8. *New York Times*, February 19, 1948.
9. *Variety*, February 22, 1948.
10. *New York Times*, March 17, 1948.
11. *New York Herald Tribune*, March 17, 1948.
12. *New York Herald Tribune*, September 16, 1948.
13. Bessie, *Inquisition in Eden*, p. 221.
14. *New York Times*, December 23, 1948.
15. Norma Barzman, *The Red and the Blacklist: The Intimate Memoirs of a Hollywood Expatriate* (New York: Thunder's Mouth Press/Nation Books, 2003), p. 70.
16. Apparently in the interests of meeting American expectations of what Italians should call themselves, she was known in Hollywood as Valentina Cortesa.
17. *New York Times*, September 24, 1949.
18. *New York Daily News*, September 24, 1949.
19. Patrick McGilligan and Paul Buhle, *Tender Comrades* (New York: St. Martin's Griffin, 1997), pp. 207–208.

# Chapter 13

────────○────────

# Attention Being Paid

JAMES CAGNEY, FREDRIC MARCH, WALTER HUSTON, and Bud Bohnen had two things in common—they were all actors and they were all considered seriously for the role of Willy Loman in Arthur Miller's *Death of a Salesman*. What they didn't have remotely in common was their appearance, and having to choose among them as physical types as much as craftsmen would prove to be the first test for dramatizing the delusions of Miller's protagonist about himself, his two grown sons, and the bitterness of life's unfulfilled promises. In the end, of course, none of the four emerged with the part that powered the most successfully realized American play of the twentieth century, but as a group they were indicative of how far the play had to travel from the page to the stage.

Cagney was Miller's idea, one that he shared with Brian Dennehy half a century after the 1949 production. "The way he explained it to me," Dennehy, who starred in a 1999 Broadway revival of the play, said, "he had always pictured Loman as a small guy, like this uncle Manny of his the character of the salesman was partly based on. Somebody who had once been a little dynamo but whose energies had begun to wear down. And who better for that in the 1940s than Cagney?"[1]

But from what Miller also told Dennehy, the Cagney idea never excited Elia Kazan, the playwright's automatic choice for a director after both had won Tony awards in 1947 for their collaboration on *All My Sons*. Kazan's initial thought was March, whom he had directed in 1942 in Thornton Wilder's *The Skin of Our Teeth* and whom he considered a close friend. But March said no, claiming he was exhausted after months of filming the costume spectacular *Christopher Columbus*. (What March didn't say, at least in Kazan's telling, was that the actor was under attack at the time for his liberal politics and wanted to stay close to Hollywood to defend his movie star standing from right-wing zealots who also just happened to have the director and Miller in their sights.) Casting their net more widely, Kazan and Miller held more than one reading with Huston, but heard none of the anxiety they deemed essential to the Loman character.[2]

The most promising candidate but one who remained was Bohnen, then still running the Actors Laboratory in Los Angeles and very well known to Kazan through the Group. According to Marina Pratt, her father went to New York "as optimistic as he ever was about anything because of the talk he'd had with Kazan on the phone after reading the script."[3] Although Bohnen's relatively slight physique appeared to mark Kazan's capitulation to Miller's conception of Loman, the playwright himself had to conclude that he "seemed to lack the size of the character even if [he] fit the body."[4] As Pratt put it, "When Daddy came back home, he had one of those little Statue of Liberty souvenirs for me, but nothing for himself."

What Kazan had not shared with Miller, Bohnen, or anyone else but his wife was that he had also sent a copy of the script to Cobb in California, knowing full well how much the actor clashed with the description of the Loman character as written but also reminded by the Huston reading how Cobb embodied all the anxiety he was looking for. "Art had [Loman] as a very small man who wears little shoes and little vests," Kazan declared gleefully in his autobiography. "His emotions, in a word, are mercurial. Which is the way Art expected the part to be cast. Not with Lee Cobb, certainly not great lumbering Leo Jacob Cobb."[5]

Cobb thought differently. Julie Cobb recalled her mother telling her, "They had people over for dinner when the script came by messenger. My father went into his study with it, and was gone for a good two hours. Then he came out and said to everybody, 'Wait till you hear this. It's the greatest play ever written!' Then he sat down and read the entire play to everybody, taking all the parts. My mother said that she and everybody else knew right away that it was a role of a lifetime."

Cobb wasted little time in flying himself to New York in his Bonanza to read for Miller. For all the work the actor had done with the

Group and other theater companies in New York and despite all his screen appearances, Miller's only clear memory of him to that point was from the Turkish bath scene in Shaw's *The Gentle People*. He admitted to having been impressed by that performance, but what did a Rabelesian reading of a bankrupt businessman in a towel have to do with a brooding salesman in a musty vest? And then there was that other factor that always seemed to pop up with Cobb: his age. At the time he was only thirty-eight, twenty-three years younger than the part called for and more like the age of Loman's older son Biff.

But Cobb was not about to be deterred, certainly not after two decades of playing older men more often than those his own age; adding years, especially burdensome years, had never been one of his character exploration problems. "This is my part," he told Miller without preamble in producer Kermit Bloomgarden's office. "Nobody else can play this part. I know the man." Miller had heard that kind of self-confident declaration before, including from some who had read for Loman, but he began to sense more than braggadocio when he and others went downstairs to a coffee shop with Cobb. As he drily described it, "He looked up at the young waitress and smiled winsomely as though he had to win her loving embrace before she could be seduced into bringing him his turkey sandwich and coffee—ahead of all the other men's orders, and only after bestowing on his unique slice of pickle her longing kiss."[6]

Still, more days passed when Miller's best argument for casting Cobb remained Kazan's reassurances he would be right for the part. Then one night in the playwright's living room: "Lee looked down at my son, Bob, on the floor and I heard him laugh at something funny the child had said. The sorrow in his laughter flew out at me, touched me; it was deeply depressed and at the same time joyous, all flowing through a baritone voice that was gorgeously reedy. So large and handsome a man pretending to be thoroughly at ease in a world where he obviously did not fit could be moving."[7]

Kazan's attitude toward Cobb going back through the Group years was hardly all flattering, but precisely for that reason he said he thought of him as the perfect Loman. "Our friendship had started close, but like many actors' friendships, it thinned out. I knew him for a mass of contradictions: loving and hateful, anxious yet still supremely pleased with himself, smug but full of doubt, guilty and arrogant, fiercely competitive but very withdrawn, publicly private, suspicious but always reaching for trust, boastful with a modest air, begging for total acceptance no matter what he did to others. In other words, the part was him. I knew that Willy was in Cobb, there to be pulled out."[8]

How much of that intuition was Kazan writing forty tumultuous years after the fact is open to question, but there is no denying that Cobb had by then acquired a reputation among some as a wound constantly seeking a bandage; that is, even as a Group veteran, he was regarded as more difficult than most when it came to dealing with directors and producers. But what Kazan's list of virtues and vices really betrayed for better and worse was *size*—a personality able to embrace not just anxiety but all manner of moods to the epic degree that not even Miller realized for a while was the director's objective. Although he never quite admitted it, Kazan needed *all* the emotional and intellectual attributes he ascribed to Cobb for his vision of *Salesman*, and they were not easily found in other actors.

Cobb was not the only casting problem with *Salesman*. Strictly in terms of hiring, Arthur Kennedy, who had costarred in *All My Sons* on the stage for Kazan and Miller and for the director on the screen in *Boomerang*, was brought in without much trouble as the son Biff. One reason for the quick agreement was a commitment to give Kennedy equal billing with the actor playing Willy. But when Kennedy realized that the actor signed to play his father would be only three years older, he began having second thoughts about everything, including the quality of Miller's play. The confidant for his agitation was usually Cameron Mitchell, playing the younger son Biff. As Cameron Mitchell Jr. told it, "Dad said Kennedy never stopped. The play was going to be a disaster. Cobb was going to be a disaster. No one would ever buy him as Cobb's son, no matter what the makeup people did. Dad said the only reason Kennedy didn't quit was because Miller had so much faith in him."[9] According to actress Laurie Kennedy, though, her father had some very concrete reasons to be concerned, and they were more about the play than the casting of Loman. "They didn't really get the critical second act together until they almost went on in Philadelphia," Kennedy said, "so, sure, Pop was very worried. But everybody was, including Kazan."[10]

Mitchell's problems were of another order—a political hostility from Kazan that was slow to burn itself out even though it had been sparked by a false assumption on the part of the director. "Dad had read for *All My Sons*, the part that ended up going to Kennedy," his son, also an actor, recalled.

> A little while later, he runs into Kazan in a restaurant, says something polite about the reading, but Kazan just gives him the cold shoulder and walks away. Dad says screw him, but then along comes the script for *Salesman* and Dad's agent insists he go up to Connecticut to a hotel where Kazan and Miller are working and do some personal lobbying for the part of the younger brother. All the way up to Connecticut Dad's trying to talk himself into getting off the train and going back to New York. Why the hell should he be making so much effort to work for that bastard Kazan?
>
> He gets to the hotel, they call up to Kazan's room, and Kazan, cold as ever, tells Dad to go into the restaurant where Miller is, he'll be down in a few minutes. The good part of this is that it gives time for Dad to do some politicking with Miller for the role. Then Kazan comes down and as though Dad isn't there at all, he asks Miller to go for a walk with him on the grounds so they can talk about some script point. Dad walks along with them, by now ready to strangle Kazan because the guy isn't even acknowledging him. Then just when Dad's about to stalk off back to the train station, Kazan suddenly whirls on him and asks, "Are you fucking Hedda Hopper?"

As Mitchell learned to his dismay, the question had been precipitated by articles the Hollywood gossip columnist had written months earlier urging Fox to sign the actor for the role of a Jewish serviceman in *Gentleman's Agreement*, the picture about anti-Semitism that had gained an Oscar for Kazan. That part had ended up going to John Garfield, a frequent target for right-wingers in Hollywood like Hopper who found him too leftist for their taste. When Mitchell said that he barely knew the columnist, let alone had been sleeping with her, Kazan was dumbfounded, having wasted many months of political animus. Miller then stepped in to say that, as far as he was concerned, Mitchell would be fine as Hap.

Mildred Dunnock's path to the role of Loman's wife, Linda, also had its hurdles. A first reading went nowhere when Anne Revere was given the part. When Revere backed out of the play to make a film, Kazan went to Ruth Nelson, another Group compatriot who had already played Cobb's wife in *Jonah* for the Actors Lab. But Nelson said no because she wanted to remain with her husband, director John

Cromwell, then under attack by witch hunters in California. Dunnock, who had already established herself on Broadway in such plays as *The Corn Is Green* and *Another Part of the Forest*, volunteered to understudy other roles if she could play Linda. Out of courtesy for such an offer, Kazan and Miller invited her back for another reading, but that didn't go anywhere, either, mainly because the two men couldn't get over their preconception of the actress as the school teacher she had been before turning to acting and that she had also played in *The Corn Is Green*; for Miller and Kazan, this made her exactly wrong for a character identified as one who "lived in a house dress all her life" and who was "less than brilliant." But Dunnock didn't give up, returning for readings several times and in various dressed-down fashions. Then, just as she was about to give up, she was hired, to at least a contributing degree because the delays in casting her role had begun to jeopardize rehearsal and booking schedules.

Such unpromising beginnings slouched into unpromising middles. While the other cast members got off book quickly and responded to Kazan's blocking directions in rehearsals, Cobb remained within his own sphere. "Lee seemed to move about in a buffalo's stupefied trance, muttering his lines, plodding with deathly slowness from position to position, and behaving like a man who had been punched in the head," as Miller recounted it.[11] After more than a week of this behavior, Cobb had not only planted a deep dread in Miller that the wrong actor had been chosen, but had also begun to make Kazan sound brittle in his reassurances that everything would work out fine. When they couldn't be overheard by anybody, the two men began to refer to the actor as the Walrus. Then on the twelfth day of rehearsal, with the looming possibility of having to recast the Loman character, the revelation came:

> Lee stood up as usual from the bedroom chair and turned to Mildred Dunnock and bawled, "No, there's more people now. . . . There's more people!," and gesturing toward the empty upstage where the window was supposed to be, caused a block of apartment houses to spring up in my brain, and the air became sour with the smell of kitchens where once there had been only the odors of earth, and he began to move frighteningly, with such ominous reality that my chest felt pressed down by an immense weight. . . . Kazan behind me was grinning like a fiend. Gripping his temples with both hands, and we knew we had it—there was an unmistakable wave of life

moving across the air of the empty theater, a wave of Willy's pain and protest.[12]

There would be other problems during rehearsals, but once Cobb had vindicated his casting instinct, Kazan too showed more imagination in resolving them. One handy vehicle was the Philadelphia Symphony Orchestra, which held concerts directly across from the Locust Street Theatre where *Salesman* was scheduled to have its out-of-town premiere. First Kazan took Dunnock there to tell her he didn't like her delivery of the play's noted "attention must be paid" curtain speech and to warn her that he would be rehearsing her through it with a baton as frenetically as the conductor in front of them was leading his musicians. When she protested this would compromise the speech's nuances, Kazan brushed aside the objection and in fact proceeded over the next couple of days to reduce her to tears by whirling a baton in the air until she had eliminated all temptation to be mawkish about the speech. Only with that taken care of did they go back to retrieve the nuances Dunnock had worried about.[13]

On the afternoon of the Philadelphia opening, Kazan also brought Cobb to hear the orchestra, specifically Beethoven's Seventh Symphony. "We sat on either side of him in a box," Miller, who went along, related, "inviting him . . . to drink of the heroism of that music, to fling himself into his role tonight without holding back. We thought of ourselves . . . as a kind of continuation of a long and undying past."[14] As with the accolades Dudley Nicholas had bestowed on him after his Actors Lab performance of Chekhov, the Beethoven comparison was hardly geared toward humility.

Opening night in Philadelphia set a precedent that would be followed many times there and on Broadway—the final curtain coming down to a funereal silence except where there was audible crying. "People crossed the theater to stand quietly talking with one another," Miller wrote. "It seemed forever before somebody remembered to applaud, and then there was no end to it."[15] In a 1989 interview with James Grissom of blogspot.com, Dunnock recalled, "When Willy died in the play and I had to come out and make my speech at his grave, you could feel—I could feel—that the oxygen had left the theater, the city, the world. A death had happened, and it was someone everyone recognized and feared who had died."

As soon as the first Philadelphia reviews hit the newsstands, the play was sold out for its local run before going on to New York. When it opened at the Morosco Theatre on February 10, 1949, many in the audience had already seen it, having followed wildfire word of mouth down to Philadelphia. The daily and weekly critics in New York were beside themselves. Howard Barnes of the *Herald Tribune* started his review by declaring that "a great play of our day has opened at the Morosco," predicting that the drama would "make history." As for Cobb, he was credited with contributing "a mammoth and magnificent portrayal."[16] Atkinson of the *Times* agreed: "Mr. Cobb's tragic portrait of the defeated salesman is acting of the first rank. Although it is familiar and folksy in the details, it has something of the grand manner in the big size and the deep tone."[17] Linking Cobb's performance more explicitly to the social grounding of the play, John Mason Brown of the *Saturday Review* said it was like watching "a great shaggy bison of a man seen at that moment of defeat when he is deserted by the herd and can no longer run with it. Mr. Cobb makes clear the pathetic extent to which the herd has been Willy's life."[18]

Starting with Kazan's first reaction upon reading the play, that Willy Loman reminded him of his own father in many ways,[19] *Death of a Salesman* hit the nerves of a lot of families with an Uncle Manny. Strikingly, numerous actors who credited the play with pushing them toward their profession spent awkward evenings at the Morosco with their own fathers. "I lived in Long Island," George Segal remembered, "and we all went—my father, mother, and brother. There was this tremendous silence driving back home after the play. My father was also a salesman, and he had the same kind of roaring personality as Loman did. I knew all about those explosions Cobb got into."[20]

Actor-director Mark Rydell had a similar experience:

> My father was a stockbroker who played handball with Cobb in a health club. Cobb gave him tickets to the Morosco, and we ended up with front row seats in the orchestra. I'll never forget that climactic scene between Cobb and Kennedy. Their tears were literally bouncing off the stage into our laps. I was paralyzed. Because I was having problems with my father, so much of it registered with me personally. There was a lot of anger and resentment in my family, just like in the Loman house. When the play ended, there was total silence in the theater. I looked over at my father, and he couldn't get

up from his seat. The play had been talking to him as personally as it had been to me.[21]

Gene Wilder was another who made sure his evening at the Morosco didn't end there. "I went down from Poughkeepsie to see it. I really didn't know what acting was until that night. There was all this realistic talk going on, for god sake! Who knew? Over the next few years, while I was still a teenager, I played every conceivable character in that play—Willy, the two sons, Linda, Howard, anybody who was a character I ended up doing at women's clubs, schools, summer schools, Milwaukee, the University of Iowa. First the play just floored me, then it consumed me."[22]

Once they had digested their triumph, Miller and Kazan went off in different directions to express niggling doubts, then reconverged in agreement that Cobb was letting the play—*their* play—get away. Miller's first second-guess was that he should have said something about Kazan's Method approach to the play. "The production concept had somehow softened the edges of my far more aseptic original intention," he would write. "I knew nothing of Brecht then or of any other theory of theatrical distancing; I simply felt that there was too much identification with Willy, too much weeping, and that the play's ironies were being dimmed out by all this empathy."[23]

Kazan never specifically acknowledged that criticism. To have done so would have been to fuel a debate over a vision of the play that had indeed conflicted with Miller's from the moment he had brought in Cobb for the leading role. By going for the burly "Leo Jacob Cobb," as he called him, instead of the physically slighter actors Miller's approach would have accommodated, the director had aimed with Willy Loman for a god that had fallen off its pedestal in postwar America rather than, as Miller would have had it with a more fragile, introspective protagonist (and that he *did* have years later in a production with Dustin Hoffman), a patient who had rolled off a psychiatrist's couch. Paradoxically, in other words, while Kazan may have gone Method and Miller may have posed more intellectual arguments in subsequent writings and in interviews about the wider social and political implications of the play, it was the Kazan tack that ended up producing an epic drama equally relevant to those not named Loman. In the words of Richard Watts Jr. of the New York *Post*, "Only the most fatuous observer could think of *Death of a Salesman* as a propaganda play, and yet it manages to go deeply enough into contemporary values to be valid and frightening social commentary."[24] It was also undoubtedly in this context of believing he had made a greater personal contribution to the finished product that Kazan referred to *Salesman* as his "favorite play," but not the best written; that is, insofar as any play can be regarded as such just on the page, he preferred Tennessee Williams's *A Streetcar Named Desire.*[25]

For the most part, Kazan saved his Monday morning quarterbacking for the self-importance waved before the eyes of those acclaimed for their part in the production. "The great success of the play certified our worth. Truth was soon out of sight; we all puffed up. . . . [Our producers], Lee Cobb, Arthur Miller, and Elia Kazan were never the same again." Co-defendant or not, he saved his sharpest jabs for Cobb, asserting that the actor had given his finest performances in Philadelphia. "After we opened on Broadway, he began to share the audience's admiration for his performance and their pity for the character he played. Life on Broadway would not, because it could not, satisfy this man's hunger for unqualified recognition."[26]

Miller agreed. Dropping into the Morosco now and then after the play had begun its run, and echoing Strasberg's criticisms during *Clash by Night*, he said he "could drive a truck through some of Lee's stretched-out pauses, which were tainting his performance with more than a hint of self-indulgence. With Kazan off to a new project, Lee had taken to re-directing Arthur Kennedy and Cameron Mitchell and to enjoying rather than suffering the anguish of the character."[27] Kennedy's daughter said that if that was true, her father never complained about it. "The main thing that used to bother Pop about Cobb was the gin rummy games he was always playing for money before the show with people from the crew," Laurie Kennedy said. "If he won, you could be pretty sure he would give a good performance that night. If he lost, things weren't going to be so great. That's why everybody in the cast was curious about those games."

As for Cobb, his identification with the role was so complete that it took time even for him to understand some of the refinements he put into his performance. Julie Cobb: "He told me he was already doing it for weeks before he wondered why he was giving this very slight limp to Loman. Then finally he realized why: There had been an old street vendor in his neighborhood who had limped. Vendor equals salesman!" But Cobb's personal triumph also generated an unstable mix of hauteur and insecurity, leading to some gratuitously nasty scenes with other members of the cast. In retrospect, Miller connected his antics to the rehearsal day when the actor had persuaded everyone he was right for Loman. "I ran up and kissed Lee, who pretended to be surprised. 'But what did you expect, Arthur?' he said, his eyes full of his playful vanity. My God, I thought—he really *is* Willy!"[28] There was also a foreshadowing of self-righteousness in the *Playbill* bio Cobb was asked to supply for the theater handout. Said the program (in part) for his entry: "He has stubbornly refused to be a victim of the Philistine practice of typecasting and has fought his way to a variety of roles."[29] *Philistine* was not a word common to such notes.

Don Keefer, the longest surviving member of the original production's cast, recalled "a lot of tension over how Kennedy had the right to be on the marquee the way he was. That one seemed to come out of nowhere. Kennedy's name had been up there a long time. Before that Lee seemed to be into one thing or another with Kazan. He was really very childlike, kept saying they were using him very badly. I asked him a couple of times what he meant by that, but I could never figure it out."[30]

What some of it had to do with, according to Vincent Cobb, was his father's futile efforts to rehearse more after the opening of the play. "He became distressed because he felt they needed additional rehearsals a while after they opened and the producer Bloomgarden made a typical management decision that they wouldn't have any because they couldn't get any more people into the theater, so what would have been the point? Guess how that attitude made him feel."

However keenly Cobb might have felt about the added rehearsals, though, there was much more conflict around his demands for more time off, arguing that Loman was an excruciating physical and psychological grind. Even those not sympathetic to his situation couldn't help noticing the toll the nightly performances were taking on him. According to Garfield's daughter Julie, for instance, "Daddy was in a play at the same time Cobb was doing *Salesman*. Whenever he walked into Sardi's, he found Cobb sitting alone and depressed, and could never figure out why. He told my mother: 'What the hell has he got to be depressed about? I'm barely hanging on with my play and he's got a big hit, but he's the one who's depressed!'" Leonard Lyons, Earl Wilson, and other Broadway columnists reported similar sightings of Cobb sitting alone in Sardi's over the spring and summer.

At least one academic, Andrew B. Harris, has suggested that was all but inevitable since Cobb's role was unique. "Loman has as much stage time as any of Shakespeare's major tragic heroes," Harris, a theater department chairman at several universities, observed, "and whereas the structure of Shakespeare's plays usually provides for a fourth act rest allowing the actor a little time to recover while the consequences of his actions catch up with him, Willy is in the thick of it from the moment the lights come up in Act One."[31] Others have pointed out that apart from the sheer time the Loman character is on the stage, he is on an emotional roller coaster, going from present to past and back to the present again in wildly different moods. Making matters yet worse, the New York summer in 1949 was miserably hot, and understudy Robert Simon didn't dare take his phone off the hook. It was not the kind of grind that made for many laughs among cast members. "Pop and Mitchell gravitated toward Millie Dunnock as if she really were their mother," Laurie Kennedy recalled being told. "But outside of that, the biggest laugh they all had was probably the night Thomas Chalmers, who was playing Uncle Ben and who sometimes staggered on stage, was supposed to deliver the line 'The jungle is dark but full of diamonds, Willy.' Instead it came out through his slurring as 'The jungle is dark and full of Willys, Diamond.' Pop said everybody had to turn upstage so the audience wouldn't see their roaring. But that sounded very much like the exception to the mood around the cast."

Shakespeare or no Shakespeare, emotional roller coaster or not, Kazan showed little patience with Cobb's complaints. "We all saw he was dramatizing . . . beyond measure. He said he was on the verge of a breakdown and demanded that I consult with his analyst. I did: we had a bad scene. I still don't know how serious Lee's trouble was; he was a very good actor and determined to prove that he had to leave the show."[32]

Dennehy, who played the part fifty years later, said that he was initially baffled by his discovery that Cobb had remained with the show only until early fall. But then he began to feel the weight of his daily encounters with Loman, too.

> Soon after we opened, I got to thinking, "Oh, my god, do I have to go through this every night for god knows how long?" It was Jerry Orbach who straightened me out. One night he came in to see me after the show and I closed my dressing room door and told him I had a

problem, that I just didn't think I'd be able to keep going physically or psychologically. Getting out of bed in the morning was getting harder and harder. Jerry laughed like hell. He'd been in a lot of long-running shows. This is one of the greatest experiences of your life, he said to me, but right now you're still in the opening phase of it where you think of it only as work. Once you get over that, you'll get to a place where you can't wait to get to the theater. And he turned out to be absolutely right. I think Cobb's real problem with the role was that he was never able to get past the work part.

Brother Norman Jacob said he had come to somewhat the same conclusion. "Basically, I think Lee was frightened by Willy Loman. The character called for so much every performance that it really wasn't all that under control, not the way Lee was putting absolutely everything into it every night. Of course he was exhausted. He refused to pull back on it. It was like he was caught between a rock and a hard place—not enough and it might get away from him, too much and it might get away from him. I think he was just plain scared every night he was doing it."

It didn't hurt Cobb's iconic identification with the role that when he finally left the play in early fall his immediate replacement was the diminutive Gene Lockhart, familiar from the screen largely for wheedling or cowardly characters. "Dad said Lockhart almost had a nervous breakdown," Cameron Mitchell Jr. related. "He was terrified. He knew he was miscast. He kept flubbing lines and everybody in the cast had to cover for him. He was really relieved when they brought in Albert Dekker and then Thomas Mitchell because Mitchell had a bigger name than Dekker for a road company tour." The only positive side of all the changes, Laurie Kennedy said, was that it kept her father interested in going to work in the evening. "He said he wouldn't have lasted as long as he did without different Willy Lomans to have to deal with. In an odd way, all the changes refreshed him."

Despite the clamorous reviews he received for his performance, Cobb was shut out from the Tony awards, the Best Actor prize for the year going to Rex Harrison for *Anne of the Thousand Days*.[33] The snub was all the more noticeable when Miller, Kazan, Kennedy (supporting actor), and set designer Jo Mielziner all carried home trophies. If Cobb was disappointed, he never said so publicly. And he was to have considerable practice in that self-discipline because, despite a couple of Oscar nominations in the 1950s, he never walked off with one of the entertainment industry's big prizes. Did that bother him? Vincent Cobb: "I really don't think he gave a shit about any of that. I can't say it might not have stung to see somebody walk off with something he thought should have been his, but he really didn't believe in all that competition for awards. And I'm absolutely positive that even if he had won an Oscar or a Tony, it wouldn't have ended up on some mantelpiece like a shrine to his glory. He wouldn't have wanted the reminder of what had been. First and last it was the work in front of him."

Which wasn't to say Cobb ever lost sight of the singular importance of the Willy Loman role in his career. In the 1970s, Mike Livingston, his agent at the time, asked if he had any regrets about his career. Cobb's reply was, "Yeah, I never found another part like Willy Loman."[34] On other occasions, he was quoted as denying the greater social significance of *Salesman*, contending that it was basically a love story between Loman and his older son Biff: "Willy Loman is nobody's hero, but we are all his bereaved."[35]

Instead of awards Cobb ended up with the kind of admiration playwrights have seldom showered on actors. Despite all his criticisms of the pace of performances after *Salesman* had been running a while and sharing Kazan's disapproval of Cobb's behind-the-scenes antics, Miller could write six years after the opening,

> I think of Lee Cobb, the greatest dramatic actor I ever saw, when he was creating the role of Willy Loman in *Death of a Salesman*. When I hear people scoffing at actors as mere exhibitionists, when I hear them ask why there must be a theater if it cannot support itself as any business must, when I myself grow sick and weary of the endless waste and the many travesties of this most abused of all arts, I think then of Lee Cobb making that role and I know that the theater can yet be one of the chief glories of mankind.[36]

## NOTES

1. Interview with author, December 3, 2012. Subsequent quotes from Brian Dennehy are taken from this interview.

2. This didn't prevent Kazan from trying twice more to get Huston for the role—first as a replacement after the play had been on Broadway for some months and then as the head of a road company tour. Both times Huston said no, claiming previous film engagements.

3. Interview with author, January 22, 2013. Subsequent quotes from Marina Pratt are taken from this interview.

4. Arthur Miller, *Timebends: A Life* (New York: Grove Press, 1987), p. 186.

5. Kazan, *Elia Kazan*, p. 356.

6. Miller, *Timebends*, p. 186.

7. Ibid., p. 187.

8. Kazan, *Elia Kazan*, p. 362.

9. Interview with author, June 24, 2012. Subsequent quotes from Cameron Mitchell Jr. are taken from this interview.

10. Interview with author, April 26, 2013. Subsequent quotes from Laurie Kennedy are taken from this interview.

11. Miller, *Timebends*, p. 187.

12. Ibid., pp. 187–188.

13. Andrew B. Harris, *Broadway Theatre* (London and New York: Routledge, 1994), p. 60.

14. Miller, *Timebends*, p. 190.

15. Ibid, p. 191.

16. *New York Herald Tribune*, February 11, 1949.

17. *New York Times*, February 11, 1949.

18. *Saturday Review*, February 26, 1949.

19. Kazan, *Elia Kazan*, pp. 357–358.

20. Interview with author, June 4, 2012. Subsequent quotes from George Segal are taken from this interview.

21. Interview with author, July 30, 2011.

22. Interview with author, October 23, 2011. Subsequent quotes from Gene Wilder are taken from this interview.

23. Miller, *Timebends*, p. 194.

24. *Post* (New York), February 11, 1949.

25. Kazan, *Elia Kazan*, p. 355.

26. Ibid., p. 362.

27. Miller, *Timebends*, p. 194.

28. Ibid., p. 188.

29. *Playbill*, Morosco Theatre, February 1949.

30. Interview with author, December 22, 2012.

31. Harris, *Broadway Theatre*, p. 63.

32. Kazan, *Elia Kazan*, p. 362.

33. Until the early 1950s, the Tonys publicized no nominees, only category winners.

34. Interview with author, April 4, 2012.

35. *New York Times*, February 12, 1976.

36. Arthur Miller, *Holiday* 17 (January 1955), p. 93.

# Chapter 14

———————◯———————

# The Actor:
# Studio of the Stars

METRO-GOLDWYN-MAYER LIKED boasting in its heyday that it had
under contract "more stars than there are in heaven." But in fact the
single greatest concentration of Hollywood elite was to be found over
the second half of the twentieth century within the linoleum-smelling
rooms of a reconverted Presbyterian church on West Forty-fourth
Street in Manhattan. It was there in 1955, after moving around from
one part of the city to another since its founding by Elia Kazan and
Robert Lewis eight years earlier, that the Actors Studio took over from
the building's most recent tenant, the National Amputation Foundation, to establish its permanent quarters. Unlike the Group Theatre,
and for reasons extending beyond its celebrated membership, it would
brew few complexes over who met the definition of a leading man and
who didn't.

Although Kazan and Lewis were its primary movers, the Studio
was not another attempt by the pair to refloat the Dollar Top production company they had pursued briefly after the demise of the Group.
From the beginning they and third partner Cheryl Crawford were to
be heard rejecting any notion of a producing organization. All three
partners were simply too busy—Kazan as an award-winning director
on both Broadway and in Hollywood, Lewis as a theater director of
such hits as the musical *Brigadoon*, and Crawford as the producer of
a number of Broadway successes. But that still left time for tackling
what all three felt was an ongoing problem even in ventures where
they were lauded for their achievements; indeed, the sharpest spur for

what would become the most famous acting center in the world since the Moscow Art Theatre was plain aggravation. As David Garfield put it in his study of the Studio, "Whatever Kazan achieved as a director was inevitably accomplished in spite of the mélange of acting styles and abilities he had to contend with. Under the typical commercial pressures of the New York theater, he was unable to use actors to their fullest potential, or to create the kind of ensemble playing he had participated in with the Group. There was neither time nor place to explore and experiment with the actor. Kazan had to make do."[1] Garfield quoted Kazan: "We want a common language so that I can direct actors instead of coach them . . . so that we have a common vocabulary. It's not a school. Actors can come and actors can go. It's a place to work and find this vocabulary."[2] Or, as the director declared more succinctly in reference to a Midtown hangout where performers at the time exchanged gossip and job leads, "I just want to get young actors out of that goddamn Walgreen drugstore."[3]

Kazan's antidote to Walgreens was a series of fixed workshops divided into two categories. One would be for beginners who knew little or nothing about the Method; he would preside over that one himself. The second, headed by Lewis, would be for established actors who didn't want their skills to atrophy between jobs or while doing low-demand work. (This was their equivalent to what Stanislavsky had divided into beginners and "experienced and spoiled" actors.) As with the Group, Crawford was responsible for business and administrative matters. Working members were expected to contribute two dollars a week toward basic expenses. That was the blueprint, anyway.

As might have been expected from the people involved, the Group saturated the Studio's DNA, for both positive and negative impulses. Even before the first workshop was organized, personal resentments and self-aggrandizements from the tense old days were on parade, with Harold Clurman claiming that the Studio idea had been his and that Kazan had run off with it as his own, and Kazan saying he didn't know what Clurman was talking about; they had merely traded general ideas. Apparently enamored of the mythic continuum of the lunch between Stanislavsky and Nemirovich-Danchenko that had spawned the Moscow Art Theatre and the Clurman-Strasberg conversations in New York cafeterias that had ultimately given birth to the Group, Crawford took to insisting that the Studio came out of a talk she had with Kazan in a Greek restaurant—at least until she conceded she wasn't all that sure and who cared anyway. Once past those debatable particulars, Kazan and Lewis made it a first principle that, aside from not mounting public productions in the Group manner, their workshops would be free of the Strasberg stresses in the Method that had so divided the 1930s company. Another Group attribute, political contentiousness, was regarded as so irrelevant to the Studio's purpose that it wasn't even addressed.

Then realities kicked in. The first goal discarded was for a maximum of twenty veterans in the Lewis workshop and fifteen in the one conducted by Kazan. As soon as word got out about the Studio, there was a stampede by actors, both fledgling and established, to attend the sessions that, apart from offering training in Method techniques, could not help but provide important contacts for paying jobs on both the East Coast and West Coast. This networking calculation forced far more intensive screening procedures for candidates, including rigorous auditions for those with small résumés, than the founders had envisioned. But screenings or not, there were almost ninety full-time members by the early 1950s.[4] Such unforeseen numbers led to more than one organizational breakdown and the onset of perennial financial woes, and also prompted some on-the-fly regulations for reimposing order. One early rule, for instance, called for dismissal of a member after two consecutive absences for any reason but a competing professional engagement. However much the founders wanted to deny they were running a school, the Studio certainly had a principal's office.

Lewis's first workshop included Marlon Brando, Montgomery Clift, Herbert Berghof, Mildred Dunnock, Tom Ewell, John Forsythe, Patricia Neal, E. G. Marshall, Maureen Stapleton, Eli Wallach, David Wayne, and one-time Group members Karl Malden and Sidney Lumet. Among those selected for Kazan's first class were Brando's sister, Jocelyn; Arthur Miller's sister, Joan Copeland; Betsy Drake; Julie Harris; Steven Hill; Cloris Leachman; Nehemiah Persoff; and James Whitmore. It was a taste of things to come and to keep coming. While the Group had produced only Tone and Garfield as stars in a Hollywood sense, the Studio went on over the next few decades to add through audition or invitation James Dean, Paul Newman, Joanne Woodward, Lee Remick, Eva Marie Saint, Richard Boone, Steve McQueen, Shelley Winters, Jon Voigt, Rod Steiger, Anthony Franciosa, Christopher Walken, Ben Gazzara, Sally Field, Geraldine Page, Walter Matthau, Anne Bancroft, Ellen Burstyn, Jack

Nicholson, Jane Fonda, Robert Duvall, Dustin Hoffman, Al Pacino, Harvey Keitel, and Robert De Niro. If the Group had carried the image of a fractious dissident right down to its final days, the Studio's membership—notwithstanding the skittish personalities projected by some individually—added up to a show business Establishment. Not even the Actors Lab in the heart of Hollywood and with the constant coming and going of big movie names came close to the star power generated by the Studio.

Hardly surprising in view of the talents attracted to the Actors Studio, one of the ongoing debates within the membership concerned the founding resolve of Kazan, Lewis, and Crawford not to undertake productions. That determination was dented as early as 1948 by Kazan himself, when his search for a workshop piece that could include his thirty-odd students led him to Bessie Breuer's *Sundown Beach*, a full-length play about U.S. Air Force pilots convalescing in Florida after the war. Before he knew it, he was mounting a full-scale production and getting into tangles with running Broadway shows because some actors with bit parts in them were quitting in favor of the play they were work-shopping in their off-hours. The decision to press ahead to a major commercial staging was abetted by cordial reviews of the play in pre–New York tryouts in Westport and Boston. Optimism was high enough to ignore the response by the *Christian Science Monitor* critic, arguably the first to complain in print about the mumbling of Studio actors.[5]

When the play opened in New York at the Belasco on September 7, the *Monitor*'s reaction seemed comparatively benevolent. Tepid was as good as it got. Atkinson of the *Times* tore into it twice, in his first-night review chiding it for giving "an impression of breathlessness as though it were running very fast to stay in the same place" and being "full of violent physical interludes that had no particular meaning,"[6] then coming back four days later to go specifically after the direction, asserting that the actors gave "a public exhibition of technique under pressure, like some of the Group Theatre's overwrought works."[7] The show, with a cast that included Nehemiah Persoff, Julie Harris, Martin Balsam, Cloris Leachman, Steven Hill, Edward Binns, Phyllis Thaxter, Vivian Nathan, and Alex Nicol, closed after seven performances.

The ramifications of the *Sundown Beach* flop were to be felt for decades, first of all around Kazan's relationship with the Studio. Already for some months he and Crawford had been going it alone after

Lewis's resignation over some hanky-panky about directing a musical entitled *Love Life*; according to Lewis, Kazan had first advised him to stay away from the script, then had sneakily agreed to direct it himself.[8] One of the numerous he-said-but-who-remembered-exactly disputes that dogged Kazan's career, he rejected the idea of taking over as the Studio's full-time artistic director. Instead, after failing at attempts to bring in Josh Logan and Sanford Meisner, he turned to more unexpected candidates. The first was Clurman, who regarded the request as amusing given the to-do about who had first come up with the idea for the Studio. The second—Strasberg, he of the Method approaches to be avoided—might have found it equally amusing if he had been known for a hearty sense of humor. But lacking that, he said yes. From that point on, and even though he did not become artistic director officially until 1951, the Studio became synonymous with Strasberg and his teaching methods.

Strasberg embodied the hesitations about having the Studio function solely as a workshop or as a vehicle for commercial productions. On the one hand, he developed his teaching role with an austere fervor, adding to a reputation already in place through his presence on the faculties of the American Theater Wing and the Dramatic Workshop. He had also come away the worse for wear from a couple of Broadway directorial chores that had persuaded him to remain on the production sidelines for a while. At the same time, however, he professed astonishment that Kazan and Lewis had opposed productions in light of the talents at their disposal at the Studio. "For me," Garfield quoted him as having told Kazan, "something like this is the basis for the building of a theater. Otherwise it has no purpose."[9] And the Studio did have periods under his direction and after his death when doing its own plays appealed as the fastest way of resolving financial difficulties. Indeed, the lowest point in the turbulent relations between the men came in the 1960s, when Strasberg ripped into Kazan for not using his influence to have the Studio named as the performing arm of the Lincoln Center Theater. Kazan admitted as much: "The reason I didn't was that I didn't believe Lee was qualified to be a producing director."[10]

As far as Strasberg's teaching was concerned, more than ever he pushed the emotional memory button, often leading to an inversion of its original purpose. Studio-trained actors were regularly accused of having their stage and screen characters submit to their personal emotions rather than vice versa, making for the paralyzed actions

Stanislavsky had warned Stella Adler about in Paris. In the course of fixating on those inward moments some performers—the kind Meisner had worried about—felt insecure physically and, with their imaginations frozen from recalling what had often been traumatic events, resorted to the gratuitous scratching, muttering, or wincing that struck them belatedly as necessary movement. In such an egocentric state Stanislavsky's exhortation that actors question the motivation of their characters' actions could lend itself to the ridiculous. One of the emblematic incidents of the kind occurred years later during the shooting of the film *The Marathon Man*, when Dustin Hoffman protested to director John Schlesinger that he had no motivation for a simple piece of action and costar Laurence Olivier blurted, "Act, Dusty. Just *act*."

It was with such episodes in mind that Lewis, whose antagonism toward Strasberg predated their successive tenures at the Studio and which was reflected in the title of one of his books, *Method—or Madness?*, quoted approvingly from Vera Soloviova, an early Moscow Art Theatre player, then a teacher of Stanislavsky's system: "Stanislavsky practiced psychology," he cited Soloviova as having said, "Strasberg practices psychiatry. Stanislavsky's emotion came from the heart, Strasberg's comes from the *kishkas*."[11] Arthur Miller, who worked frequently with Studio actors, used some of the same terminology: "I think Strasberg . . . is a great force which is not good for the theater. He makes actors secret people and he makes acting secret, and it's the most communicative art known to man; I mean, what's the actor's *supposed* to be doing. . . . When you eliminate the vital element of the actor in the community and simply make a psychiatric figure on the stage who is thinking profound thoughts which he doesn't let anyone know about, then it's a perversion."[12]

But however mocked some of the performing procrastinations and exaggerations of Studio people,[13] however their craft remained a work in progress for some years, their recognition factor was extremely high by the early 1950s. This owed not just to Strasberg and the Studio, but to the burgeoning entertainment medium of television that had a convenient well for casting. As the home of weekly regular live drama series that were aired nationally, such as Studio One and the Philco Playhouse, New York was able to offer young actors more possibilities than those to be found on Broadway and Off-Broadway. And once those performers began attracting attention also in Chicago and Los Angeles, Hollywood pounced. It had some unusually pressing reasons for presenting young new faces to the public, and one of them was very political.

## NOTES

1. David Garfield, *The Actors Studio: A Player's Place* (New York: Collier Books, 1980), p. 45.
2. Ibid., p. 54.
3. *Show Business Illustrated*, February 1962.
4. Incomplete records from the Studio's first years make this more of an estimate than a precise figure.
5. *Christian Science Monitor*, July 27, 1948.
6. *New York Times*, September 8, 1948.
7. *New York Times*, September 12, 1948.
8. Lewis, *Slings and Arrows*, pp. 187–188.
9. Garfield, *Actors Studio*, p. 80. Cobb appeared to agree. According to daughter Julie, his aversion to strictly teaching situations as opposed to actual performance kept him away from the Studio even during his time in New York doing *Death of a Salesman* and despite knowing so many of the principals.
10. Kazan, *Elia Kazan*, pp. 607–608.
11. Lewis, *Slings and Arrows*, p. 281.
12. *Paris Review* 10 (Summer 1966), pp. 71–76.
13. Some extravagances were also soon to be seen in non-Studio actors exposed to West Forty-fourth Street habits, such as with a newly acquired verbal writhing by Glenn Ford in the mid-1950s.

# Chapter 15

═══════════════○═══════════════

# The Un-American
# Dream

ONE LEADING ROLE COBB did not seek was in the postwar congressional witch hunt unleashed by the House Un-American Activities Committee (HUAC) behind the banner of anti-Communism. But seek it or
not, he was cast as a prominent target, and what turned out to be the
most negligible consideration for both him and the politicians adding
him to a movie industry list of undesirables was that he had never regarded himself as a formal member of the Communist Party. It was all
about naming names, thereby making headlines for HUAC and making it possible for him to keep working; facts and rights were secondary
when not altogether irrelevant. His response to the harassment marked
him psychically, socially, and professionally for the rest of his life.

A HUAC forerunner, the Special Committee on Un-American
Activities, had been nosing around Hollywood already in the late
1930s. Chaired by Texas congressman Martin Dies, it was a product of the political opportunity provided by the Stalinist purges in
the Soviet Union and of the corporate animosity to the stands taken
by numerous motion picture figures on behalf of the loyalist cause
in the Spanish civil war—a no-no for those who profited from doing business with General Franco's backers in Nazi Germany and
Fascist Italy. Although it fell over its own feet in California, the
Dies body exerted appreciable influence by setting precedent for
farcically wild congressional accusations pivoted around the word
*Communism,* an exercise in demagoguery emulated years later by both
HUAC and Wisconsin senator Joseph McCarthy. One Dies claim was

that there were "not less than 2,000 outright Communists and party liners still holding jobs in the government in Washington"; another that the New Deal's Work Progress Administration (WPA) was a Communist conspiracy hatched by Franklin Delano Roosevelt; a third that actors Humphrey Bogart and Fredric March were Communists. Before folding his tent Dies had to retract all those absurdities and throw in his concession that there was "no credible evidence of Communist activity in the movie industry," but tactics had been hatched.[1]

World War II and the American-Soviet alliance against Germany kept HUAC on the sidelines for a while, but it came roaring back to investigative life after the conflict. Its resumed interest in Hollywood in 1947 under Chairman J. Parnell Thomas differed from the Dies fishing expedition in critical ways. For starters, it returned to movie matters at the covering invitation of the right-wing Motion Picture Alliance for the Presentation of American Ideals (MPAPAI), thereby preempting criticism from within the industry town that it was an outsider just hunting publicity. The MPAPAI had largely been the creation of director Sam Wood (*Goodbye, Mr. Chips*; *Kitty Foyle*; *The Pride of the Yankees*) who would almost literally drop dead from his phobia of Communists in suffering a fatal heart attack in 1949 after prolonged raging at actress Margaret Sullavan for not firing a leftist writer on one of her pictures. Among the prominent organization members allied within the Wood crusade were John Wayne, Ward Bond, Walt Disney, Robert Taylor, Ginger Rogers, Barbara Stanwyck, Clark Gable, and Kazan's favorite gossip columnist, Hedda Hopper.

Another major difference in the California probes of the Dies and Thomas committees was in the attitude of studio executives, who had no interest in having their moneymaking stars, directors, and writers branded as Reds but everything to gain from having some industry craft union leaderships denounced as part of a foreign conspiracy. If the studio heads had been forced to reach a modus vivendi with the guilds for actors, directors, and writers back in the 1930s, they continued to oppose postwar attempts by dissident workers of the Conference of Studio Unions (CSU) to displace the Mob-controlled International Alliance of Theatrical Stage Employees (IATSE) because they found it much cheaper to pay off the hoods and accept their quid pro quo of supportive muscle than to accede to the pay and benefits demands that loomed as an alternative. They didn't like having outsiders witness their reliance on IATSE thugs and hose-wielding police for breaking up picket lines, either. When Actors Lab board member Rose Hobart made the mistake of seeing the police hoses in action outside the Warner Brothers Burbank studio in 1945, a war of words ensued that ended with Lab members taking to the streets in solidarity with the CSU and studio chief Jack Warner demanding back all the props and sets he had donated for the theater's stage productions. From then on the trade press, especially the *Hollywood Reporter*, went after the Lab, charging that if it wasn't Communist, it was at least sympathetic to the thinking of the American Communist Party.[2] There was more than one reminder that Bohnen, Carnovsky, and other members had come from the Group Theatre, producers of *Waiting for Lefty* and other antimanagement plays. This put the Lab on a collision course with the MPAPAI's published guidelines to the studios that their pictures should not disparage the free enterprise system, deify the common man, criticize success, glorify failure, or smear industrialists. A lot of people very quickly forgot how important the Lab had been to the thriving of theater in Hollywood.

The first big national splash from HUAC came when, after a "fact-finding mission" in California, the panel opened hearings in Washington in October 1947. To endorse its objectives it paraded before radio mikes and newsreel cameras several recognizable "friendly witnesses" who had had belatedly suspicious thoughts about some of the equality and fraternity dialogue they had recited in pictures made during the war. With the exception of Gary Cooper, the friendlies were a little worn at the edges, not exactly riding the crest of box office popularity. Ginger Rogers, for example, had long left behind both Fred Astaire and *Kitty Foyle*, while Robert Taylor was deep in a career valley between his prewar romancing of Greta Garbo and Vivien Leigh and his brief rebound in the 1950s as Ivanhoe and assorted knights of the realm. Richard Arlen had been a leading man only in B pictures, and hadn't even been that for a while. Three others, Ronald Reagan, George Murphy, and Robert Montgomery, were already on their way over to television as a transition to Republican Party careers. It might not have been a Hopalong Cassidy cast, but it wasn't an A list, either. As for Cooper, his handlers had felt the need for some public clarification after the actor's name had circulated in a comedy of errors as a backer of a Latin American Communist Party he had never actually heard of. On the other hand, such MPAPAI members as Wayne, Stanwyck, and Gable avoided the hearings, and, friendly or not, for reasons that gave

priority to their still thriving careers. As actor Robert Vaughn, author
of a book on the blacklist, once told the author,

> The attitude of the Cohns, Warners, and the rest was very pragmatic.
> They didn't really give a damn if some actor wanted to testify to say
> that he had been a Red or to say the Committee was doing a won-
> derful job. Uppermost to them was that an actor not be associated
> with the Committee *in any way* since that would make their image
> in the mind of the public hazier down the road in a few years. After
> a while, would the public remember *how* an actor had testified, or
> would it simply remember that he had, that he had been mixed up
> in some kind of political thing that undermined whatever generic
> image a studio was banking on at the box office? The apprehensions
> of the studio bosses were first and last apprehensions about dollars
> and cents.[3]

But if the committee was sensitive to the box office reasons a
macho star like Wayne didn't want to be filmed complimenting a
wrinkled, gray-haired congressman for being a greater American hero
than he was, it had little patience with witnesses who could not be accused of friendliness. The fall hearings in fact became a short subject
when ten of the first nineteen witnesses subpoenaed showed up only
to announce they had no intention of cooperating. The so-called Hollywood Ten, present or past members of the Communist Party, were
director Edward Dmytryk, director-screenwriter Herbert Biberman,
producer-screenwriter Robert Adrian Scott, Cobb friend Alvah Bessie,
and fellow screenwriters Lester Cole, Ring Lardner Jr., John Howard
Lawson, Albert Maltz, Sam Ornitz, and Dalton Trumbo. When they
maintained their positions on various constitutional grounds, not to
mention pointing out how there was nothing illegal about having party
membership, they were prohibited from making any further statements
in the hearing room and then charged with contempt of Congress, after which HUAC adjourned the session behind Thomas's face-saving
warning that "this is only the beginning." Three years later, after being
fired by their studios or told to forget scheduled projects and put on a
blacklist, the ten had their sentences of up to one year upheld by the
Supreme Court and went to jail.[4]

To what end? Had HUAC spared the American public subtle
Communist propaganda in scripts turned out by the indicted writers? Had it established the ground for stronger legislative protections

against anti-American attitudes seeping into the mass entertainment media? As Victor Navasky has noted, that had never been the point.

> Even if the subversive-hunting committees had been interested in collecting information for legislative purposes (and the evidence is that they weren't), the request that each witness name names as a test was not in pursuit of such legitimate ends. . . . The purpose of the hearings, although they were not trials, was clearly punitive, yet the procedural safeguards appropriate to tribunals in the business of meting out punishment were absent: there was no cross-examination, no impartial judge and jury, none of the exclusionary rules about hearsay or other evidence. And, of course, the targets from the entertainment business had committed no crime: "whistle blowing" in this context injured only the innocent.[5]

For a few years after the scene with the Hollywood Ten, HUAC hovered in the wings while various government and private groups exerted pressures on the studios to keep their distance from leftists. In California a state legislative committee chaired by John Tenney took particular aim at the Actors Lab, summoning Bohnen and fellow directors Rose Hobart, Will Lee, and Joe Bromberg to repudiate their alleged Communist ties. When the witnesses refused to testify, they were cited as "critics of the committee," by now in itself an implication of subversive intentions. That put an end to the Lab's access to GI Bill credits and to its arrangements with Fox and Universal for teaching contract players.[6] Even with those setbacks the Lab had built up enough of a reputation to push ahead for a few months with plans for a television series, but then on February 24, 1949, Bohnen, the Lab's all-but-indispensable chief administrator, dropped dead of a heart attack while performing, and the factionalism he had been keeping at bay swamped the group to its demise. His daughter, for one, never doubted the connection between his death and the hounding from Tenney. Marina Pratt: "He'd never had heart problems. What he had were witch-hunting problems."

If the Tenney committee wore the mantle of elected government while determining who was politically acceptable, others did not. In addition to the MPAPAI and studio executives who acceded to its recommendations with little resistance, the American Legion and the Catholic War Veterans joined in the vetting, sending their newsletters on the politically suspect to hundreds of posts around the country, making it clear to the studios that noisy boycotts from Maine to New Mexico could follow from their displeasure with a picture or those appearing in it. Lawyers and even psychiatrists found nothing unethical about betraying the confidences of clients for racking up Americanism credits. Then there was American Business Consultants, Inc., of importer and Chiang Kai-Shek lobbyist Alfred Kohlberg. Its claims of expertise for political litmus tests rested on former FBI agents heading its investigations, the insinuation being that they still had access to the files of that anti-Communist of anti-Communists, FBI director J. Edgar Hoover. Kohlberg's outfit was also conspicuous in the repentance system that behind the veneer of "clearing," the accused consolidated the blacklist's legitimacy. For those desperate to get off the proscription rolls, entities such as American Business Consultants facilitated closed-doors sessions with Washington investigators where the accused were encouraged to name others who had been present at Communist Party or leftist meetings, including those of a united front character during the war; to make effusive declarations of loyalty to the United States at some public forum; to make under-the-table payments to dubious funds purportedly carrying on the patriotic work of the investigators and their employers; to work on anti-Communist features in front of or behind the camera; or to do all of the above.

In the August 1947 issue of *Esquire*, film critic Jack Moffitt surveyed the atmosphere sardonically in a column entitled "The Muse Discards Her Mask," declaring in part, "These words are written from a Hollywood in turmoil. Magazine correspondents are alighting from every train to probe allegedly Communistic activities in the movie capital. The Federal Bureau of Investigation is said to have had so many agents planted in the Actors Laboratory that audiences aren't quite sure whether they're applauding J. Edgar Hoover or J. Edward Bromberg."

For a while the blacklisting (always denied by the blacklisting studios themselves) mostly had to be inferred by the public at large through the absence of some familiar face from the screen or from the writings of George Sokolsky, Walter Winchell, Louella Parsons, and other syndicated columnists who took on the task of stipulating which Hollywood personalities were Red, which "pinko," and which just not sufficiently red, white, and blue. It was all too much for some, notably Edward G. Robinson, who went out of his way on two occasions to rebut charges of Communism that not only weren't true but that had never really been leveled against him except as tendentious gossip circulated by Hearst newspaper hacks. But in the paranoid smog choking the industry that was enough of an indictment to get someone like Robinson on a "gray list"—no specific Communist ties and therefore of no use to those seeking more names, but still politically irritating and undeserving of a part if it could go to a true blue American instead. Among the others who found it necessary to declare their patriotism were Jose Ferrer, March, and Bogart, the last two the targets of the original Dies committee. In the March 1948 issue of the fan magazine *Photoplay*, for example, Bogart apologized for previous criticisms of HUAC in an article entitled "I'm No Communist" and asserted that "I'm about as much in favor of Communism as J. Edgar Hoover."

On March 21, 1951, HUAC returned to the fore by opening another round of Washington hearings that carried through on Thomas's warning about "only the beginning." It wasn't Thomas, however, who was there to fulfill his vow since in the meantime he had been imprisoned on corruption charges for packing too many of his relatives on the House payroll. It fell to his successor as HUAC chairman, John S. Wood, to subpoena new witnesses, starting with Larry Parks.

Parks, best known for his portrayal of Al Jolson in *The Jazz Singer*, had actually been one of the original nineteen subpoenaed by the Thomas panel in 1947 but had never gotten to testify because of the fracas with the Hollywood Ten. His summons had hardly been surprising since he had never denied membership in the Communist Party during the war years and had expressed his willingness to talk about the reasons why he had joined. But that wasn't enough for the committee; as always, it was primarily interested in more names for suggesting the kind of widespread conspiracy that would justify continuing its own inquisitions. At first Parks held to the position that he would talk only about his own past as a Communist, but when he saw that wouldn't satisfy the panel's demands, he made a plea that would be paraphrased by many witnesses following him: "I chose to come and tell the truth about myself. . . . Don't present me with the choice of either being in contempt of this committee and going to jail or forcing me to really crawl through the mud, to be an informer. For what purpose?"[7]

He needn't have bothered to ask. Persuaded that he would not be blacklisted if he identified others who had attended Communist-organized meetings in Hollywood homes during the war, Parks rattled off a roster of actors who had comprised the featured casts of some of the biggest pictures in the 1940s—Bromberg, Bohnen, Carnovsky, Karen Morley, Dorothy Tree, Anne Revere, Marc Lawrence, Gale Sondergaard, and Lloyd Gough. And Cobb, with whom he had appeared in the Lab production of *Noah*. It didn't help Parks personally: he was blacklisted anyway, the verdict of Wayne, Hopper, and other MPAPAI eminences being that he had waited too long to say what he had to say to the congressmen. The actor spent much of the rest of his career touring the country with his wife, Betty Garrett, in minor stage efforts and earning a reputation among former friends as the quintessential rat.

Prior to being named by Parks, Cobb had had no more political visibility than scores of others he had worked with in the New York theater in the 1930s, at the Lab, or within actor union caucuses; given the intensity of his work schedule between New York and California, he might have had less. But if Parks had never seen any reason to deny his membership in the Communist Party, Cobb had seen yet less reason to disassociate himself from workingman values that went back to the Bronx and the Jacob family. Before he was told to apologize for it, he had subscribed to various leftist initiatives, including being an early investor in Keynote Records, a label that got its start in 1941 with "Tragala," "Marineros," and other loyalist protest songs from the Spanish civil war before going on to feature giants of the jazz world. His few public political forays had been unexceptional—joining in the demonstrations outside Warner Brothers for the overthrow of the corrupt IATSE leadership, signing petitions along with thousands of others for the Cultural and Scientific Conference for World Peace in 1949 (at a time when the very notion of peace or antinuclear militancy was considered a Soviet propaganda ploy),[8] and so on. If he had one moment in the spotlight, it was at an Actors Equity meeting in 1942, when he introduced a motion to table efforts to ban Communists, Fascists, and other ideologues from executive union positions for the duration of the war lest it be interpreted as a slur on a United States ally. It went without saying that he wasn't afraid of slurring Italy or Germany. In any case, the motion was withdrawn before a full-membership vote.[9]

But modest as these activities might have been, there were plenty of other reasons for HUAC to have had a dossier on Cobb with or without Larry Parks. Just his attachments to the Group and the Lab would have been worth a few entries. Then there was his refusal to do *The Iron Curtain*. And he hadn't converted too many HUAC members to the glories of the theater with *Death of a Salesman*—not merely because of his association with Miller and Kazan, but because the play itself had been deemed so "anti-American" in excitable quarters that when the already diluted film version was released nationally in 1951, it was preceded by a short subject in which an actor was shown reassuring salesmen that their jobs reflected American core values and that characters like Willy Loman were nothing more than aberrations in the capitalist system. And then there was his friendship with Reuven Dafni, a Croatian partisan during the war who had fought with Marshal Tito and had then gone on to become an important fund raiser for the state of Israel. That put Cobb in the proximity not only of somebody who had fought with the Communist Tito, but of one who was being noisy about being Jewish—not a recommended association in the eyes of gavel wielders who could live with accusations of being anti-Semitic without much trouble.

"Nobody in our family ever made a secret of being on the Left," Norman Jacob observed,

> and we didn't see any reason why we should have. My father was what you would call a Norman Thomas socialist, really just a New Dealer. Both Lee and I were to the left of him, I suppose. I remember the time I was sick, the time I found out about my other brothers and sister, he was always giving me this private newspaper the Englishman Claude Cockburn turned out. I think it was called *The Week* and it was a fairly Communist take on world events. Lee always had a mimeograph copy of it and gave it to me after he was finished with it. I was only 12, but I loved reading it! Another time, it must have been early in 1941, my father was talking about getting life insurance, and Lee blew up. "We're about to get into a war," he yells, "and by the time it's over the capitalist system will be gone and there'll be no need for life insurance!"

Once Parks had stopped talking, Cobb began to feel the practical consequences of thinking along such lines. Less than a year away from one of the most applauded performances in American theater history, he found himself on a career slide that would keep him for several years in low-grade pictures that few people saw and fewer critics liked. What started off as a place on the gray list of studios neared full blacklist status the longer he waited to hop in front of a microphone.

As he told Navasky in 1974, "When the facilities of the government of the U.S. are drawn on an individual it can be terrifying. The blacklist is just the opening gambit—being deprived of work. Your passport is confiscated. That's minor. But not being able to move without being tailed is something else. Phone taps are expected, but the interception of the grocery bill? After a certain point it grows to implied as well as articulated threats, and people succumb. My wife did, and she was institutionalized."[10]

Beverley's decline, which included substantial drinking, anticipated the worst of the HUAC hounding but was gravely exacerbated by government fingers on her grocery bill. According to her daughter, the actress had suffered from "a misdiagnosed and a poorly treated anxiety disorder which resulted in her being over-medicated." In son Vincent's view, misdiagnoses and bad medicines were part of the problem but not all of it. In fact, her stay in a sanitarium in 1952 for a few months ("I visited with my father once. It was like something out of a movie—all rolling lawns and stately structures.") was followed over the years by a series of stays in conventional hospitals where her treatments included electroshock therapy. "That was really primitive in those days, and just the possibility of having to go through with another round terrified her, only made her anxiety worse. What she really suffered through was a cyclical depression that today would probably be diagnosed as a bipolar condition."

Julie Cobb has remained dubious about that conclusion. "Her 'depressions,' as I understand them, always resulted from her use of prescription drugs which were either prescribed incorrectly or misused by her. During her last hospital stay the doctors felt that convulsive shock therapy was indicated. In order to proceed, they had to wean her from various medications. Once she was 'clean,' her depressive symptoms had vanished and she was discharged without the other treatment."

Asked if Beverley's condition might have also been a consequence of her stalled career, her daughter said, "She was not an ambitious actress. While she was gorgeous and very gifted, I believe she lacked the blind drive that other actresses in her generation possessed. So I don't think she mourned the fact that her career was less than she was capable of." And as for whether her father had supported his wife's career: "It's been so long, I'm no longer certain about his feelings regarding her professional life. I think it's safe to say he was mixed. He had great regard for her talent and we know he attempted to connect her with people in Hollywood who could further her career. However, when I was very young, he told me in no uncertain terms that 'a woman cannot have both a career and a family.' I absorbed those words and was somewhat stymied by them my whole life. I now disagree with him, but times have changed a great deal."

Cobb's correspondence with Beverley in the early 1940s supports Julie's view that he had tried to interest Hollywood in her abilities; they also suggest that, though most of the studios were run by Jews, there were jitters about somebody who had come out of Yiddish cinema and its characters. Thus in a November 26, 1940, letter to Beverley, Cobb recounted his endeavor to bring her together with Norman Taurog, the director of *Men of Boys Town*: "He saw *The Light Ahead* in a private projection booth. Just we two. He was *extremely* enthusiastic and interested. Mind you, he took the trouble to see the picture at 8 p.m., after a very difficult day's work. He doesn't think anyone else should see that picture because they might not be as inclined to be as sympathetic to the truly ugly types of people that are personified in the film. He thinks that might be very damaging to you if it fell in the wrong hands." A clear edginess of his own in touching on some of the characters in the Yiddish picture precluded any Cobb opinion on Taurog's attitude. In any case, the screening did not lead to anything for Beverley.

As for Vincent, he rejected the notion of career having been a major factor in his mother's illness. "I don't think any of her basic problems could be attributed to anything or anyone outside herself. What I do know is that my father encouraged her later on to get back to work, that it would be her salvation. And she did do a few things with me and another little Yiddish playlet. She was always really, really good in what she did."[11]

By the time Cobb was encouraging her to get back to acting, though, Beverley had already filed for divorce, from the sanitarium of her first hospitalization. He did not contest it. Under the terms of the divorce the children initially lived with their mother, but then when he reached his teens, Vincent moved in with his father for a brief period before then going away to college.

If Cobb had "mixed" feelings about his wife's career, he had them about other things, too. When Bessie refused to cooperate with HUAC, the actor sent him a telegram declaring, "You've raised our spirits and filled our hearts with pride by the magnificent stand you have taken for the preservation of our freedom. Please convey these sentiments to Albert [Maltz] and the others. Love."[12] But when the screenwriter dropped by the Cobb home a couple of years later to ask for a five-hundred-dollar loan to help him feed his family and meet legal expenses, he was turned down. Bessie was so stunned by Cobb's refusal, from his "hero," that even writing about it years later, he adopted the distance of a screenplay form to recreate their conversation. When all Cobb offered was to feed the writer's wife and daughter or pay for some groceries, Bessie cursed him, to which Cobb was recorded as having replied, "I can understand how a man like you, who's been through what you've been through and who's going to prison, can say a thing like that to an old friend. . . . I hope you'll come to see me again. . . . You're a revolutionary, you know. Go on being a revolutionary. Go on being an example to me."[13]

Bessie's flair for the pompous would normally cast doubt on the veracity of this screenplay "dialogue," but in fact similar remarks were attributed to the actor in other encounters with people who broke with him because of HUAC. In trying to put Cobb's unexpected refusal to lend him money into perspective, Bessie traced it back to what Group colleagues had encapsulated as Herr Moody. "He was capable of bottomless moods of depression that put my own to shame, for he did not emerge from them for days, and during those days he would not say a word to anyone, including his wife and [Vincent]. I had even flown with him when he was in these moods and had touched earth again with a shattering sense of liberation from certain death."[14]

In his 1974 interview with Navasky, Cobb voiced pride that, despite the emotional and professional price he and his family paid, he had kept HUAC at bay for more than two years. "I was one of the most effective resisters to the terror for two and a half years. That isn't well known because the purpose of the game was to keep it from being known. The cat-and-mouse game was that they couldn't put me on the stand. We'd meet—two representatives of the Committee and me—but I was of no use to them unless I cooperated, so to speak. I thought I was stalwart, brave, in adamantly refusing cooperation. I had the dubious honor of being admired by them."[15]

But that was in retrospect. By the middle of 1951, the Red Scare storm in Hollywood had become a tornado, with one ex-Communist or claimed ex-Communist after another eagerly naming names in order to get off the blacklist. Screenwriter Martin Berkeley, perhaps the most disparaged of all witnesses even by neutral observers, took the occasion of his September 19 appearance to name 161 people, some of whom had apparently been only guilty of once seeing the *Daily Worker* on a newsstand. Even his committee interrogator William Wheeler had to ask Berkeley, whose biggest credits were such schlock as *Revenge of the Creature* and *The Deadly Mantis*, to stop talking because he was naming too many people. Cobb's need to get away from this atmosphere for a while led him back to Broadway in early 1952 for the secured territory of Papa Bonaparte in a revival of *Golden Boy*, this time finally starring Garfield as the boxer-violinist. But HUAC's investigators knew where New York was, too, and they continued to press. For another year Cobb held out through more bad movies, another weak play on Broadway, and suddenly disappearing people he had thought of as friends. "All of this time I was out of touch with my colleagues— the people with whom I had shared these ideological tenets," he told Navasky. "When the chips were down, you were abandoned. They ran when I was named. The very people I was protecting were beneath contempt. I called my lawyer and told him I was in political trouble, and he said, 'Don't come up here, I'll meet you in the car.' He wouldn't suffer to be seen with me coming into his office. . . . They would sympathize with me as I died—*that* human they would allow themselves to be. There wasn't a single exception to that statement. I'm talking about breakfast, not moral support."[16]

Taking Cobb at his word, that made for a lot of hypocrites who went out of their way to attack him for betraying fellow actors, writers, and directors after he finally succumbed to the HUAC pressures. The problem was, aside from the reference to his attorney, he did not specify who had been avoiding him prior to the testimony he agreed to give in Room 1117 of the Hollywood Roosevelt Hotel on June 2, 1953. "The very people I was protecting" would at least insinuate that those accused of avoiding him before his testimony were some of the same who denounced him for having surrendered their names afterward.

"It was they who made the deal with me," he said of the investigators. "I was pretty much worn down. I had no money. I couldn't borrow. I had the expenses of taking care of the children. You are reduced to the position where you either steal or gamble, and since I'm inclined more to gamble than to steal, I gambled. If you gamble for stakes you must win, it's suicidal. You lose. And that's what happened."[17]

He had help with the gamble. Not even Kohlberg's American Business Consultants played a more important "clearing agent" role at the time than Martin Gang, an entertainment lawyer who had been a ubiquitous Hollywood presence for years in divorces, assaults, and suits of various kinds involving such clients as Luise Rainer (the Odets divorce), Susan Hayward, Wallace Beery, and Bob Hope. By the late 1940s, however, Gang had come to specialize in HUAC targets and on a trajectory that went from the feisty defense of the rights of the original Hollywood nineteen to the rationale that, as an attorney obligated to represent the best interests of his clients, that "best" was advising them to testify so they could get off the blacklist ("walking the Gang plank," as it became known). After a while, he absented himself from the defense table in the hearing room, satisfied that he had acquitted his duty in prior backroom agreements on testimony with HUAC agents, most often the William Wheeler who had asked Berkeley to stifle himself. Among those accepting that arrangement were Sterling Hayden, Lloyd Bridges, and Cobb. On that technicality Cobb was able to tell his HUAC questioners that he was appearing before them without counsel.[18]

The main themes of the actor's testimony were his membership or nonmembership in the Communist Party, the talking points at meetings he had attended, and the naming of names. On the first point he insisted to Navasky twenty years later, "I was never even in the Party—but what use would it be to them, the Committee, if I said that? Besides, if you lived through the 1930s you had to be a Communist; no one feels injustice as keenly as the young. I was never a revolutionary except in spirit. And the American Communist Party [members] were a laughingstock—they were idealists, children. None of the revolutionaries of the world had any respect for the American Communist Party. However, we had been friends, not strangers, drawn [together] by revolutionary principle."[19]

Short of an outright lie to Navasky, what was apparently at work here was the actor's academically caressed sense of the literal—the same propensity that enabled him to deny without fear of contradiction that he hadn't been a formal member of the Lab although he had been very active on both its stages and in its teaching rooms. Certainly, "I was never even in the Party" had not been heard at the Hollywood Roosevelt Hotel. To the direct question from HUAC interrogator Wheeler "When did you join the Communist Party?" Cobb offered no challenge to the assumption, but simply replied, "I joined in 1941, I believe. 1940 or 1941. . . . I attended a couple of meetings as a visitor and subsequently accepted the fact that I was a member. I put it that way because there didn't seem to be any formality involved such as the signing of a card or indoctrination of any other kind."[20] More often than not, the actor testified, the meetings in the early 1940s were held at the New York apartment of former Group colleagues Carnovsky and Brand, with the talking points usually being about some development in the war. When he moved to California and attended other gatherings of Communists, he disclosed, Beverley had also been present, and for discussions that sometimes verged on the esoteric. One that he recalled was a project spearheaded by screenwriter John Howard Lawson to align the teachings of Stanislavsky with Party precepts. "The project failed miserably because the moment we departed from the text as published by Stanislavsky, we destroyed the most important part of it."[21]

Prompted by Wheeler to talk about his financial contributions in both New York and Los Angeles, Cobb indicated that as a sign of his casual relations with the party. At the gatherings hosted by the Carnovskys, he said, his donations had literally been small change; in California he had rebuffed attempts to get him to volunteer a percentage of the salary he was making from the studios. "No more than five or ten dollars," he said of his last eight months at the meetings after the war.

As for the names, aside from Carnovsky and Brand, he identified Gerry Schlein, the wife of artist Charles Schlein, as the principal organizer of the Hollywood meetings. To the list provided by Parks he added actors Jeff Corey, Rose Hobart, Ludwig Donath, and George Tyne, as well as a couple of minor screenwriters and radio writers. "We were thorns in their sides," he said of himself and Beverley, "because we didn't subscribe more and more to the requirements and the general pattern of acquiescence." Asked to elaborate on the acquiescence (the same motive he gave for losing interest in the Group) that he said finally drove him away, he replied, "A big point was made of adhering to a spirit of democratic centralism, and it was so obvious that the centralism attained and the democracy was only given lip service to."[22]

His appearance itself aside, what disconcerted many about Cobb's testimony was the total abjectness of his characteristically ornate parting remarks to the committee: "I would like to thank you for the privilege of setting the record straight, not only for whatever subjective relief it affords me, but if belatedly this information can be of any value in the further strengthening of our Government and its efforts at home as well as abroad, it will serve in some small way to mitigate whatever feeling of guilt I might have for having waited this long. I did hope that, in my delay to speak earlier, others of the people I had mentioned might have availed themselves of this opportunity for themselves to do likewise."[23]

As in numerous similar cases worked out between Gang and Wheeler, Cobb's closed-doors testimony was supposed to have remained behind closed doors; as in an equal number of cases, it didn't for very long. By the end of September the wire services and dailies all over the country were not only reporting his appearance but listing the other actors he had named. In fact, this only made public what had been in the wind throughout the summer, this causing several awkward scenes with people who refused to believe he had agreed to name names. One of the most embarrassing was with Dassin. "When there were rumors that Lee Cobb was going to cooperate," the director told Patrick McGilligan,

> I said, "Over my dead body." I just could not believe it. These rumors were persistent. People were calling me because they knew we had been very close. I was living in Europe by then. I had just gotten my passport back, and I went to New York to see Lee. Interestingly enough, I saw him at a party with a group of old friends. I got Lee aside and said, "Lee, there are rumors . . ." He said, "I just want to know one thing. Do you believe them?" I said, "Of course I don't believe them." And the night before was when he had done it all! That, I think, was the one that broke me the most. That was the toughest one. . . . I turned my back on him.[24]

Cobb's version was different, and with a self-serving timeline that, ignoring the director's arrangement with Zanuck for shooting *Night and the City* years earlier, had Dassin running off to Europe rather than returning from there on a visit. He told Navasky, "One of my closest friends pleaded with me not to do a thing like this, as he ran to catch the boat for England. He was fleeing the country, but I was the coward. We haven't spoken since—and he became a well-known director."[25]

Norman Jacob later added a footnote to the encounter between his brother and Dassin.

I was walking along the street in New York and ran into Julie at that same time. And the first thing he says to me is, "It's not true, is it?" I really didn't know what he was talking about at first, but the more he explained, the more indignant he got. "It better not be true," he said, or something like it. And suddenly I'm getting indignant, too, at the thought of Lee testifying and I go home and do something I've never been able to forgive myself for. I write Lee a letter with the same indignation Dassin had shown me, asking him to deny all the rumors. Of course he never answered me, and he shouldn't have. He was going through hell. He didn't need me making it worse.

One who didn't regret making her feelings known more than once was Adele Ritt, wife of the director Martin Ritt, a Group Theatre member who was blacklisted from television for most of the 1950s behind charges that he had once donated money to a cause linked to Chinese Communists. According to producer Norman Lear, he once invited the Cobbs and Ritts to the same dinner party, and the offended director's wife "was furious and sat staring at the wall all night."[26] Brian Dennehy reported a similar scene at another party, when the Ritts walked in the front door, saw Cobb, and immediately left.

The reaction of the people specifically named by Cobb was predictably bitter. Carnovsky "always referred to him as *merde*-face," said son Stephen Carnovsky, a retired English teacher.

You have to remember that in those days they really didn't know if a concentration camp was waiting for them if they found themselves named. Of course they understood that the people testifying all did it with different motives. Some wanted to advance their careers, others wanted to buy a house, others again just needed desperately to get back to work. But what it always came down to for my parents was what you did, no matter the reasons for it, and in Cobb's case they couldn't forgive. They went back together too long sharing many of the same experiences.[27]

Jeff Corey, blacklisted for twelve years, was another who dismissed the hardship argument as a reason for giving in to HUAC pressures. "I could've gotten out of it, too, by naming names. It was rough, you know. I had three kids to support. I'm very proud of the way we coped. I didn't go around bellyaching, just did what I had to do." But Corey, who used his time on the blacklist to establish himself as one of the country's most respected acting teachers, developed more complex feelings in later years after Cobb's death. "One afternoon in the 1970s I was doing a pilot at the Columbia ranch and the Irish actor Dan O'Herlihy and I were both badmouthing Lee because of the rotten work this onetime great actor did. And I got in my car to leave the ranch and I heard that Lee was declared dead on arrival at an emergency hospital. And like a crazy man, I addressed the radio and said, 'I forgive you, Lee.'"[28]

Sometime afterward, according to Corey, he found himself working with Julie Cobb and told her that story.

> She threw her arms around me and thanked me and began to cry. I spent the next hour comforting her. Cobb had once told her he was very hurt when he said hello to me one day on the Universal back lot and I walked past him. She said he had once told her that she had no idea how anxiety-making it was to have every arm of the government zeroing in on you and I told her, "Julie, you have no idea how exhilarating it is to tell every arm of the government they're behaving poorly and to go fuck themselves." And she looked at me as though, Jesus, she'd never thought of that.[29]

Rose Hobart said that she called Cobb directly after being named by him.

> He said he had been in my house at a meeting of the Communist Party, where I was present. A bloody lie! I called him and said, "I want to talk to you!" It turned out that he knew damned well that I hadn't been there because I hadn't. What he said was, "I never would have mentioned you had they not brought it up." I thought, how stupid can you be. Obviously, they would con people into telling things. He said it had been January or February, and sure enough, I was in the Aleutians and could prove it![30]

Julie Cobb found out about the HUAC testimony the hard way. A student at San Francisco State in 1965 at the height of the political turmoil then enveloping Northern California universities, she sensed that some of her fellow marchers behind the Free Speech movement and against the war in Vietnam simply didn't like her.

> Some of those folks were "friends" of mine who felt compromised by associating with me. I was quite naïve and didn't connect the dots. Frankly I didn't even know there were dots to connect. Finally a

friend told me people resented me because of Dad's cooperation with HUAC. On a visit home I asked Mom about it and she suggested I talk to Dad. We sat in my car one day after a lunch date and he told me his version of those awful events. He wept over lost friendships. And he told me there was no way to imagine what it's like when the U.S. Government decides it wants something from YOU. He maintained that he did not provide names, but rather affirmed names the committee already had. Some people never believed that. I choose to believe his version.

Vincent Cobb never had any such conversation. "I tried to bring it up with Dad. He would not talk about it and deflected the conversation in another direction. We never did have dialogue about that topic. I don't know whether he might have felt more vulnerable and accessible to Julie about those things or that he couldn't face me with all that. I simply don't know."

In the years after his appearance, Cobb himself was given to bringing it up at some unlikely moments and often in a tone of infinite guilt, second only to the self-contempt Sterling Hayden professed for his HUAC testimony.[31] With Navasky, however, the contempt was as directed outwardly as much as inwardly. "If I had not been in need, I'd have never cooperated. By implication I did dignify the Committee. I went through as little of the charade as I had to. My friends had the attitude, 'I would rather eulogize you dead than have you as an imperfect contemporary alive.' There's a need to see people that way: The little man grows in stature, ennobles himself, by saying he hasn't done what you did; the least in jeopardy are the most intransigent nonunderstanders—I was going to say nonforgivers. Some people need me so I can be anathema to them."[32]

## NOTES

1. Michael Freedland (with Barbra Paskin), *Witch-Hunt in Hollywood: McCarthyism's War on Tinseltown* (London: JR Books, 2009), p. 23.

2. Salvi, "History," pp. 100–101.

3. Dewey, *James Stewart*, p. 290. Vaughn's point was reinforced by the subsequent blacklisting of Adolph Menjou, up to then one of the busiest actors in Hollywood but also such a frenzied right-wing critic of President Roosevelt (accused of stocking American gold reserves for the Soviet Union) that he too

was considered as having forfeited his character versatility by imposing such a pronounced image on the public.

4. An eleventh charged witness, German playwright-screenwriter Bertolt Brecht, fled to Europe between his noncooperative testimony and the Court ruling.

5. Victor Navasky, *Naming Names* (New York: Hill and Wang, 1980), p. xiv.

6. Salvi, "History," pp. 178–179.

7. Freedland, *Witch-Hunt in Hollywood*, p. 127.

8. *New York Times*, March 24, 1949.

9. *New York Times*, January 10, 1942.

10. Navasky, *Naming Names*, p. 271.

11. Beverley's career wound down in the 1950s and early 1960s with small roles in *The Robe*, *The Shrike*, and *Ada*, and a couple of TV series appearances.

12. Bessie, *Inquisition in Eden*, p. 243.

13. Ibid., p. 245.

14. Ibid., p. 244.

15. Navasky, *Naming Names*, p. 271.

16. Ibid., p. 271.

17. Ibid., p. 271.

18. *Hearings*, p. 2345ff.

19. Navasky, *Naming Names*, pp. 271–272.

20. *Hearings*.

21. Ibid.

22. Ibid.

23. Ibid.

24. McGilligan and Buhle, *Tender Comrades*, p. 214.

25. Navasky, *Naming Names*, p. 273.

26. Interview with author, January 26, 2010. Subsequent quotes from Norman Lear are taken from this interview.

27. Interview with author, January 8, 2013.

28. McGilligan and Buhle, *Tender Comrades*, p. 187.

29. Griffin Fariello, *Red Scare: Memories of the American Inquisition* (New York: Avon Books, 1995), p. 285.

30. Anthony Slide, *Actors on Red Alert* (Lanham, MD, and London: Scarecrow Press, 1999), p. 45.

31. Sterling Hayden, *Wanderer* (New York: Avon Books, 1977), p. 358ff.

32. Navasky, *Naming Names*, p. 273.

# Chapter 16

———————◯———————

# Going Door to Door

WILLY LOMAN WOULD HAVE BEEN familiar with Cobb's trudging from one dim prospect to another at the dawn of the 1950s. Even at rumor level there were scant indications of a major Hollywood opportunity following his Broadway triumph in *Death of a Salesman*. Initially, this wasn't due only to studio wariness about hiring him because of his politics. Having pulled out of *Salesman* in November 1949 "on the advice of his physician,"[1] and notwithstanding Kazan's skepticism, he gratefully embraced a few months of rest in a new home in Beverly Hills. It wasn't until April 1950 that his name was tied to a specific project, one in which he not only would have starred but also made his debut as a film director. But even that undertaking, a crime drama entitled *No Tomorrow* and with a plot that sounded a lot like *The Dark Past*, would have been under the aegis of B-level producer Sam Wiesenthal.[2] *No Tomorrow* turned out to be aptly named; instead, Cobb's first engagement after *Salesman* was an equally modest melodrama entitled *The Man Who Cheated Himself* and in which he only acted. His consolation prize was that it was the first feature in which he received top billing.

The actor tried to win from publicity interviews for the picture what he couldn't get from what was on the screen. A drab-looking exercise directed by Felix E. Feist, *The Man Who Cheated Himself* cast Cobb as a police detective who helps a seductive wife cover up the supposedly accidental shooting of her husband and who then futilely tries to keep his younger brother, also a detective, from pursuing clues suggesting premeditated murder. As hinted at by the title, Cobb's cop is the last one to realize how he has been ensnared by the wife. While most critics were noting that Jane Wyatt was critically miscast as the siren and that John Dall as the younger brother had the wrong vowel in his surname, Cobb took the opportunity of meetings with the press to make it clear he would have been happier with *No Tomorrow* or any other project that would have initiated him as a director. Without reference to Feist, whose major credits to that point had been for short subjects, Cobb told one interviewer,

> A director's is the most rewarding job in this medium. I have ideas—ideas that I hope and believe will be fresh. For one thing, you always hear people putting emphasis on the director "who knows what he wants." This is intended as high praise. But it's only half the point. How does he get the *actor* to know what he wants? Is he able to appeal to the actor in a way the actor responds to his purpose? I may be wrong, but I believe I'd have a good avenue of communication with other actors, to establish the proper empathy with them.[3]

The want ad went unanswered: he never did get an official credit as a motion picture director. But especially while working for a series of minor talents like Feist in B and C pictures in the 1950s, he was reported as having taken over sets as the culmination to disagreements, shot scenes to his satisfaction, then returned to his actor role. He confirmed as much in his interview with Roy Pickard for *Films in Review*, but declined to identify the pictures. For the record, his only direction credit after his early years at the Pasadena Playhouse and then at the Actors Lab was for television some time later.

For his next two films Cobb's employer was Humphrey Bogart and the latter's independent Santana Productions. Both pictures echoed past Bogart successes even more than *No Tomorrow* had been cut from the cloth of *The Dark Past*. The first of them was *Sirocco*, which the star and his company would have been "shocked! shocked! shocked!" to hear was a lame attempt at invoking *Casablanca*. This time Bogart is a cynical gun runner in Syria who gets himself caught between the French colonial army and nationalists and ultimately pays for it with his life. Cobb plays a high-minded French colonel who gives up his life first. Crowther spoke for the majority in terming the picture "torpid" and "conspicuously without charm," asserting that the studio-bound production was "no more suggestive of Damascus than a Shriners convention in New Orleans." Cobb's performance was characterized as one of "glowers and grumbles."[4]

He had a lot more to glower and grumble about with *The Family Secret*, strongly reminiscent of Bogart's *Knock on Any Door* but without the social commentary ambitions of the older film. As in *Door*, John Derek plays a callow kid who commits a killing, though this time accidentally. His lawyer-father (Cobb) urges him to confess everything, but his mother argues against that and the son is only too happy to accept her advice. Then the second plot intervenes, dragging along a third and fourth with it. The police arrest another suspect, the wife of the suspect comes to Cobb to defend her husband, and the suspect drops dead of a heart attack before he can be cleared. The critical verdict, what there was of it, was that the family secret should have remained in the attic. As little as *Sirocco* and *The Family Secret* did for Cobb, they did less for Bogart, hastening the decline of Santana Productions.

Doing a revival of *Golden Boy* in New York not only gave Cobb a breather from his domestic and professional problems in California, it also reunited him with Group people who were being tracked politically as much as he was. They included playwright Odets, who was doubling as the director, and cast members Art Smith and Tony Kraber. But the most prominent was star Garfield, the biggest name to that point in the House Un-American Activities Committee's (HUAC's) sights. Already, Garfield had answered one committee subpoena to justify his early support for the Hollywood Ten and his membership in united front groups during the war; at that hearing session he had weaved more artfully than Joe Bonaparte to avoid naming any names. His payoff was to be blacklisted on radio and television anyway, to the point that the Defense Department voided a commitment to use him as the narrator on a recruitment film. Already weakened by a heart condition and for living it up at night, the actor listened to advisors counseling another session with HUAC to clarify any doubts about his aversion to Communism. In the meantime he spent many hours away from *Golden Boy* cobbling together the (unpublished) article "I Was a Sucker for a Left Hook," a mea culpa piece recommended by his East Coast counterpart to Martin Gang, attorney Arnold Forster.[5]

Having achieved the status of a golden oldie from that other age on the far side of World War II, *Golden Boy* was received more respectfully than the original Group presentation and far more enthusiastically than the film version. This was true even of critics who, like John McClain, confessed to never having accepted the play's central premise of Joe Bonaparte having to choose between the violin and the boxing ring. ("My personal peeve with the story is that I was never convinced the boy was going to be a new Heifetz in the first place, so what's so terrible if he goes out and makes $700,000 at the expense of a swollen knuckle?") This time, though, McClain allowed as how he was taken by Garfield's "forceful" performance and by how "Lee J. Cobb succeeded . . . in getting me aroused to the great problem of what to do with resin, if your boy is going to put it on his feet or on his violin bow."[6] Less flippant were other critics, including Atkinson, who directed most of his praise toward Garfield for "giving one of his most forceful performances, purged of the overeager mannerisms that used to mar his acting."[7] The limited-run presentation, which those in the know referred to as "Garfield's Revenge" because of the bad feelings stirred within the Group over the original casting of Luther Adler in the lead role, ran for fifty-five nights. The play gave significant boosts to the careers of Jack Warden, Jack Klugman, and Arthur O'Connell.

Then the other shoe fell. In April, Kazan returned to the HUAC microphones for the second time in four months to name names, all from his days with the Group. A month later, it was Odets's turn. The first person the playwright named was Bromberg, who had died a few months before and for whom he had delivered the funeral eulogy. Then he fingered Smith and Kraber, the *Golden Boy* cast members he had just directed. The day after Odets finished testifying, Garfield collapsed of a heart attack at the age of thirty-nine. As in the case of Bromberg, the HUAC pressures he had been struggling under for long months were given a key supporting role in his death.

Within the hearing of others anyway, Cobb never addressed the Odets testimony or the stress wearing down Garfield, least of all the probability that the subject of the political witch hunt had come up at some point among them during *Golden Boy*. On the other hand, even more than twenty years later and in the face of his own appearance before the committee, he confessed to Navasky that he had been dismayed by Kazan's naming of names. "I was shocked. I was offended. I wasn't in as deep. I thought, If I were in his boots I'd die before they'd break me. But Kazan acted out of principle. If I didn't think so, I could ask him, 'How could you name

Tony Kraber—a selfless man, a Band-Aid if you scratch yourself?'
... It didn't sit well."[8]

There wasn't much that sat well with him when he returned to
California after *Golden Boy*, either. In case he needed a reminder of
what might have been, he got it with the release of the movie version
of *Clash by Night*, with Paul Douglas in the role of the cuckolded husband Cobb had sought. The casting of the rugby ball–faced Douglas,
no more of a classic leading man than he was, continued to rankle for
years. As for his own options, they remained very few, and with even
the Kazan and Odets pins having fallen, his politics were very much a
factor. The project he chose—*The Fighter*—might have looked promising on paper, but what came out was a dime store *Viva Zapata!* shot in
less than three weeks.

Yet another teaming of Cobb with Richard Conte, *The Fighter*,
based on Jack London's "The Mexican," tells of a peasant (Conte) who
crosses the border and makes enough money in the ring to pay for the
arms that a revolutionary leader (Cobb) back home needs for battling
the Diaz dictatorship. The picture was directed by Herbert Kline, a
documentarian who had been one of the first to film the battles of
the Spanish civil war and also one of the first to reject cooperation
with HUAC. The production values were barely at the level of a TV
western, and Conte, too asphalt and fire hydrant for his role, walked
through it catatonically. By contrast, Cobb seemed to relish his extroverted Pancho Villa type, and it was later suggested, especially in view
of Kline's limited experience with fictional features, that *The Fighter*
was one of the films where he had had some directorial say. Among the
more charitable critics was Archer Winsten, who said that "the good
things in *The Fighter* are reminiscent of better films."[9]

Like many of the period who had been trained on the stage and
then forced to make most of their income from motion pictures,
Cobb would have preferred to leave television out of the discussion
altogether; "the theater is the actor's medium, film is the director's
medium, and television is nobody's medium," as he was wont to say.
But it was also television that helped keep him afloat economically for
a couple of years in the early 1950s, at least until the blacklist came
to dictate its hiring policies, as well. Moreover, in both his earliest
flirtation with the medium and later on, it provided him with roles
that weren't confined to ethnic stereotypes. His very first foray, for
NBC's Somerset Maugham Theater on April 30, 1951, was as Charles

Strickland, Maugham's Anglicized version of Paul Gaugin in *The Moon and Sixpence*—material he had been familiar with since the Pasadena Playhouse. After that, in October of the same year, he played a furtive businessman who killed his lover (*The Veil* on the Lights Out series) and a megalomaniacal magnate who financed his own flight to Mars (*Test Flight* on the science-fiction Tales of Tomorrow series).

*The Tall Texan*, the actor's last released film before his HUAC testimony, didn't need help for its banality to be noticed, but got it anyway. Trying to cash in on the 3-D wave set off in late 1952 by *Bwana Devil*, the humble Lippert Pictures paired the western around the country with the fairly brief and hastily thrown together *A Day in the Country*, shot in the new optical process. As described by the *New York Times*, moviegoers who walked into theaters to see *The Tall Texan* were "supplied with a pair of cardboard glasses with a red lens and a green one, but *A Day in the Country* merit(ed) a gas mask." This made it all the easier for the *Times* man and other reviewers to wonder why anyone would have wanted to see *The Tall Texan*, a fourth-rate copy of *Stagecoach*, in the first place, since "it is hardly less foolish or tiresome" than the 3-D short. Despite conceding a "good cast" featuring Cobb, Lloyd Bridges, Marie Windsor, and Luther Adler, the consensus was that the western "showed little talent or imagination on either side of the camera."[10] Bridges would be one of those named by Cobb before HUAC a few months later.

Given the dismal film alternatives in Hollywood, it didn't take much to get Cobb back to Broadway, and by the end of the year he was once again in New York, this time rehearsing George Tabori's *The Emperor's Clothes* under the direction of Harold Clurman. Set in Eastern Europe in 1930, the play had many of the political particulars that tantalized the America of the 1950s in the blush of the cold war—a professor (Cobb) forced into premature retirement by a dictatorship, a son (Brandon de Wilde) heading for a big fall because of British- and American-influenced fantasies depicting his father as a hero, a neighbor who takes the fantasies too literally, and the professor's arrest and torture at the hands of police goons. If the Budapest-born Tabori was trying to be subtle by laying the play in a period when the only dictatorship to worry about in his homeland had been that of the fascistic Admiral Horthy and not the Communists, that went out with the wash. What especially irritated the critics was that the playwright, already blacklisted on radio and television because of collaborations in Europe with Bertolt Brecht, continually shifted moods to indulge whimsy and gallows humor in extended monologues for a subject they thought should have been treated somberly and tersely. For Walter Kerr the play's "virtues (were) drowned in a sea of suffocating words."[11] For the *Variety* reviewer, Tabori's "gabfest . . . destroyed the play's urgency."[12] Similar reactions came from Atkinson[13] and McClain.[14] As the spouter of most of the words and the source of many of the abrupt mood changes, Cobb was generally saluted for trying to maintain the drama's balance but was ultimately viewed as defeated by the play's structure. Only *Variety* demurred, evoking the old Strasberg criticism of the actor by saying that he "plays with intense concentration and emotional power, but his plodding pace makes an already gabby role seem interminable."

Cobb made four pictures in the immediate aftermath of his HUAC testimony. Two of them were programmers but marked his gradual reintegration into the industry and its commercial priorities; a third was back to the nickel-and-dime financing of inertia, but became an evergreen for the religiously inclined; and the fourth was the most controversial of the period and the most important of his career.

With *Yankee Pasha* the actor returned to heavy makeup as a Moroccan sultan who makes life difficult for an American adventurer (Jeff Chandler) who has journeyed to North Africa to rescue his fiancée (Rhonda Fleming) from the Arab pirates who have abducted her. For Universal-International the tale was incidental to the fact that the picture was the studio's first in CinemaScope and to Fleming's harem outfits. That was just as well since it was generally written off as "an Oriental western . . . that despite its exotic splendors, burnooses, turbans, and Arab stallions . . . is closer to Eagle Pass than the Barbary Coast."[15]

What Rhonda Fleming did for diaphanous pants in *Yankee Pasha*, Anne Bancroft did for mesh stockings in *Gorilla at Large*. Here again the publicity focus (by a subsidiary company of Fox) was supposedly elsewhere than on provocatively dressed women—in this case on the 3-D process. But the story of a disenchanted police detective (Cobb) investigating murders at an amusement park came at the wrong time for a decidedly dyspeptic Crowther. "There is something almost evil about the content and structure of this film," the *Times* man railed. "It is such an evident pander to unintelligence. The menace is animalistic, and the notion that a person might don the costume of a gorilla and go around killing is as high as it goes."[16] Most other reviews preferred just to say that the picture was a bill filler for double features.

Evil was about the only accusation not leveled at *Day of Triumph*, a shoestring-budgeted account of the last days of Jesus Christ. In his best biblical robes and diction, Cobb played Zadok, leader of the Zealots, who explains for the length of the picture why he decided against trying to draft the Messiah as a figurehead for his anti-Roman political band. Made as part of a projected religious series by Irving Pichel, *Day of Triumph* availed itself of far more unlikely casting than Cobb—for instance, Mike Connors as a fellow Zealot, Joanne Dru as Mary Magdalene, and western regular James Griffith as Judas. But as tepidly as the picture was received, it still reached the market before such epic productions as *King of Kings* and *The Greatest Story Ever Told* so that it became staple TV viewing around Easter for a few years. Ultimately, far more people saw it than the CinemaScope of *Yankee Pasha* and the 3-D of *Gorilla at Large*.

And then there was *On the Waterfront*.

## NOTES

1. *New York Times*, October 18, 1949.
2. *New York Times*, April 17, 1950.
3. *Los Angeles Times*, May 14, 1950.
4. *New York Times*, June 14, 1951.
5. Nott, *He Ran All the Way*, p. 298ff.
6. *New York Journal-American*, March 13, 1952.
7. *New York Times*, March 13, 1952.
8. Navasky, *Naming Names*, p. 272. In an interview with the author on September 6, 2012, Karl Kraber, son of Tony Kraber, said he wrote to Kazan after his father's death in September 1986. Said Kraber, "He replied that my father had forgiven him, but I have no idea where he got that from, certainly not from my father."
9. *Post* (New York), June 1, 1952.
10. *New York Times*, April 13, 1953.
11. *New York Herald Tribune*, February 20, 1953.
12. *Variety*, February 23, 1953.
13. *New York Times*, February 20, 1953.
14. *New York Journal-American*, February 20, 1953.
15. *New York Times*, April 19, 1954.
16. *New York Times*, June 12, 1954.

# Chapter 17

<hr/>

# On All Fronts

THE IDEAL PREPARATION FOR the making of *On the Waterfront* were the psychodramas from the Group Theatre. Artistically, politically, and psychologically, the picture was bathed in enmities and resentments that still managed to yield the most dynamic Hollywood film of its time, leaving behind endless controversies about its intentions and speculations about the relationships among its cardinal figures.

Although Cobb was not aware of it at the time, an offer from Kazan to play the union mob boss Johnny Friendly followed years of second, third, and fourth thoughts by different studio heads for going ahead with the project; it also preceded months more of nerve-wracking tensions, some of them very physical, that would dog every phase of the shoot. When there weren't threats from organized thugs who wanted to block the picture about corruption on the New York docks, there were bureaucratic maneuvers aimed at the same end and ongoing hostilities among the director and his volatile players. Just the relationship between Cobb and Kazan after the director's criticism of the actor's behavior during *Death of a Salesman* represented more baggage than was normally welcomed for a collaborative project. Vincent Cobb has characterized his father's relationship with Kazan as "complex," but it was a complexity far from the skeptical compatibility of John Huston's relationship with Humphrey Bogart or the gruff paternalism of John Ford's with John Wayne. There had already been both too many bouquets and too many hurts exchanged between them for business as

usual. And that was without even going into their testimonies before
the House Un-American Activities Committee (HUAC).

While Kazan, at the urging (and with the writing) of his wife Molly,
took out a full-page ad in the *New York Times* to defend his testimony
with preemptive aggressiveness, Cobb paced the opposite shore beating himself up for having caved into the two years plus of hounding
by the congressional committee. But what he couldn't shake even in
that glum state, as he indicated to Navasky, was the feeling that there
was something amiss about Kazan's claims of acting on principle—a
perspective based in good part on a misery that he personally had fallen
so short of any such nobility. "I didn't act out of principle," as he told
Navasky. "I wallowed in unprincipledness."[1]

There was every reason to believe that Cobb drew that contrast
with more than a little irony. He was no more in the dark than anyone
else in the film business about the booster rocket reenergizing Kazan's
career after his April 1952 testimony, owing no little to a lucrative contract with Fox that had been jeopardized when he had been the target
of HUAC's investigation into his political past. Tony Kraber, one of
those named by both Kazan and Odets, put it more directly when, during his own committee questioning on August 18, 1955, he was asked
about being cited by the director, and replied, "Is this the Kazan that
signed the contract for $500,000 the day after he gave names to this
Committee? Would you sell your brothers for $500,000?"[2] Although
Kazan would challenge that allegation in his autobiography, he did so
only to the extent of admitting that Zanuck had given him an ultimatum to name names or not be paid for a picture owed by an already
existing contract. Nor had it seemed mere coincidence to anyone that
the director's first film after stepping away from the HUAC witness
table had been a propaganda melodrama (*Man on a Tightrope*) about
the efforts of an Eastern European circus to escape the Soviet bloc and
reach freedom in the West.

But if there were as many thorns as rose petals in their creative
past, Cobb also knew he was in no position to reject Kazan's offer. He
needed the money and needed the exposure a Kazan project could give
him. The reality was that he hadn't been part of a major film production since he had been supporting Tyrone Power and James Stewart
immediately after the war and before his move to Broadway. Neither
did he have to be jabbed in the ribs to appreciate the mockery in having had his long-sought ambition to be a leading man in the movies

realized only with the likes of *The Man Who Cheated Himself* and *Day of Triumph*.

The Continental Congress didn't have more forefathers than *On the Waterfront* did. One genesis tale said it was Kazan in 1951 who broached the subject of the rugged, often brutal world of New York City longshoremen with Arthur Miller, urging him to attack it as a screenplay rather than as a stage drama. The more generally accepted version, though, is that it was Miller who brought the subject to the director, having been working on a script since *Death of a Salesman* had opened. The protagonist of what was entitled *The Hook* is a stevedore who battles waterfront union corruption after some prodigal detours of his own. The playwright was said to have been attracted to the theme by the story of Pete Panto, a longshoreman murdered in 1939 when he sought to battle Joe Ryan's International Longshoremen's Association (ILA), infamous for its ties to mobster Albert Anastasia. Miller's protagonist doesn't end up in a New Jersey swamp the way the real Panto did, but neither does he emerge all that victorious thanks to the friends he had counted on in a union election voting against him at the eleventh hour in fear for their own lives. Although he thought Miller's treatment of the subject needed work (something he said automatically to everybody after his first reading of a script), Kazan was sufficiently intrigued to tote the playwright with him to California to meet with Zanuck at 20th Century-Fox, counting on their combined Broadway credits to carry the day until they could get back to the typewriter. But Zanuck said no, being more concerned with the director's commitment to shooting *Viva Zapata!* with Marlon Brando so Fox could make some of the money Warner Brothers had been piling up with the star from *A Streetcar Named Desire*.

When Kazan and Miller next went to Harry Cohn at Columbia, they ended up being shunted off to meetings with Roy Brewer, president of the International Alliance of Theatrical and Stage Employees (IATSE). This was not exactly a meeting of the minds insofar as it hadn't been all that long since the IATSE had been organizing hoods to break up the Conference of Studio Unions protests in Burbank, making it as close as any group in Hollywood to the ILA profile being denounced by *The Hook*. And not only that: Brewer doubled as chairman of the Motion Picture Industry Council, a pressure group that had as its sole claimed purpose keeping Communist propaganda out of motion pictures. Somewhere in the discussions among Brewer, Kazan, and Miller, the idea of substituting Communist subversives for mob racketeers as the heavies in *The Hook* was floated, and everything went downhill from there. Later on, there would be conflicting versions about who pulled out first, if the Communists as villains had been a serious proposal or just Brewer's teasing of the leftist intellectuals, or if Kazan or Miller were repulsed by Brewer and his flaunted ties with HUAC and the FBI. The main thing was that *The Hook* was scuttled as another collaboration between the director and the playwright (it would come back to at least partial life in 1955 with Miller's *A View from the Bridge*, but without Kazan as the director).

While all this was going on, Budd Schulberg, yet another who named names before HUAC and the son of long-time Paramount production chief B. P. Schulberg, was researching his own screenplay on the criminal activities of Ryan's ILA. Up to then, Schulberg's most noted accomplishment was as the author of the novel *What Makes Sammy Run?* about a ruthless movie industry insider. His chief sources of inspiration for the New York docks story were a series of articles that ran in the *New York Sun* and a waterfront priest who claimed to have done more than be interviewed by the writer of the articles and who would figure prominently in getting *Waterfront* going. The reporter, Malcolm Johnson, won a Pulitzer Prize for distinguished local reporting in 1949 for a twenty-four-article series published in November–December 1948 that appeared under the title of "Crime on the Waterfront." This was followed up by another series in January 1949 in which Johnson singled out some of the forces at work trying to combat the Ryan-Anastasia hold on the Hudson River piers. The most energetic crusader was Jesuit John "Pete" Corridan, who had not only pointed Johnson in the direction of much of the material for the *Sun* series but who also, at least by his own assertion, had practically written the second series in January under the reporter's byline. (This claim Johnson found immodest in the extreme, but he never completely dispelled it, either.)

Shortly after collecting his Pulitzer, Johnson sold the rights to his story to an independent outfit called the Monticello Film Corporation, specifically set up for the occasion. The company's driving force was Joseph Curtis, nephew of Columbia head Cohn. When Curtis hired Schulberg to do the screenplay, it was with the understanding that the director would be Robert Siodmak, the Germany-reared maker of such black-and-white features as *The Killers* and *Cry of the City*; according to Curtis, Siodmak's experience with hard-edged subjects and ease about shooting in city locations made him ideal for the project.[3] Schulberg needed more than that, though, and wasted little time looking up Corridan for more practical details. Both sides later acknowledged that the priest was initially cool to the idea, especially coming from a writer whose background gave him more Dream Factory than Pier 45 credentials. Fearful that the distractions of movie glamour would sidetrack his reform efforts, the Jesuit told the writer that "there's no percentage for us helping you turn this into another Hollywood movie."[4] But Schulberg persisted, pointing out that he had written not just *What Makes Sammy Run?* but also *The Harder They Fall*, a novel set in the sleaziest corners of the boxing world. Persuaded that the writer knew more about life than what was encountered on a back lot, Corridan turned him over to a stevedore named Arthur Brown who bore the marks of years of beatings from union mobsters for questioning their authority. It was Brown who, behind warnings to Schulberg to keep his mouth shut, guided him through shape-ups and the other daily travails of longshoremen that provided the realistic details that would eventually suffuse *Waterfront*.

But the picture was still an elusive goal in April 1951 when, with Corridan, Curtis, and Siodmak all signing off on it, the finished screenplay was sent to Cohn for final approval and budgeting. Before Cohn ever pronounced himself on the merits of the script, Schulberg appeared before HUAC on May 23, 1951, to admit his one-time membership in the Communist Party and to confirm the memberships of most of the Hollywood Ten screenwriters. For some of those engaged in the debate over the implied political thrust of *Waterfront*, the fact that the writer had sent the script off to Columbia prior to his appearance refuted a widespread impression that the film's informer-hero personified an elaborate rationalization by Schulberg (and Kazan) for why they had named names before HUAC—a valid point if it could be presumed he had never given a moment's thought ahead of time to what he was going to say in front of the congressmen. But whatever the importance of its delivery date, the script ended up at the bottom of Cohn's slush pile. The West Coast reason was waiting to see if the HUAC testimony would make Schulberg a hero or a pariah, while the East Coast one was threats from Ryan to sue anyone who sought to libel him or his local.

Fast-forward to the fall of 1952, after the Miller-Kazan treatment of *The Hook* had already been shot down by both Zanuck and Cohn.

Corridan, who had no intimate knowledge of the Miller script and would have been unlikely to endorse it for a grocery list of reasons starting with its cool moralistic tone, began pressing Schulberg to revive their project. It was only then that he learned that the writer had been laying low because (he said) the producer Curtis had decided that the smartest way to rescue the script from oblivion was by adding more sex and violence. Corridan didn't have a chance to be apoplectic since in the same breath Schulberg informed him that Curtis's option was about to run out on the property and that he had already told Johnson he himself would buy the series and try again with Hollywood. And indeed that was what occurred, and this time with Kazan and not Siodmak attached as the director.[5]

Whenever he was questioned about the coincidence of working with Kazan on the same kind of material Miller had been earlier, Schulberg was quick to note that he had begun his version (in 1949) before the playwright had started his own and that he never even met the director until a year after *The Hook* had been dropped as a viable project. Leaving aside the extraordinary self-discipline by Kazan that would have called for, there would seem little reason to doubt him. Although features of the two works are similar, they are largely of the generic nature of a hero seeing the light against mobsters he had thought of as family and the nuts and bolts of daily stevedore work. Even the odd specific parallels, such as an episode when a loading sling collapses in a ship hold and kills a worker, ultimately underline differences more than similarities. In Miller's script the death is an accident that typifies how the union doesn't protect its workers, while in Schulberg's it is a murder aimed at shutting up an informer. If Miller's approach to the subject was that of reflective denunciation, Schulberg's was of visceral exposé.

More striking in familiarity was the trip Kazan made to Hollywood in May 1953 with Schulberg—essentially to run the same studio gauntlet as he had with Miller. This time, though, the director went west with more than hopes since he had already squeezed some development money out of Zanuck for keeping Schulberg going through numerous drafts of the screenplay and had exchanged more than one enthusiasm with the Fox chief on the telephone. During their conversations Zanuck had gone so far as to suggest actors for the lead roles, coming down insistently for Brando as the protagonist Terry Malloy and going along with Kazan's choice of Karl Malden for a priest character patterned after Corridan. As for the part of Johnny Friendly, the names bruited included Paul Douglas and Broderick Crawford, who, despite more limited range, were comparably heavy-jowled actors getting the middle-age lead roles Cobb thought he should have been getting for years. When the time came for final casting, however, Kazan would stress another criterion that had nothing to do with the star roles collected on a résumé and that would suggest Cobb had been his target from the start. In the meantime, the Schulberg script he took on the train to Los Angeles, he assured his traveling companion, was the best he had seen since *Death of a Salesman* and *A Streetcar Named Desire*, and he had every reason to think Zanuck agreed with him. Steeped as he was in the whims of Hollywood studios through his early years in California, Schulberg admitted not going far beyond hope during the trip.

The good news for Kazan at Fox was that Zanuck was no longer fixated on *Viva Zapata!* The bad news was that he didn't understand how anyone could still be thinking about making social issue black-and-white dramas on a traditional screen when his company was ushering in the future with the CinemaScope color epic *The Robe*, to be followed soon after by *Prince Valiant*. Oh, and aside from that, he hated Schulberg's script. Or, as Kazan later quoted the one-time producer of *The Grapes of Wrath* as saying, "Who's going to care about a lot of sweaty longshoremen?"[6] The only room the studio head left even for hope was another conference if Kazan and Schulberg could guarantee a commitment from Brando as their star. It was not a promise they could make, and that too had to do with the HUAC experiences of the principals.

When Cohn also passed (for the third time, counting the Miller submission), the project looked dead. That it remained alive was in good part due to the coincidence that Kazan and Schulberg had taken a room at the Beverly Hills Hotel on the same floor as Sam Spiegel. An Austria-born independent producer with a picaresque past as a youth in Palestine and a fugitive from Nazi Germany, Spiegel had never seen a dollar he couldn't spend in high style, for the most part on himself. Sometimes he didn't wait to have the dollar, and his notorious wiliness in dealing with people led Kazan to say he never did anything that wasn't "tactical." But his personal carriage (and penchant for calling himself S. P. Eagle on credits because "it sounds American") camouflaged his taste for screen challenges, whether in subject matter or production logistics. One of his most critically acclaimed "small" films had been *The Stranger*, with Edward G. Robinson playing a Nazi hunter who pursues his quarry to a postcard New England town where a former Gestapo officer (Orson Welles) has set up a respectable new life. He had had even more success with Huston's *The African Queen* with Bogart and Katharine Hepburn, the shooting of which in the Belgian Congo became a cautionary tale of location filming. But Schulberg, who had been acquainted with Spiegel through his family, caught the producer at the right moment, after he had produced a couple of flops and was in dire need of a picture that would get him out of near bankruptcy. Having Kazan's name connected to the project was enough for him to invite Schulberg to his room to read the script, after which Spiegel immediately said he would take it on. In mere days he worked out a deal at Columbia with Cohn, who suddenly forgot about his previous rejections, including the submission made by his nephew Curtis.

No sooner had Spiegel agreed to shepherd the film than HUAC once again raised its head. The producer, the director, and the screenwriter all agreed with Zanuck—that the lead role of Terry Malloy was made to order for Brando. What wasn't made to order for Brando were Kazan and Schulberg. (Cobb hadn't yet been signed.) Although he had studied with the director at the Actors Studio and owed much of his stage and film triumphs in *Streetcar* to him, he told one and all that he couldn't accept working with somebody who had named names before the congressional committee. "He hurt lives doing that," as he was quoted by one friend as lamenting. Decades later in an autobiography he said the same thing:

> I was reluctant to take the part because I was conflicted about what Gadge had done and knew some of the people who had been deeply hurt. It was especially stupid because most of the people named were no longer Communists. Innocent people were also blacklisted, including me, although I had never had a political affiliation of any kind. It was simply because I had signed a petition to protest the lynching of a black man in the South. My sister Jocelyn . . . was also blacklisted because her married name was Asimof and there was another J. Asimof. In those days stepping off the sidewalk with your left foot first was grounds for suspicion that you were a member of the Communist Party.[7]

Brando's was hardly an isolated opinion, either in New York or Hollywood, but in the actor's case it was strengthened further by his relations with Stella Adler, his most influential acting coach, and her Group Theatre contemporaries who were in no mood to forgive Kazan for outing Carnovsky and the others. When the actor appeared resolute in his refusal to work with Kazan, Spiegel offered Terry Malloy to Frank Sinatra, then in his dramatic renaissance with an Oscar from *From Here to Eternity*. Sinatra wasted no time in accepting.

And nobody was really happy. Although formally committed to Sinatra, Spiegel continued his pursuit of Brando through third parties. For his part, Kazan had been informed of Brando's antagonism toward working with him, and that fed more than one declaration that he was overjoyed to have Sinatra as his leading man. But those claims aside, he also let his dissatisfaction with the casting be known by asking Malden to quietly direct a screen test with Paul Newman for showing it to Spiegel. Spiegel didn't want Newman, but Kazan's evident lack of enthusiasm for Sinatra made him increase his efforts for Brando. With the help of the actor's psychiatrist, who counseled him to do the picture, Spiegel got his star, though with trickle-down ego effects lasting years. When Sinatra didn't get the part of Malloy, he demanded that of the priest that had already been promised by Kazan to Malden. What the crooner ended up settling for was a painting from Spiegel's highly regarded collection and the animus that would mark his relations with Brando when the two of them appeared together in *Guys and Dolls* a year later. As for Kazan, despite his contradictory statements, he asserted in his autobiography, "I always preferred Brando to anybody." He also admitted that the actor never let him forget his objections to the HUAC testimony and the reason he had reluctantly agreed to take on the Malloy role anyway. At some point during practically every day of shooting, Kazan said, Brando stressed that he had said yes only to remain near his New York–based analyst rather than have to accept another offer in California.[8]

The signing of Brando led Kazan pretty directly to Cobb for the role of Johnny Friendly. Although there was conjecture the casting was a gesture of solidarity by one HUAC cooperative witness with another, nothing in the director's subsequently voluminous writings hinted at anything of the kind. But what Kazan did note more than once was the Stanislavsky training of all the principal players—Cobb and Malden from the Group Theatre, Rod Steiger and Eva Marie Saint from the Actors Studio, and Brando from both the Studio and Stella Adler. Even the relatively small roles of the crime commission investigators were given to Group player Leif Ericson and Studio student Martin Balsam, while other Studio aspirants like Pat Hingle and Nehemiah Persoff were assigned bits. Such rumored alternatives to Cobb as Paul Douglas and Broderick Crawford for the Johnny Friendly role didn't have that background, and while Kazan never rejected out of hand non-Method actors (most vividly working with the ultra-technical Raymond Massey in *East of Eden*), he never disguised his preference for Group colleagues and Studio students because of their commonly developed sense of performance (the chief motivating factor behind his creation of the Actors Studio). Cobb was also in trimmer shape than the other mentioned candidates for the physical scenes the mobster Friendly had with Brando's Malloy—one of the major motifs of the film. Given Kazan's working methods, it is not entirely out of the question, either, that he exploited Brando's resentment of the cooperative HUAC witnesses to add an edge to his character's ultimate defiance of Cobb's Johnny Friendly. Repeatedly throughout his career, the director exacerbated rather than played down antagonisms between actors (between Massey and James Dean in *East of Eden* and between Brando and Anthony Quinn in *Viva Zapata!* to cite two examples) in the interests of greater screen electricity. "Dad always said Gadge would do anything to get the most out of actors," as Vincent Cobb said, "and while he never thought Brando's attitude toward HUAC was the main reason he was hired, he knew Kazan would use it to the maximum. I think he was very ready for it."

The *Waterfront* script kept going through revisions up to the start of the shooting in November. In itself this was not unusual, and it did not affect the general dramatic line of the ex-boxer-longshoreman Terry (Brando) waking up to the fact that he has been used by his father figure of Johnny Friendly (Cobb) and his older brother Charlie (Steiger) for helping them maintain their hold on the West Side docks. His decision to break with them and testify before a crime commission comes through his love for Edie (Saint), whose brother he unwittingly helped murder, and under pressures from the priest Father Barry (Malden). But what did not remain the same from Kazan's initial contact with Cobb were the scale of the production and where it was shot.

Although the talents involved were from the A list, Cohn had made it a condition of taking on the picture from Spiegel that every cost would be spared, from the length of the shooting schedule to salaries to basic special effects devices employed on major productions. Cohn's Columbia might not have had its CinemaScope epics like *The Robe* (and wouldn't for some time) as priorities, but it shared Zanuck's worries that audiences seeking black-and-white social dramas would be more likely found in front of their TV sets than at movie theaters. On the issue of salaries, for instance, Kazan claimed in his autobiography that he took down a hefty six-figure fee in addition to a percentage of the net, but other indications were that the director, Schulberg, and Spiegel all realized most of their payments through profit sharing. With the exception of Brando, who banked a reported $100,000, the actors were even easier to handle—Cobb needing the job (and, according to one of his sons, getting only $5,000), Steiger and Saint among the most luminous members of Kazan's Actors Studio but the former with only one screen credit and the latter with none at all, and Malden a sturdy but not especially famous Hollywood supporting player.

A more critical change, affecting the personal safety of the director and his actors, was in the shooting location. In the fall of 1953, Ryan's ILA was expelled from the AFL (American Federation of Labor) following months of public hearings, investigative news reports, and Corridan's unflagging aid to both. But even as a new local was being put together, Ryan's goons continued their intimidating ways by threatening longshoremen to sign loyalty oaths to the discredited union or face the consequences. Moreover, the New York Shipping Association, which had always turned a blind eye to the ILA's activities as long as its commerce wasn't compromised, remained in contract negotiations with Ryan, creating total confusion among both longshoremen and shippers about how effective the expulsion from the AFL was and what was supposed to replace it. When some of Ryan's thugs began drifting around the Chelsea locations on the West Side chosen for exteriors, Spiegel and Kazan had second thoughts about shooting in Manhattan. It was no last-minute trepidation. Already, Schulberg had been writing a little less specifically about the Manhattan setting in later drafts. The story was obviously still about the Hudson River docks, but not so explicitly that an especially attentive viewer would wonder why this structure looming up in the background was on the east rather than on the west. In other words, eyes had been drifting west to the New Jersey city of Hoboken long before the announcement that this would be the main location for the film.

Corridan, hired as a technical advisor at Schulberg's urging, made his most important contribution by brokering permission for the film to be shot on Hoboken's Pier 1. The move to New Jersey still wouldn't have been possible, though, if there hadn't been another waterfront investigation on the west bank of the Hudson implicating Mayor Fred DeSapio and his friends in seamy places in various harbor irregularities. When an election forced out DeSapio in favor of John Grogan, the filmmakers had their ideal mayor because Grogan was also president of the Marine and Shipbuilding Workers of the CIO (Congress of Industrial Organizations) and had several incentives for encouraging the *Waterfront* shoot.

Tony DiNicola, one of the numerous longshoremen hired as extras on the film, recalled that Grogan had everything to gain and nothing to lose by welcoming the film crew to Hoboken. "The same hearings that took some of the air out of DeSapio also brought up Grogan's name as just one more guy on the arm," DiNicola said, "but as a pretty minor player. Still, when he took over as mayor, he had his other job as president of Local 15 and he wanted everybody to know he ran a clean union. So what better way than to bring in a movie that's all about cleaning up dirty unions?"[9]

Even then the shoot wasn't invulnerable to those who didn't want any part of the picture. For starters, there were the physical threats, and nobody was more exposed to them than Cobb and his projected characterization of a Ryan-like figure. "I'd say the one advantage he had was that most of his scenes were indoors, so he didn't need to be in Hoboken as much as Brando and some of the others," DiNicola recalled. "Still, even with that, Kazan got him some extra protection."

The extra protection was in the surrounding muscle that appears in most of Johnny Friendly's scenes. Rather than go to Central Casting, Kazan hired real tough guys—former boxers Tony Galento, Tami Mauriello, and Abe Simon. A fourth member of the phalanx was Roger Donahue, who had once killed an opponent in the ring. Had Cobb requested the additional muscle? According to Vincent Cobb, "He laughed about it, but that was years after the fact and he certainly never complained about it. One tip-off was that he could be enormously patient with other actors who, let's say, weren't ready or able to do a scene, but he too had his limits. With guys like Galento and Mauriello you had a situation much worse than that because even when they knew their lines, they didn't always get them out very articulately. Dad had a lot of exchanges with them, but he always gave me the impression that he was fine for the tradeoff of more takes for more protection."

Kazan also opted for special protection. As he recorded in his autobiography, "The 'mob' was always around, watching what we were doing. . . . I decided I'd be easier and work better if I had a bodyguard: he was a fine fellow named Joe Marotta, the brother of the chief of police. Joe carried a pistol and was never more than six feet away from me throughout the picture. One day some hoods pushed me up against a wall and, holding me there, began to berate me, their point being that I was making the people of Hoboken look bad—yes, they were that civic-minded. But then Joe walked up, and they walked away."[10]

Not all the harassing came from ILA toughs. The Hoboken agencies still staffed by loyalists to the former DeSapio administration made sure shooting permits expired at the end of just about every shooting day, necessitating regular reapplications through the municipal bureaucracy. When Spiegel lived up to his reputation for doling out dollars a penny at a time, holding up payments to the longshoremen hired as extras for two dollars an hour, they went after production manager Charlie Maguire, dangling him out over the Hudson until he guaranteed them payment by the end of the day. Then there were Spiegel's unannounced visits to the set. Totally oblivious to the damp, freezing weather endured by the crew every day of the six-week shoot, the producer would drive up in a limousine, advise his arm candy for the day to stay warm in the car, then call everyone together to complain that they were costing him a fortune by working so slowly. Kazan finally had enough and threatened to shut down everything for good if Spiegel didn't stay over in Manhattan. There were no more limousine visits.

But there was still the save-money-at-all-costs deal between Spiegel and Cohn, and that accidentally helped enshrine a *Waterfront* scene for generations. When Kazan came to the moment when the Brando and Steiger characters meet in the back of a taxi, where Terry suggests he might inform against Friendly before the crime commission and Charlie accepts his part of the blame for his brother's humpty-dumpty existence, the director was astonished to discover that, because of all the economizing, he couldn't have the standard rear projection device for indicating the cab's progress through New York streets. Defying the personal experiences of tens of millions of taxi fares over the years, he had to go along with a proposal by cameraman Boris Kauffman to get some Venetian blinds from the nearby Myers Hotel and use them to cover the back window, eliminating the outside traffic problem.

But while the blinds provided an amusing talking point for the scene, it was the actual back-and-forth between Brando and Steiger that etched it in the minds of filmgoers. In one way or another, Schulberg, the Friendly henchman played by Roger Donahue, and Cobb all had a role in it, though none were on screen.

If *On the Waterfront* bequeathed a single line of dialogue to rival the "Frankly, My Dear, I don't give a damn" ending of *Gone with the Wind*, it was Terry Malloy's lament to Charlie in the back of the cab that "I coulda been a contender." According to Schulberg, the line ended up in the script thanks to Donahue. Complimented by the writer after a sparring session, the boxer smiled sadly and pressed his finger down hard on his white cheek, immediately raising too much color. "Irish skin," he told Schulberg. "Bleeds too quick. Without that, I could've been a contender."

Cobb, meanwhile, was cited by Malden as the unknowing cause of one of the more contentious episodes during the filming, again stemming from the taxi scene. Until the day he died in 2002, Steiger never tired of accusing Brando of "not being professional" for his refusal to feed off-camera lines to him during single-shot close-ups, leaving that task to Kazan. The director himself provided only a semi-apology for Brando's brusque departure from the set as soon as he was off camera by saying he was late for his psychiatrist's appointment—an explanation that only infuriated Steiger more. According to Malden, however, Brando's exit had nothing to do with his analyst, and reflected his anger with Steiger. Actor Robert Walden recalled Malden telling him,

> When Rod first came on the picture, he couldn't brag enough that he was playing Marlon Brando's brother and that he was working with Lee Cobb, the actor who created Willy Loman. You never saw anybody so excited. But as the picture moved along, he was doing most of his scenes with Lee, and nobody ever accused Lee of playing small if he didn't have to. Especially as this Johnny Friendly character, he was large, large, large. Well, the more Rod was exposed to that, the more he started emulating Lee. When they get to the cab scene, there he is still doing it, even breaking out in tears, and Marlon was livid. He did just about everything small, and as far as he was concerned, there was no scene that needed small more than that

one. When Gadge didn't rein in Rod enough to his liking, Marlon just finished what he had to do and took off. He accepted the large from Lee because that's who the character of Friendly was, but not from Steiger.[11]

Brando himself backed Malden's account during a 1957 interview with Truman Capote. "There were seven takes because Rod Steiger couldn't stop crying. He's one of those actors who loves to cry. We kept doing it over and over."[12]

But that story differed not only from Kazan's, but also from that of the only other actor required on the set for the taxi scene—Nehemiah Persoff, who was shown briefly at the conclusion as the driver who transports Steiger to certain death for betraying Friendly.

I don't know where Malden got that story. I was sitting around there all day on Fifty-eighth Street waiting for my shot. I was at the Actors Studio at the time and Kazan hired a lot of us for small roles, I think it was for seventy-five dollars. And I can say that Brando marched off because he'd made an appointment with his therapist and that seemed to have been part of the agreement he had with Kazan before shooting started. Did Steiger make him angry because of a reading? That would have certainly been in Rod's DNA, but I don't remember that from that day.

Whether it was the Malden-Brando version or the Kazan-Persoff one, Steiger rarely let Brando off the hook when asked in succeeding years about his experiences on *Waterfront*. "We were generous to each other as actors and technicians," he typically commented to biographer Tom Hutchinson. "We knew it was going to be a fine movie. Except of course for Mr. Brando; generosity was not the name of his game."[13]

In his later years, Steiger told a Cobb story that hasn't survived serious reflection. According to the actor, he was so in awe of the man who had played Willy Loman that it took him some days to work up to inviting him around to his apartment one evening for a simple spaghetti dinner. When Cobb accepted without hesitation, Steiger described himself as "being on cloud nine." But the very morning Cobb was due to come over, he said, he learned about how he had named names before HUAC. "What was I supposed to do? I couldn't stand the idea of somebody doing that. But I couldn't just walk up to him and say the spaghetti's off. So we went through with it. He came over and we had to invent conversation for a couple of hours. It was one of the longest nights of my life."[14]

The anecdote was consistent with Steiger's lifelong criticism of the cooperative witnesses before HUAC; among other things, he was one of those most vocally opposed to the Motion Picture Academy of Arts and Sciences giving Kazan an honorary Oscar for lifetime achievement in 1999. What it was not consistent with was the calendar. Since the invitation for the spaghetti had to have been extended in late November or early December 1953, he would have had to have gone almost six months without hearing of Cobb's June testimony, though it was fairly widespread news within the industry even before newspapers had reported the appearance in September. Moreover, he seemed not to have been too bothered politically by working under Kazan or, for that matter, by costarring shortly afterward with Bogart in Schulberg's *The Harder They Fall* screen adaptation. "Rod could be a very exciting actor," Vincent Cobb said, "but he could be as difficult to deal with on a personal level as most said Brando was. He himself admitted having serious depression issues. Dad said once that you never knew what was going to come out of his mouth if the words weren't already on the page for him. I don't know if the spaghetti dinner is true. It may have been or it may have been completely made up. Or, a third possibility: They actually had the dinner, and only afterward Rod put all the HUAC stuff around it."

The motion picture to emerge from the personality conflicts, financial restrictions, mobster threats, and political miasma was their sum, but also considerably more. No surprise, it attracted criticism of every conceivable tone. Leading the positive reviews was that of Weiler in the *New York Times*, who declared in part, "A small but obviously dedicated group of realists has forged artistry, anger, and some horrible truths into *On the Waterfront*, as violent and indelible a film record of man's inhumanity to man as has come to light this year." Terming it "movie-making of a rare and high order," Weiler lavished praise on the director, the writer, the cameraman, the musical composer Leonard Bernstein, and every member of the cast, from Brando's "shatteringly poignant" Terry Malloy to Cobb's "muscularly effective . . . absolute unregenerated monarch of the docks."[15] Other New York dailies followed suit, the *Herald Tribune* calling the film "a director's triumph,"[16] the *Post* saying it was "a credit to all who participated in its making,"[17] and the *Daily News* awarding it its highest four stars (if also mumbling that Brando remained an "uneven" actor because he wasn't always intelligible). Few major dailies around the country disagreed, and from coast to coast the picture swooped up critics' circle prizes, as well as being named best film of the year by the National Board of Review and other national bodies.

But there were also dissenters. *Time* magazine, for one, took Zanuck's snob view that there was nothing of "heroic, classic-style drama" in the problems of longshoremen and gave it only the backhanded compliment of being similar to the "screen journalism" of such 1930s gangster pictures as *Little Caesar*.[18] And essayists with more time to think about it than daily or weekly reviewers were much sterner. The ideologically entrenched could not have been expected to skate past the parallels of the HUAC testimonies of Kazan and Schulberg and Malloy's decision to testify against Friendly, and they didn't. John Henry Lawson, one of the blacklisted screenwriters named by Schulberg before HUAC, charged that the picture was "antidemocratic, antilabor, antihuman propaganda," and that this was inevitable having been "concocted by men who wear the livery of the informer."[19] For Eric Bentley, it was bad enough that *Waterfront* depicted the act of informing as virtuous but absolutely "appalling" that the picture was "created in the first place to point up this virtue."[20]

But literal readings as either a Schulberg-Corridan exposé of corrupt unions or a Schulberg-Kazan rationalization for naming names have always been undermined by the film's primary focus on the personal relations among the chief characters rather than on investigative revelations or political apologies. No doubt the messages have been there for the finding, so much so that attempts to divorce the actions of the Malloy character from the HUAC appearances of Kazan and Schulberg have mainly illuminated the fantasy life of those doing the attempting. Even Kazan acknowledged the parallel. Concerning the climactic scene on the barge when Malloy screams at Friendly "I'm glad what I done!" the director told an interviewer, "That was me saying with identical heat that I was glad I'd testified as I had. I'd been snubbed by friends each and every day for many months. . . . The scene in the film where Brando goes back to the waterfront to 'shape up' again for employment and is rejected by men with whom he'd worked day after day—that too was my story, now told to all the world. So when my critics say that I put my story and my feelings on the screen, to justify my informing, they are right."[21]

What jobs he didn't get because of his testimony Kazan didn't get around to specifying. But the larger issue is that even if the parallels were there, they hardly added up to any sense of triumphant vindication for squealing on the screen. The tinniest notes in the picture were in fact struck precisely with its lapses into bravado. One came at the very end when the dock workers were credited with shoving Cobb's Johnny Friendly into the drink. Two more occurred earlier within the same scene—when Malden's priest slugged Malloy for telling him to go to hell and then he demanded a beer with the quaking accomplishment of a schoolboy deciding he had earned his first adult beverage. However different the final version of *Waterfront* was from *The Hook*, it echoed the Miller work in its profoundly pessimistic view of working as a dock loader on the Hudson. That sense of foreboding weighed so heavily that not even Malloy's climactic "Calvary Crucifixion walk" completely dissipated the feeling that the day after the film's narrative, things would return to the way they were. The dockers as a whole were presented as so passive, even cowardly, that Jesus Christ would have had to labor up the Alps to shake them out of their torpor.

That this did not make for 108 minutes of unrelieved depression owed to Kazan's crystallization of the film's two competing motifs and the extraordinary embodiment of both by Brando—the violence between Malloy and Friendly and the tenderness between Malloy and Edie. Every one of the scenes between Brando and Cobb was fraught with physical combat, sometimes casual, sometimes not so casual—an opening scene in the back of the bar where Cobb was all over Brando as his "boy" and then went on to slap around another character; the street scene where the irate Cobb paternalistically took a chunk out of Brando's cheek after reading him the riot act; the courtroom scene where Cobb worked himself up to a volcanic eruption after Brando had testified against him; and, finally, the climactic punch-up on the barge. For these sequences to have worked, the Johnny Friendly on the screen had to have been played by somebody not only with the gravitas of a mob boss but also with a physical fitness not intimidated by the character of an ex-boxer. "It was really one of the few times where Dad was as needed for what I can only call his physical strength as much as for his acting abilities," Vincent Cobb noted. "He liked it, too, especially because Kazan was always egging him on to be physical. He liked joking with Galento and the others that they would be the next ones he would be taking on."

Alternating with the violences of the Cobb scenes were those between Brando and Saint, which Kazan himself called his favorites in the picture.[22] With the help of an alternately frenetic and sumptuous score by Bernstein that foreshadowed his music for *West Side Story*, they made *On the Waterfront* as much of a love story as a crime drama—an objective the director said he had had from the beginning. If initial reviews largely emphasized the latter over the former, subsequent critiques reevaluated the picture for the contrasting rhythms of the Malloy who had to overcome his docility before the overbearing Johnny Friendly and the Malloy who had to overcome his own street brutalities for the sensitivities represented by Edie. Next to the killing of Charlie that Kazan indicated as the basic reason for Malloy's testimony against Friendly, and not his own a priori attitude that all squealing was justifiable, it was his love for Edie, not the moralistic lectures of Father Barry about cleaning up the union, that had the greatest impact on him. Down to it, and in spite of the pivotal role of the real Pete Corridan in helping to put together the picture, the most marginal of the major characters was Malden's Father Barry. As even Weiler noted amid his lavish praise of the film, the Malden priest was "accorded a mite too much emphasis."[23] But against the more visceral impact of the Malloy-Friendly and Malloy-Edie relationships, not as much long-lasting importance. To this extent, Corridan had a point in his original distrust of Hollywood landing on the Hudson.

If anyone remained extraneous to all the tensions around the picture, it was Saint. "I really just heard all those stories afterwards," she said.

> I'm glad because I haven't had to make up my own stories over the years to all the people asking me about it. I was too involved in my role. In the morning, sometimes with Marlon, I'd get the train over to Hoboken from West Ninth Street. As for Lee, we all considered him—I know I did—the great actor of his generation. Between takes he was the sweetest man in the world. There was nothing but warmth about him. And then you'd see the character he was playing and you were reminded what great acting was all about.[24]

When the awards season came, Brando, Kazan, Saint, and Schulberg, as well as a number of technical contributors, marched through the Oscars as victoriously as they had through metropolitan critics' circles. Cobb, Malden, and Steiger were less fortunate because they were competing against one another in the supporting player category, allowing a fourth nominee from outside the picture to sneak through (Edmond O'Brien from *The Barefoot Contessa*). Cobb was hardly dispirited, however, and he went to as many celebratory luncheons and dinners as he could to show the flag. As he was quoted by one companion at the luncheon for announcing the Academy Award nominations, "It feels good to show my face again and not get the feeling people want to slap it."

What was to linger long after the awards and become immaterial to all the textual and subtextual analyses of the film's intentions was Brando's performance. Starting with Kazan, it has ever since been regarded as a landmark elevation of realism, if not by *New York Daily News* reviewers, by the tens of thousands of actors and directors who have worked in the profession. Cobb was among them. Amid all the disenchantments he expressed for his motion picture career in *Films in Review*, he also allowed about *Waterfront* to Pickard, "I suppose it was okay. As a film it was a good example of the Method, of the virtues of having a popular cast speak the same language, of being motivated by the same school of acting. Brando was very easy to work with. A very formidable talent."[25]

In a 1990 blogspot.com interview with Grissom, Brando repaid the compliment and then some: "There was no bullshit with Lee. None. He was there to work and to work well, and he was fierce in his devotion to the work at hand. He couldn't make a false move because he was so firmly walking toward the truth. He could not be moved."

## NOTES

1. Navasky, *Naming Names*, p. 272.

2. Eric Bentley (ed.), *Thirty Years of Treason: Excerpts from Hearings before the House Committee on Un-American Activities 1938–1968* (New York: Thunder's Mouth Press/Nation Books, 2002), p. 486n.

3. According to Nott (*He Ran All the Way*, pp. 296–297), there was also a parallel initiative to adapt the Johnson series with Garfield projected as the star under director Robert Rossen. This was denied by Kazan and others despite substantial evidence it was true.

4. James T. Fisher, *On the Irish Waterfront: The Crusader, the Movie, and the Soul of the Port of New York* (Ithaca, NY: Cornell University Press, 2009), p. 124.

5. Fisher, *On the Irish Waterfront*, p. 193.

6. Ibid, p. 243.

7. Marlon Brando (with Robert Lindsey), *Brando: Songs My Mother Taught Me* (New York: Random House, 1994), p. 78.

8. Kazan, *Elia Kazan*, pp. 470–471.

9. Interview with author, October 11, 2010. Subsequent quotes from Tony DiNicola are taken from this interview.

10. Kazan, *Elia Kazan*, p. 521.

11. Interview with author, March 14, 2011. Subsequent quotes from Robert Walden are taken from this interview.

12. Truman Capote, "The Duke in His Domain," *New Yorker*, November 9, 1957.

13. Tom Hutchinson, *Rod Steiger* (New York: Fromm International, 2000), p. 82.

14. Conversation with author, April 30, 1991.

15. *New York Times*, July 29, 1954.

16. *New York Herald Tribune*, July 29, 1954.

17. *Post* (New York), July 29, 1954.

18. *Time*, August 9, 1954.

19. As quoted by Fisher, *On the Irish Waterfront*, p. 290.

20. Eric Bentley, *What Is Theatre? A Query in Chronicle Form* (Boston: Beacon Press, 1956), pp. 98–102.

21. As quoted by Hoberman, *Bridge of Light*, p. 267.

22. Kazan, *Elia Kazan*, p. 525.

23. *New York Times*, July 29, 1954.

24. Interview with author, November 9, 2011.

25. Pickard, "The Self-Preservation Gene."

# Chapter 18

―――――――――――――――――○―――――――――――――――――

# Matters of the
# Heart . . . and Head

ON THE WATERFRONT opened the door for Cobb to resume the film career he had been developing before going east for *Death of a Salesman* and before having to deal with the blacklist. Once through it he didn't waste much time, committing himself to one picture after another interspersed with television appearances. But the price tag was heavy: none of the pictures was another *Waterfront* and his reach for quick cash in a couple of cases amounted to little progress from *The Man Who Cheated Himself*; his reinforced celebrity from the Kazan film brought attention more easily to his HUAC (House Un-American Activities Committee) appearance; and his exhausting work schedule came close to killing him, very literally. As a bachelor moving around in Los Angeles apartments, he would have never been cited for his healthy eating habits, either: doughnuts didn't have to be roasted before being served.

With *The Racers*, he was back at Fox with Zanuck and with the journeyman of journeymen directors Henry Hathaway, who had called the shots on *Call Northside 777* and on such other studio staples as *The House on 92nd Street*, *Kiss of Death*, and *The Desert Fox*. The picture offered the perks of extensive location shooting in France, Monaco, and Italy and, of particular pleasure to Cobb, the opportunity to discuss his passion for cars with the top racing drivers of the day, hired for cameos. But then there was the film itself. In a four-wheeled reprise of his heel role as the boxer in *Champion*, Kirk Douglas played an Italian bus driver (!) determined to win the Gran Prix di Napoli, no matter how many men and women he had to run over to reach that finish line. Making the predictable, one-note affair more oppressive was that the central woman in his life was played by Bella Darvi, the latest in a long line of Zanuck mistresses the producer stuck into big pictures until their lack of talent prompted too many catcalls to be ignored. Cobb played the manager of the Douglas racing team with an accent picked up from doing Papa Bonaparte too often. At that, he was spared such dialogue as that from a dying Gilbert Roland to Douglas: "My crankcase is leaking." There was no critical dissent from Crowther's evaluation that Cobb, Roland, and the rest of the cast "go through the motions without seeming to know why."[1]

More noteworthy, if for the wrong reasons, was another Fox picture—*The Left Hand of God*. Directed by Edward Dmytryk, it tells of an American pilot (Bogart) who is downed in China during the war, gets rescued by a warlord (Cobb), goes around marauding for a couple of years, then slips into the clothes of a slain priest to get away from the bandits. When he is taken for a real cleric at a mission, he goes through some priestly motions for a while, knowing all along that the warlord will be coming after him and that the devoutly Catholic mission nurse (Gene Tierney) would also like to go after him but is prevented from doing so by his collar. Nothing really gets worked out at the end except that everybody knows the priest is a fake because he tells everyone he is. *The Left Hand of God* had a lot in common with such other Fox productions of the 1950s as *Love Is a Many-Splendored Thing*, *The House of Bamboo*, and *The Inn of the Sixth Happiness*—it was set in Asia and gave work to lots of Asian-American actors, employed primary colors in CinemaScope and a lush musical score in Stereo Sound to obliterate memory of the studio's days producing black-and-white semi-documentary crime dramas, and depended on bird trills from the sound effects department to fill up long silences between characters conversing while spaced too far apart on the wide screen. Cobb played the warlord like a Chinese Johnny Friendly who laughed too much; or, in Crowther's words, "rumbles, roars, and grimaces."[2]

Although laid during what was described as a civil war, the picture made no specific mention of Chiang Kai-Shek's Nationalists or Mao Tse-Tung's Communists, leaving the impression that Cobb's warlord was simply in battle with rivals. On the other hand, Catholic and Protestant cleric characters made it clear that the Chinese villagers on the screen needed a Western God in their lives. The director Dmytryk was the only one of the Hollywood Ten who got off the industry blacklist by walking out of jail to a HUAC hearing room where he named the names (twenty-six of them) he had refused to for years. It all made for messages not so much mixed as pureed. On a more ominous personal note, all three cast principals went about their business in extreme discomfort—Bogart with the back pains that would lead to tests and discovery of the cancer that would kill him after only two more pictures, Tierney on the edge of a nervous breakdown that would prevent her from working again for seven years, and Cobb with a laboring cardiac condition.

Cobb's urgent need for cash was underlined by the fact that he accepted an offer from minor-league Republic Pictures in between his two roles for Zanuck. Being a Republic western, *The Road to Denver* with John Payne was relegated in most cities to a Saturday morning opening and barely attracted reviews. Its appeal to Cobb, aside from the paycheck, was that his role as a town boss getting between two brothers called for him to do just about all his dialogue in a saloon set over very few days while most of the rest of the cast had to do a lot of location work in Utah. It was the kind of convenience he would negotiate for frequently in the future.

His most significant appearance in the first part of 1955 was on television. Thanks to his inclusion on the *Red Channels* proscription list, that income avenue had dried up for him for a while. Even with his HUAC testimony, the networks and their sponsors had stayed away from him as too controversial for people who might have read headlines as well as bought soap. The one exception between *Waterfront* and May 1955 was an NBC Ford Theater role in April 1954 that marked the one and only time Cobb might have been considered as working with his estranged brother, Norman. For a few years, Norman had been peddling story ideas around to the networks trying to break in as a writer. Later on, he would be accepted on the circuit as a contributor to several western TV series and to the medical drama *Ben Casey*, but in 1954 he was credited only with the story for a suspense outing entitled *The Night Visitor*, in which Cobb largely supported his *Salesman* costar Arthur Kennedy. The lugubrious melodrama had Kennedy as a suspended cop who, sure he is going to be dropped from the force for good and with his pregnant wife (Martha Vickers) symbolizing even more bills he won't be able to pay, pulls off a desperate jewel burglary while fellow cop Cobb is at his home reassuring the wife that the suspension will be revoked. His dialogue is big on the virtues of honest men no matter their difficulties, and Kennedy ultimately vindicates his confidence by returning the jewelry without getting caught and is indeed reinstated. *The Night Visitor* had the two major pieces for promoting the story as a reunion of the leads from *Salesman*, but NBC left them on the table since by then the play ("Weren't there Communists involved in it?") was not regarded as the ideal fare for that average viewer in Peoria. The show came and went so quickly that even Laurie Kennedy, who spoke with her father often about his work, said she had never heard of it.

The show did not bring the Cobb brothers any closer, and this didn't surprise Norman. "In spite of everything I always thought there was a deep loving between us," he told his nephew Jerry in their recorded talk.

> That was certainly true for me and I always thought it was true of Lee, too. But a lot of patterns, I have always thought, were set down years ago when we were in the Bronx. The most obvious one, of course, was the eleven years between us. That's not easy for any pair of brothers to bridge. Then there was the attitude of my parents toward Lee—that he was this wonder and that I should feel the same way toward him. And the truth is, I really did feel that way toward him. I admired him enormously. Was it a distance that maybe he got used to over the years? Did Lee require that mystique my parents had encouraged? I think that's a possibility. He was certainly sensitive to the static between us. One day, for instance, I was in his house in Beverly Hills. I don't remember exactly what we were talking about, but what I do remember him saying with this oddly serious look was 'there are times when brothers can do great damage to one another.' Even then it felt like some kind of warning, but I didn't have the slightest idea about what.

Unlike *The Night Visitor*, there has never been an obscurity problem for *Darkness at Noon*, a novel published in 1940 by the Hungarian-born Arthur Koestler that became the most noted example of the "God That Failed" literature by Communists who deserted the party during the Stalinist purges in 1938. A stage adaptation by Sidney Kingsley won Claude Rains a Tony in the early 1950s and, illustrative of its appeal to anti-Communists, the ferociously harassed Edward G. Robinson took it on the road expecting it would help make his case as a loyal American with HUAC. Something of the kind could not have been far from Cobb's mind when he took the lead in a TV version produced by NBC's Producers Showcase on May 2, 1955; for sure, there was no secret about the political weight being given the broadcast once it was announced that it would be accompanied by remarks from Vice President Richard Nixon.

In *Darkness at Noon* the middle-aged apparatchik Rubashov finds himself imprisoned for crimes against the state after another whimsical turn of the wheel in a politically paranoid society identified in everything but name as the Soviet Union (Koestler actually based many of the details of the story on his imprisonment not in the USSR, but in Franco's Spain). The play is divided pretty much into three parts: sessions with Rubashov's interrogators (Oscar Homolka and David Wayne); attempts at communicating with a prisoner (Joseph Wiseman) in an adjoining cell; and flashbacks with his lover (Ruth Roman) when he had been the one doing the persecuting and before she was executed as a traitor.

Cobb, Homolka, and Wiseman on the same set offered potential for a Tournament of Flamboyance, but as directed by Delbert Mann, that didn't happen, at least on May 2. Where it happened, and continually, was in the rehearsals leading up to the network airing. More than half a century later, Nehemiah Persoff, who played a prison guard in the play, could still laugh about it.

> It was hilarious. First you had Homolka who could have done an entire play just with his cigarette holder, and he's using that and everything else on this desk of his. And finally Lee has enough of it, and says to Mann that if Homolka's going to keep playing around like he is, he's going to stand up and drop his pants. Message received. Then you had Wiseman, who was very high strung. There's this whole thing about how these two prisoners are supposed to tap-tap-tap between their cells for communicating, and Wiseman starts going crazy that Lee is only tapping twice when he should tap three times or vice versa, whatever it was, and Lee can't understand why this is infuriating Wiseman, so that only seems to entertain him more. "All I want is a fucking cue and he won't give me one!" Wiseman keeps yelling, and Mann assures him he'll work it out with Lee and everything will be perfect. Well, of course, when it comes to the actual performance, Lee hears how many taps Mann tells Wiseman to expect and does a different number. Wiseman was livid but by then he couldn't do anything about it.

"The only thing I can remember my father ever saying about Cobb," Martha Wiseman, a professor at Skidmore University, said in an e-mail to the author, "is that he didn't like him much."[3]

It was Persoff who, unwittingly, prompted a more melancholy measure of Cobb's state of mind doing the play.

> There's a scene where I'm escorting Rubashov back to his cell after an interrogation session and my commanding officer orders me to push him inside. I get this inspiration to improvise the line "I wouldn't touch this scum," and Rubashov just goes into his cell. Years later—I mean *years* later—I'm doing something else with Lee, and one day he comes over to me and says, "That was because I named names, wasn't it?" I didn't know what he was talking about. "That *scum* line," he says. "That's where it came from. That's what you were thinking of me for testifying." I finally understand and I say, "No, Lee. I was doing the guard who doesn't want to be associated with Rubashov even to touch him." It was only then that it seemed to dawn on him that I'd been improvising strictly in terms of the play. Did he believe it? I don't know. He was a very troubled man.

Most TV critics praised the show, and especially the performances of Cobb and Homolka, though except for Wiseman's raving flights here and there, Mann avoided the *Alice in Wonderland* aspects of the political persecutions vivid in Koestler's novel. In appearing on the screen after the drama's conclusion, Nixon said that NBC was to be "congratulated" for "effectively documenting Communism" and warned that "we in free nations must be eternally vigilant" against the Soviet threat. For reasons not immediately evident, *New York Times* TV critic Jack Gould chided only the producers for Nixon's appearance, asserting that it was the vice president who should have been "spared such embarrassment. . . . The effect was a little like following an impressive symphony concert with a harmonica solo."[4]

But where Cobb's political vulnerabilities were concerned, there was plenty of crassness to go around, and not all of it was from the Republican White House or obtuse TV critics. Only weeks before taking on *Darkness at Noon*, he turned down an offer from Arthur Miller to play the lead on Broadway in *A View from the Bridge*. The offer was startling for more than one reason. A noncooperative witness pursued by HUAC, Miller had broken even with his long-time collaborator Kazan after the latter had named names. So why not with Cobb, too? As the playwright recounted it, the subject came up during a meeting with William Wheeler, when the HUAC investigator sought to get a sense of what could be expected from Miller in a hearing room by asking about his relationship with the actor. "I could not help thinking of Lee, my first Willy Loman, as more a pathetic victim than a villain, a big blundering actor who simply wanted to act, had never put in for heroism, and was one of the best proofs I knew of the Committee's pointless brutality toward artists. Lee Cobb, as political as my foot, was simply one more dust speck swept up in the thirties idealization of the Soviets."[5]

That condescending assessment was only the beginning. Miller went on, "As I didn't need to remind Wheeler, *View* was, among other things, about a man who informed on his own relatives to the immigration authorities. Cynically or not, I had thought that under the circumstances Lee would bring the pain of the harried longshoreman onto the stage rather than some studied impersonation."[6]

By Miller's account, Cobb wanted to do the play, but was afraid that "the (American) Legion would make it hot for him again" if he renewed his theatrical association with the playwright. So in May 1955, instead of being in New York doing the twisted dockworker character of Eddie Carbone for Miller and only a few days after the broadcast of *Darkness at Noon*, he was in Houston playing an oil swindler for director William Castle in *The Houston Story*. The picture was one of a loose series churned out by Columbia's B unit purporting to expose rackets in major American cities; it had been preceded by the forgettable programmers *The Miami Story* and *Inside Detroit*. Although carrying top billing and a contractual promise that he would only have to spend a few days shooting in Houston's sweltering heat, Cobb was a physical mess from the moment he arrived in Texas. As Castle would note later on, "Houston, Texas is intolerable in August[7]—especially if you're going to make a picture in the oil fields. The humidity was oppressive. Filming a fight sequence in the oil fields was tough enough without having an exhausted star. Cobb was pale and haggard. Something was wrong. Watching him rehearse a scene where he was supposed to lift a man bodily and throw him to the ground worried me."[8]

Castle had cause to worry. Later that night he was summoned to Cobb's room at the Shamrock Hotel. "He was on the floor clutching his chest, writhing in pain. 'My chest,' he moaned. 'Call my father.'"[9] Instead, Castle called for an ambulance and, still dressed in his bathrobe, accompanied the actor to Hermann Hospital. When the initial diagnosis of exhaustion came in, he saw no reason not to persuade producer Sam Katzman back in Los Angeles just to wait a few days until Cobb recovered. In the meantime, he saved the day at least for himself by exploiting an error a nurse had made seeing him sitting in the hall in his bathrobe outside Cobb's room. Because the two men had similar builds, she assumed he was the actor and scolded him for being out of bed—an error that inspired him to replace Cobb in a couple of long shots for the location part of the production. But that didn't resolve the central problem, and in fact Cobb's heart problems were only beginning. Within a couple of weeks of flying the actor back to Los Angeles, it became clear that he wouldn't be able to return to work anytime soon. If nothing else, this provided Castle with the ingredients for one of his favorite stories—how Cobb, he himself, and permanent replacement Gene Barry had all ended up on the screen playing the same oil swindler.[10]

The most graphic account of what befell Cobb after his return to Los Angeles came from the actor himself in a first-person account given to *Pageant* magazine two years later. In a recorded session with writers-reporters N. and M. Rau, he admitted that he was still counting on returning to *The Houston Story* after the two months of rest ordered by his doctors. He had been so optimistic about his recovery that he appeared on a heart drive telethon to warn viewers against ignoring telltale signs of an attack. But then one night, alone in his apartment:

> You're awakened by pain. You say, "I don't feel well. Something's wrong." You feel hot, and the pain gets worse, but it's 3:30 A.M. And you think: "I'm not going to be an alarmist. I'll wait and see. Tomorrow, I'll tell the doctor . . ." [But] the pain gets to be too much, so you take one of the nitroglycerin pills that are supposed to give relief in five seconds. It has no effect. You take a second pill. Nothing.
>
> You know it's serious. The hotness of the pain and the way it's moving make it a terrible thing. It spreads and goes down your left arm early, then both arms, then up the neck. First it's a hot coal in your chest. Then it's a throbbing kind of thing, it's hard to breathe. . . . I was alone on the upper floor of an apartment building with the door locked. I'd have to call the doctor. And I'd have to let him in. I started dialing the number. But after the first two digits I knew I couldn't complete it. The pain was too much. So I dialed the operator instead and she put the call through.

Then there was the problem of opening the door for the doctor.

So you start for the door. You stumble a few feet, you crawl, you inch along. All the while there's the pain, the excruciating pain that never lets up. And as you drag yourself along you think: "This is it, all right." There's no bargaining with it. You've got to die. But why does it have to be in agony? Why can't you just go in your sleep? . . . With this pain you're so completely overcome that you've no time to philosophize, and you're torn between alternate compulsions to pray for life or pray for death—any kind of deliverance. There's extreme fear, but it's not fear of death. The worst thing is the pain, and that's the thing you fear.

When his doctor arrived nearly a half hour after the onset of the attack, he found Cobb on the floor, shot him up with morphine, and got him to the hospital. What exasperated the actor over the next few days, he told the *Pageant* reporters, were the constant reassurances along the lines of "You're going to be all right. Don't worry—you'll find a way to live sensibly, and you'll live longer than all of us." For Cobb that was not a reassurance. "To be told you're going to live if you take it easy, which would mean never again using that [acting] potential to the full—who wants to live at that price? . . . Either I'm on the stage or I'm not. . . . The kind of work I'm talking about is where you don't know where work ends and love begins. . . . If you can't aspire to that anymore, if you can't pursue your work as you pursue anything you love, without shackles, without reservations, giving it all or nothing— then what's the use of living?"

While it was touch-and-go, there was a news blackout on Cobb's condition, and even on his hospitalization. But when he was moved to a convalescent hospital, he immediately received two visitors from outside his family. The first was Frank Sinatra.

Years before I'd worked with Frank on *Miracle of the Bells*, but he wasn't a personal friend. Yet as soon as he heard I was ill, he called. "What's all this jazz?" he asked. He's the kind that plays against sentiment. "Look, how about my coming over and seeing you?" He was shooting at MGM at the time, and he came to the hospital straight from work. I don't remember the dialogue, but it pooh-poohed the whole thing. The next thing I knew, books started coming, and baskets of fruit and flowers. I felt like a gangster's well-kept moll. Frank visited whenever he could, and called when he couldn't.

But that wasn't enough. He knew I was alone and anticipated every one of my problems. He knew, for one thing, that I couldn't go back to my apartment because of the stairs. When the time came for me to leave the hospital, Frank found an apartment for me in Los Angeles, engaged a man to cook for me, and arranged everything else to keep me from being worried. You just can't even attempt to measure that kind of thing. In the hospital I'd sort of proved to myself that I could get back on my feet. Frank helped me feel that I wouldn't have to do it all alone. This reaching out a hand to another—it's a rare virtue even among kin, let alone strangers. It returns something important to you. It did to me.[11]

Among those witness to Sinatra's assistance was Mary Hirsch. A school teacher with a degree in education from the University of Southern California, the twenty-six-year-old Hirsch had met Cobb (he was then forty-four) shortly before at a dinner party hosted by their mutual friend, music editor Else Blangsted. At the time Hirsch (maiden name Bako) had been separated from her husband Lester Maxwell Hirsch, a physics professor in the California university system, and had custody of their three-year-old son, Tim. Even though Cobb had been forced to leave the dinner party early, Blangsted would say later, the actor had made it clear how smitten he was with Hirsch. It was a sentiment returned during Cobb's hospitalization. As he told the Los Angeles *Examiner*, "Mary helped me get well by coming to see me in the hospital practically every day of the five weeks I was sick."[12] She was also there for the move to the apartment Sinatra had leased. In Kitty Kelley's biography of Sinatra, *His Way*, Hirsch is quoted as saying about Cobb's move: "It was one of those places that very rich people live in—clean and beautiful, with walls that are quilted and comfortable. I don't know if Frank picked it out, or someone on his staff, but he paid for everything. He was wonderful during those critical months, and yet very elusive. He was never there to be thanked or hugged or shown any kind of gratitude. He didn't seem to like that or want that. . . . Frank had been through bad times, too, and I think he sensed a soulmate in Lee."[13]

Once back on his feet, Cobb dated Hirsch regularly. "One of the first things she did for him was simply cook, and she was a great cook," Tony Cobb related. "You left my father alone for a time, and practically the only thing he did was make sure the breadbox had enough doughnuts. His idea of fruit was an Orange Julius. And that's without

counting the Cadbury chocolates he filled up on watching television."
In early 1957 Hirsch obtained a divorce and shortly afterward, on June
27, she and Cobb were married at City Hall. Their first son, Tony, was
born on March 24, 1960, and their second son, Jerry, on September
7, 1961. According to Tony, the fact that Blangsted had known Bako
since their college days and had also had a brief fling with his father
made Cobb do odd things when the music editor came over for a visit.
"According to Else, there was one time that he actually hid behind the
couch to eavesdrop on what they were talking about, just in case it was
about him. At least that was Else's story."[14]

In later years, Cobb would talk about the "renewal" he felt with his
new marriage and new family after the inside and outside strains of the
final phase of his marriage with Beverley. As he told Patricia Bosworth
of the *Times*, "How strange and wonderful to become a parent again!
This time it's more relaxed. There is no competition, none of the ego
problems you have when you are still young and feel threatened by
children. Now I can enjoy my sons and watch them grow, accept their
love and give them back all the love in the world."[15]

Neither the Jewish Cobb nor his Catholic wife felt threatened by
their mixed religions. "I never figured out whether it was something
they agreed on between themselves and never brought up or whether
it just happened naturally," Tony said,

> but we were pretty much kept away from religion. And I mean to
> the point where two or three times we'd be out with my mother and
> she would pull over in front of a church and tell us to stay in the car
> while she went inside for a quick visit. Maybe it was because she
> was afraid that if it got back to Dad she'd taken us inside, he'd think
> she was trying to convert us or something. My grandmother, Mom's
> mother, was a very serious Catholic. But she also loved Dad a great
> deal and had already been used to Mom's first husband Hirsch, also
> Jewish, so I don't think there was any pressure on Mom from there.
> The important thing is that it never came to anything, and a few
> minutes later Mom would come out of the church without a word,
> and off we'd go.

For all the evidence, including his own words, attesting to Sinatra's intervention, Cobb in later years made some puzzling comments
when referring to it. In a 1968 interview with Patricia Bosworth, for
example, he said, "Frank and I hadn't really seen each other since

we had acted in *Miracle of the Bells* years before, but there he was saving my life. After he'd helped me he disappeared again and I don't believe I've talked with him since. I would still like to thank him."[16] The only thing wrong with that sense of regret was that in 1963, eight years after his heart attack and five years before the interview with Bosworth, Cobb spent a great deal of time with Sinatra filming *Come Blow Your Horn*.

However much help Sinatra and the woman who would be his second wife were during his recovery, Cobb also had a reminder of more hostile realities at the time when another HUAC session in New York called his name into cause for the first time in a public hearing room. It came up during the questioning of George Tyne, one of those identified by Cobb as a Communist in June 1953. Tyne had worked with Cobb in *Thieves' Highway* and had done featured roles in numerous postwar films before being blacklisted. Asked if he was aware of Cobb's testimony, Tyne threw the question right back at his interrogator, declaring, "I take no value in the word of a stool pigeon. . . . I'm disturbed by anyone who appears before this committee as a stool pigeon, curries favor, tries to get jobs and money." He was then cut off and threatened with contempt charges, but still refused to cooperate with the panel.[17]

## Notes

1. *New York Times*, February 5, 1955.
2. *New York Times*, September 22, 1955.
3. E-mail to author, March 28, 2013.
4. *New York Times*, May 4, 1955.
5. Miller, *Timebends*, p. 393.
6. Ibid., p. 394.
7. Castle's memory betrayed him here; as recorded by the *Dallas Morning News* of May 11, 1955, the episode recounted actually took place in the equally intolerable month of May.
8. William Castle, *Step Right Up: I'm Gonna Scare the Pants off America* (New York: Pharos Books, 1992).
9. Ibid.
10. Given the usual schedule and financial restraints around B pictures, it is not unlikely that Cobb's personal relationship with Cohn had something to do with the Katzman-Castle patience about recasting the role.

11. N. Rau and M. Rau, "My Heart Attack: A Famous Actor's Fight with Death," *Pageant*, June 1957, pp. 23–27.

12. *Examiner* (Los Angeles), November 17, 1957.

13. Kitty Kelley, *His Way: The Unauthorized Biography of Frank Sinatra* (New York: Bantam Books, 1986), p. 247.

14. Conversation with author. All subsequent quotes from Tony Cobb are taken from conversations with the author over the course of several years.

15. *New York Times*, November 17, 1968.

16. Ibid.

17. *New York Times*, August 16, 1955.

# Chapter 19

═══════════○═══════════

# All the Guilty Men

ON THE WATERFRONT ASIDE, Cobb made his greatest impact as a film actor in the late 1950s. His personal calendar finally caught up to the middle-aged and older roles he had been playing since applying makeup for the first time, and there was less tentativeness than there had been even in his most successful characterizations. Like such later players as Al Pacino and Tommy Lee Jones, he controlled the screen to a degree that his characters sometimes didn't. As Kazan told James Grissom in a 1993 blog interview, "He was unafraid to be big, and his bigness came not from ego or a desire to be noticed, but because he understood the importance of plays and parts and the arts." That understanding didn't necessarily make for art, but it did more often than it didn't and was almost always magnetizing. It was also in the late 1950s that he gave his most dynamic television performance in a part that offered more emotional range than any other he had done since Willy Loman.

The actor returned to work one easy task at a time after his heart problem, and it showed in a largely sedentary role in *The Man in the Gray Flannel Suit*. Based on a best-selling novel about the advertising world, the Fox production had Gregory Peck as a novice climbing the career ladder on Madison Avenue while having a conscience crisis about an illegitimate child conceived in Italy during the war. His saintly wife (Jennifer Jones doing a Bernadette in the suburbs) agrees to go with him to a judge (Cobb) to arrange payments back to Rome for the rearing of the child. The *Times* found the picture "mature, tender, and touching,"[1] not devoting much attention to the fact that, almost forty, Peck was too old and self-assured for his junior achiever role and that the plot spent far more time working out family crises than advertising campaigns for clients. Sitting behind a desk for most of his time on the screen, Cobb's judge exuded infinite approval for the decision of Peck and Jones to send money over to Italy.

Then it was back to Katzman at Columbia to close out the obligation he felt had been left hanging with his illness in *The Houston Story*. Since *The Miami Story* had done more business than either *Inside Detroit* or *The Houston Story* in the little series about city-linked racketeering, the studio returned to Florida for *Miami Exposé*, with Cobb in the role of a cop doubly bent on cleaning up an organized gambling ring after one of its thugs has killed a close friend. As with *The Houston Story*, shooting on *Miami Exposé* had to be suspended briefly for a heart attack, this one fatal to veteran actor Edward Arnold. Arnold's venal character in the picture hadn't been all that different from the one he had never gotten to play opposite Cobb in *The Houston Story*.

The biggest thing not exposed by *Miami Exposé* was *Miami Exposé*—either to critics or paying customers—and that was just as well given its tatty, penny-budget look. Box office apathy awaited Cobb's next undertaking, as well, but under radically different circumstances. Based on a television play by Reginald Rose, *12 Angry Men* sets a dozen New York male jurors in a single room to debate the fate of a Puerto Rican teenager accused of murder. The modest black-and-white production, a labor of love for leading man and producer Henry Fonda, features a gallery of established performers—Cobb, E. G. Marshall, Jack Warden, Ed Begley, Martin Balsam, and Jack Klugman, among them—playing various city types who one by one give in to the Fonda character's arguments that the prosecution did not prove its case and that the defendant has to be found not guilty. Cobb's Juror Number Three (none of the characters was identified by name until the very last scene), a bully used to getting his way, is the last holdout. His climactic crumbling, when he is shown to have been persecuting an estranged son in his mind as much as the murder suspect on trial, merits comparison to his courtroom tirade against Brando in *On the Waterfront*, in both instances his character progressively surrendering articulated rage to an incoherent, emotional eruption. It was a stellar example of Method unintelligibility as dramatic technique rather than performing tic.

From the first gathering of the cast, *12 Angry Men* was treated as a stage play, with two solid weeks of rehearsal. According to what Cobb told his son Tony, it was at one of the earliest rehearsals that the star-producer Fonda noticed something that could prove troublesome in a drama underlining the equality of a dozen men.

> Dad said Fonda came to him and asked him to take Klugman out for a drink or something because Jack was absolutely intimidated by Dad. And in fact in any interview Klugman gave over the years, he always mentioned Dad and Fonda as his greatest influences and singled out *Salesman* for the best dramatic performance he had ever seen. Well, Dad wasn't one for all that much drinking, but he got Klugman into a gin rummy game, and by the time it was over, with Dad talking about all his problems, he had broken through to Jack, and the intimidation was gone.

Initially at least, *12 Angry Men* received the kind of respectful reviews that assured attendance only by those who wanted to feel civic minded rather than moved or entertained. Taking stock of the sketched in bigot, sadist, wise guy, patriotic immigrant, and other types represented by the actors, Weiler found that the drama "clearly mirrors the mind and heart of a society of citizens in our town," concluding sanctimoniously that the picture's theme was that "man's fate is the problem of every man."[2] (Years later, Cobb would attend a theater production of the material in Los Angeles directed by his daughter Julie and admit to her that he had always found it "very preachy.") It was not until the film took the Silver Bear at the 1957 Berlin Festival and Fonda won an acting trophy in England for his performance that it began its climb toward recognition as one of the most effective dramas of the period. Of the other actors, only Cobb got an award nibble, being nominated for a Golden Globe in the Supporting Actor category.

There was plenty about the filming of *12 Angry Men* to make Cobb comfortable, starting with the no-nonsense ensemble playing by veteran performers who went about their business at more than a geographical distance from Hollywood. Not only was he surrounded by performers many of whom he had worked with more than once, but he was directed by Sidney Lumet, a one-time member of the Group making his debut behind the camera. According to assistant director Donald Kranze, it was the kind of atmosphere

> where everybody expected everybody else to know what they were supposed to do and respected one another for that. That's why Fonda cast them in the first place. They were pros with theater backgrounds. Diva histrionics had no place. You didn't screw around on a Hank Fonda set even when he was just there as only an actor. When he was also the producer, forget it. One time Sidney asked me to call Lee for a set-up, and I went over to get him. "Oh, that mechanic," he says to me, but with the kind of smile that made it clear he considered Sidney anything but a mechanic.[3]

For Lumet's part, he voiced particular admiration for Cobb, and in some of the same words used by Kazan. In a 1991 blog interview with James Grissom, the director, who had also worked with the actor in the 1957 TV drama *No Deadly Medicine* for Studio One, declared, "So many actors tiptoe toward the unpleasant nature of their characters, but not Lee. When he took on Juror Number Three, he invested entirely in his prejudice, his anger, his pettiness. When all of the anger was combined with the energy and the focus of Lee's acting talent, it was frightening—and wonderful. . . . He was there to blow some gaskets and shoot for the furthest location. It was great."

But even in that supportive atmosphere there was an incident reminiscent of Persoff's experience with Cobb over the improvised word *scum* in *Darkness at Noon*. The script coordinator for *12 Angry Men* was Faith Hubley, who with her husband John had gone into independent animation production after he had been blacklisted. She also had more than one personal connection to Cobb, first studying with him briefly at the Actors Lab in Los Angeles when she had had acting aspirations and then being drafted as a babysitter for Vincent Cobb when the actor had been serving with the Army Air Force. In what apparently happened only once but which her interview with McGilligan left a little ambiguous, Hubley recounted, "On the set Lee would look at me and burst into tears and say, 'How can you sit there looking at me? Who ever thought I would be this disgusting person and you would be watching me?' So Sidney Lumet and Henry Fonda would say, 'Take the script and go hide!' There was no pleasure in that." Almost a decade later, according to Hubley, she had a similar scene with

Cobb when she went backstage at Lincoln Center where he was doing *King Lear*. "I told him he had given a wonderful performance, and he said, 'You can't think I am wonderful. How can you? I am nothing. I am disgusting.' I said, 'Look, that was twenty years ago.'" But, Hubley indicated, that reminder did nothing to ease Cobb's tension with her.[4]

With his next project, *The Garment Jungle*, Cobb didn't need self-recrimination because others beat him to it, though not because of his testimony before HUAC (House Un-American Activities Committee). After *Miami Exposé*, Columbia chief Harry Cohn decided that Katzman's series on city rackets had run out of whatever gas it had been siphoning off. At the same time, not forgetting the financial and critical success *On the Waterfront* had brought to the studio, he wasn't opposed to a more ambitious production targeting corruption in the New York garment industry. But that didn't mean he was willing to open *all* his cash drawers, either, so when director Robert Aldrich came along with *The Garment Jungle* script, he said okay, but only on the condition that the picture be shot in Los Angeles with extensive use of studio interiors. "I don't know why Aldrich didn't say no right there," actor Robert Loggia, who had his first major role in the picture, said, "but he didn't, and that was the start of the trouble."[5]

*The Garment Jungle* cast Cobb as a Seventh Avenue manufacturer resistant to the unionization of his house and dependent on a mobster (Richard Boone) to keep labor organizers away. Even when bodies start piling up, he turns a blind eye. Finally, his son (Kerwin Mathews), newly returned from the Korean War, makes him see how he is as responsible for all the thuggery as the mobster is. This precipitates a showdown with the mobster during which the manufacturer is killed, but everything is immediately wrapped up with the invasion of one of Cohn's Hollywood interiors by the cops.

Aldrich wasn't around to see the slapdash denouement. As Loggia recounted it,

> Aldrich really thought he could do another *On the Waterfront*, at least at the beginning. But he was in fights all the time with Cohn. The need to shoot in LA instead of on the streets of New York was just the first round. What really bothered Cohn—and again a reason Aldrich should have never gotten into the thing with Columbia—was that Aldrich's previous picture had been *The Big Knife* and there was this tyrannical character of a studio head in it that a lot of people

assumed was based on Cohn. Harry Cohn wasn't the kind of guy who forgot things like that. Finally, one morning Aldrich comes in to work with tears in his eyes and says, "I'm out of here, guys." That was a disaster. Vincent Sherman was brought in to replace him. Sherman knew where to point the camera and how to do things economically for making the front office happy, but he was no Aldrich. He couldn't make contact with the actors the way Aldrich did, and you had a lot of actors—me included and Boone—who counted on that kind of contact.

And Cobb? Both Loggia and Aldrich were to suggest that matters might have developed differently if Cobb, the biggest name in the cast and with the *Waterfront* cachet, had put his foot down. In an interview with Peter Bogdanovich, for instance, Aldrich termed the experience of *The Garment Jungle* "very sad," going on, "Cobb was one of the sore points on that film. He had an old, long-standing relationship with Harry Cohn. Cobb and I just didn't get along. He's a very strong-willed actor, a wonderful actor, but . . . That could have been a wonderful picture. It just ran out of guts in the middle."[6]

Loggia was more direct:

Cobb was never supportive. He wasn't a team player. He was cantankerous, hard-willed, and unhappy. One thing I know he was unhappy about was that nobody had ever taken him seriously as a leading man. That came out more than once—how so-and-so had never had any trouble being the star, but the best he got in that vein was something like our picture. That kind of remark didn't do much for morale, believe me. He'd never even give you lines from off-camera. That went against everything I'd learned from Stella Adler, where you were there to serve the piece, not vice versa. What else can I say? He was pretty self-centered.

Curiously, for someone top billed and with a résumé of so many emphatic characters, Cobb's manufacturer was about the blandest presence on the screen, an impression reinforced by having most of his scenes in the kind of drab, generic living rooms and offices that might have been imported from Katzman's quickies; that is, a black telephone was about the only prop contrast to an oppressive grayness. He had nowhere near the force of either Loggia's union organizer and Boone's mobster or even of Wesley Addy's reptilian killer or old nemesis Joseph Wiseman's union rat who betrays the Loggia character. William Zinsser was at the high end of compliments in calling *The Garment Jungle* "a well made minor film."[7]

*The Three Faces of Eve* was another small picture, but in a much bigger container. A black-and-white Fox production in CinemaScope produced and directed by Zanuck confidant Nunnally Johnson, it was essentially a three-character play about a Georgia housewife (Joanne Woodward) with multiple personalities, her overwhelmed husband (David Wayne), and the psychiatrist (Cobb) who treats her over several years. If the premise alone didn't convince of the seriousness afoot, having Alistair Cooke introduce the story and then narrate over time bridges with constant reminders that everything was based on fact took up the task. The heart of the picture are the scenes between Cobb and Woodward as the latter passes back and forth from the mousy Eve White to the slatternly Eve Black to the solid, intelligent Jane. It was a tour de force role, and Woodward didn't let it get away from her, sweeping all the Best Actress prizes to be won, including the Oscar. The picture impressed less. As almost always for Hollywood's dramatizations of the psychotherapy profession, the story was funneled toward a climactic *eureka!*—a single childhood trauma explaining all and allowing the protagonist to live happily ever after. That was enough to drive critics already on the edge from Johnson's pedantic direction and fussy dialogue (tons of "What?" and "What do you mean by that?") off the cliff altogether. Crowther, for instance, termed the exercise "psychiatric hocus pocus" and said the ending made him "feel gypped and gulled."[8]

Woodward disagreed, at least when it came to her experience in working with Cobb. As she told Grissom in a 1990 interview for blogspot.com, "He epitomized everything I loved about the theater and everything I wanted to be. . . . I felt utterly comfortable—at such an early stage in my career—to trust him as both my character and as an actress. I grew up around him."

Over his next three pictures it was Cobb who had the tour de force roles, and, clearly back in robust health, he didn't stint on them any more than Woodward had with hers. The most lavish of the three was Richard Brooks's adaptation of Fyodor Dostoyevsky's *The Brothers Karamazov*. It was also the film that, even counting *On the Waterfront* and *12 Angry Men*, brought Cobb his most exhilarated notices. As the patriarch of a family of four jagged pieces, the actor was never so

appropriately extravagant as the lustful, diabolic Fyodor who inter-
rupted his drinking and wenching only to make sure he still had a tight
grip on the inheritances left by the dead mothers of his sons. Arrayed
against him were Yul Brynner as the arrogant Dmitri, Richard Basehart
as the saturnine Ivan, William Shatner as the pious Alexei, and Albert
Salmi as the epileptic bastard Smerdyakov, reduced to a household servant. The plotlines winnowed by Brooks from the epic novel focused
on Dmitri's cuckolding of his father with the tavern maid Grushenka
(Maria Schell), the complications that brought to his relationship with
his vengeful fiancée Katya (Claire Bloom), and the murder of the old
man.

For the picture as a whole, most critics congratulated Brooks for
doing as well as he did on what was viewed as an impossible adaptation
task. "Except for a halfway happy ending that blunts the drama's irony,"
Crowther commented, "he has done a good job of compressing the
substance of the book. The greed and love and lust are in it, and also
a little sense of spiritual compassion and intellectual sterility."[9] That
was the view of cast members, too. "I think the film came very near the
heart of that difficult and superb masterpiece," Claire Bloom said. "It
was certainly a brave attempt on Richard's part."[10] In his own fashion,
William Shatner echoed Bloom. "There was only one thing that drove
me crazy about that picture—Schell and her constant crying," Shatner
said. "Jesus, she never stopped. Every emotion meant more tears. Even
when she was laughing, she was crying, for god sake! But outside of
that, I don't think anybody has anything to be ashamed of. Brooks was
really serious about doing a serious job, and I think he got the best he
could from everybody. With one exception, of course."[11]

Nobody carped about the performance given by Cobb, who for the
first time since his Hopalong Cassidy days was persuaded to go before
the cameras without a hairpiece. "Lee J. Cobb as the bald and bearded
father is a monster of drolling lecheries, greeds, and beady-eyed suspicions," Crowther said. "He is a vastly wicked man."[12] Variety topped
that by declaring, "It is Lee J. Cobb who walks—or rather gallops—
away with the picture. The part is gargantuan and it is not a bit too big
for the actor."[13] The role brought Cobb his second Oscar nomination
for Best Supporting Actor.

Shatner, for one, also developed a personal relationship with Cobb
that Wiseman and Loggia, to mention two, had never been encouraged
to pursue.

I brought out something paternal in him. How could you not have the greatest respect and admiration for somebody who had played the lead in what was arguably the greatest American play? He lived right near where I did in Laurel Canyon. On Sunday nights the Cobbs and the Shatners went to Man Fook Lo on San Pedro Avenue. Carl the waiter clapped his hands in glee when he saw us coming because he knew we were there for the incredible Chinese Chicken Salad. The thing was filled with MSG, of course. Who knew? When we began staggering around later that night, we always assumed it was the beer we'd drunk.

But Shatner also admitted to one regret: "I think I could have been more aware of how important he was to me when I was around him. I respected him, admired him, thought of him as a dear friend, but in retrospect I've always wondered whether I couldn't have been more conscious of him. People like that don't come along every day. At least not in my life they haven't."

Cobb's second collaboration with Reginald Rose, the writer of *12 Angry Men*, was in the unlikely setting of the big-scale western *Man of the West*. There wasn't very much at all about the picture that answered to the predictable. Originally, *Man of the West* was supposed to have marked the ninth time Anthony Mann had directed James Stewart, but a falling out between the two after years of working together led to Gary Cooper's being signed for the lead. What wasn't replaced was the brutal misanthropy Mann had been injecting into his westerns (*The Naked Spur, The Far Country, The Man from Laramie*, etc.) for years, to the point of considerably darkening the screen image of his perennial star Stewart. Beyond the physical savageries (and there were plenty of those) were the cynicisms and vengeances that motivated just about every character and that defined a hero largely by his survival over others. A smile in an Anthony Mann western was something to be wiped off a character's face.

In *Man of the West* Cooper plays a reformed outlaw who happens to be on a train when it is robbed by his old gang, headed by his demented uncle Doc Tobin (Cobb)[14] and cold-blooded cousin Claude (John Dehner). Stranded by the robbery with a saloon singer (Julie London) and a con man (Arthur O'Connell), Cooper ends up at his old outlaw shack where the uncle wants to believe he has come back to join in a bank robbery. The cousin doesn't believe it, making it clear that the only reason he doesn't kill Cooper is that he doesn't want to dispel Tobin's illusions. When the gang arrives at the bank, they discover it has been abandoned within a ghost town for years and that the uncle had just been nurturing a fantasy. In the climactic shoot-outs, Cooper kills all of the gang members, including Doc Tobin. Into that platter Mann drops one bitter ingredient after another—a forced striptease of the singer; Cooper's even more violent stripping of the outlaw (Jack Lord) who led the assault on the singer; the shooting of a mute outlaw (Royal Dano) who manages his only sound on earth with a piercing scream as he dies; and the uncle's rape of the singer. For pathos, there is the panicked killing of a Mexican woman who lives in the deserted town with her husband, Cooper passing the man on his way out of town, and leaving it up to him to discover his dead wife.

*Man of the West* would have alienated squeamish critics anyway, but United Artists sealed its fate by opening it in major cities, including New York, on the same day as the even more sprawling (but much more bloated) *The Big Country*.[15] The Cooper-Mann pairing didn't have a box office chance against the millions spent on the publicity campaign for the William Wyler western with Gregory Peck, Charlton Heston, and Jean Simmons, especially when critics approved of its big shootouts in the name of pacifism while Mann's bloodshed wasn't aimed at making anyone feel good. By and large, initial reviews were along the lines of congratulating the craftsmanship expected of Cooper and Mann with their track records but wondering about all the sour views of humanity. *Variety* singled out Cobb's character as "a frontier Fagin of demonic violence and destruction."[16] Only in Europe, notably in France, where Mann was viewed as a leading American auteur, was the film taken as a major effort by the director, with then-critic Jean-Luc Godard calling it much more accomplished than all the westerns with Stewart. In the event, it turned out to be Mann's last western and Cooper's last imposing screen role.

If the French liked Mann, they were in awe of Nicholas Ray (*In a Lonely Place, Rebel without a Cause, Johnny Guitar*), the director of Cobb's next project, *Party Girl*. One of the last of the sumptuous MGM color productions from the studio era, *Party Girl* might have been a straightforward B tale of a mob lawyer (Robert Taylor) in Chicago of the Roaring Twenties who, disgusted with his successful defenses of killers, breaks with the hoods and especially his mentor (Cobb). But that was neither the MGM nor the Ray way. With Cyd Charisse playing the lawyer's lover, there were two elaborate dance numbers choreographed and directed by Robert Sidney that were as sensually provocative as anything the studio had ever produced, no Gene Kelly required. For his part, Ray made as much quick work as he could of the stolid Taylor to focus on Cobb, whose Al Capone–like character foreshadowed the turn Robert De Niro did in *The Untouchables* years later. Among other things, the gangster is introduced sitting in a chair and weeping over a photograph of Jean Harlow with the news that the actress has gotten married; he resolves that crushing blow by taking out a gun and blasting the photograph. Later on, he savagely beats to death (with a commemorative gold-plated pool cue rather than the baseball bat De Niro used) a henchman who has betrayed the mob. For Weiler's taste, "Cobb turns in a Wild Man of Borneo performance wherein he not only chews the scenery but spits it out and chews on it again and again."[17]

Ray, another who had named names before HUAC and who spent a good part of his life battling alcohol and drug problems, wouldn't have had it any other way, even before film critics on both sides of the Atlantic gradually decided that *Party Girl* had been intended as much of a grotesque look at mob life in the 1920s as his *Johnny Guitar* had been of westerns. When he wasn't driving home that point with the Cobb character, he was doing it with a sleazy killer played by John Ireland, who kept addressing Charisse's dancer as "Puss." "My father thought that was very funny," John Ireland Jr. said,

> especially to somebody like Charisse, who was supposed to be this night club dancer but who could never hide that classical ballerina look. But nobody else seemed bothered by it, so he wasn't going to bring it up. He made it sound like a picture of jigsaw pieces. You had Taylor and some of the old MGM guard. Then you had Cobb doing a lot of directing of himself and not getting much of an argument from Ray. Charisse, he said, acted like she was doing a musical, and was relieved she did a lot of her work with the studio choreographer instead of Ray. As for Dad, even though he was forty, he was hanging around with the kids like Dennis Hopper and Nick Adams and Corey Allen. Nobody ever accused him of not liking a good time, and he seemed to have had a very good one on that picture.[18]

The mild and uncertain reviews greeting *Party Girl* helped ensure its relatively quick death at the box office in the United States. But that was just the first voting bloc heard from. European auteurists didn't let Ray down, and as one of them put it, "To remain insensitive to the thousand beauties of Nicholas Ray's *Party Girl* is to turn one's back resolutely on the modern cinema, to reject the cinema as an autonomous art."[19] American critics from the same school weren't won over by the story or the acting, but they too argued against the quick dismissal of the picture. "In Ray's wild exaggerations of décor and action," Andrew Sarris asserted, "there arises an anarchic spirit which infects the entertainment and preserves the interior continuity of the director's work."[20] Two of Cobb's most significant portrayals in the 1950s didn't have an audience problem. They weren't to be found in movie theaters, either. By the middle of the decade the rationalizations of some established actors that they only did "small screen theater" when they agreed to a television project had evaporated before multi-camera filming techniques and the growing number of weekly anthology series, almost all of them shot in Los Angeles. Cobb took to the offers as much as anybody, while remaining a big enough name from the movies and the stage to star in what was left of the live theatrical series with their compressed three-week rehearsal schedules, most notably Playhouse 90 on CBS. For relatively quick paydays on film there were "special guest" billings for everything from the Zane Grey Theater to The Desilu Playhouse.

His first role for Playhouse 90 came with *Panic Button* on November 28, 1957, when he played a Civilian Aeronautics Board official looking into whether a disastrous air crash had been caused by the dead pilot or by the surviving copilot (Robert Stack). After so many years of playing both good cop and bad cop, both of which were part of his character, the role wasn't much of a stretch. But two years later, with *Project Immortality* on June 11, 1959, he had a role he seized with both hands and that represented one of his most complex performances.

In the science-fiction fantasy premise of *Project Immortality* Cobb plays Lawrence Doner, a brilliant mathematician dying of leukemia. To make sure his knowledge doesn't die with him, the government assigns an agent (Kenneth Haigh) to his home to record his scientific insights; or, in the words of one character, "suck the brain and discard the man." Inevitably, the government man gets drawn into the household problems of the Doners (wife Gusti Huber, son Michael Landon, and daughter Patty McCormack), learning that there is more to the scientist than the data he can transmit to a computer. Cobb's role runs the table—from a man trying to deny his own imminent demise, to a parent dealing with a balky son and an adoring daughter, to a husband rueful about his marital failures, to the genius-dazzling gatherings of scientists with his solutions to long-standing mathematical problems. When he wasn't spouting arcane formulas, he was regaling himself and others with limericks and puns. In the opinion of William Ewald of United Press International, he was "not only immense in his physical portrayal of a man being sapped gradually of his vigor, he was positively awesome in rounding out the man, of trotting out his insides for the screen."[21]

The actor's coworkers were more mixed about what went on behind the scenes for delivering the performance. For Patty McCormack, Cobb was

> bigger than life. We did a scene in the living room during a party where I'm supposed to sit at the piano with him and entertain the guests singing while he played. I had learned to sing "My Man" in French phonetically during the rehearsals. I had cleverly learned the words and pushed past my own shyness and was brilliant through all the rehearsals and right through Dress Rehearsal. Then the nightmare happened. The show was live, and I couldn't get past a certain verse! All the extras playing people at the party and Lee joined in, with a lot of la-la-las and I followed along. I never knew how our director Fielder Cook felt about it. It's all a horrible blank! But what I remember clearly was how kind and supportive Lee was, looking straight into my eyes and working very hard to encourage me through my little crisis in front of millions of people. I felt totally enveloped by him.[22]

For writer Loring Mandel, on the other hand, Cobb seemed bent on creating as many crises before that national audience as resolving them.

> Let there be no mistake—he had enormous vitality doing that part. And nobody could ever doubt his intelligence, either. That combination was why he seemed so right to Cook and me for the part. It was what made him unique as an actor, period. But overall I'd say he acted very badly during production, and precisely because of that intelligence which slipped over into arrogance sometimes. There was one particular line, for example, where the character of Doner is supposed to say, "In the long run the unified field theory will be

true." And Lee says no, he can't say that. And when we ask him why, he says it's because the unified field theory *isn't* true. I thought he was kidding, but he wasn't. Lee Cobb the actor knew better than Lawrence Doner the scientist or even *real* scientists did![23]

According to Mandel, Cobb had problems with some of his fellow players, as well.

Not with Patty. She loved him. And he wasn't alone in having them with Haigh, who had just done *Look Back in Anger* in London, and was a man utterly incapable of warmth. I mean, he was a real weirdo. Gusti was a thorough professional, so when Cobb tried to move her around so he had a better camera angle, she didn't complain. I think she even found it a little funny. He was always trying to direct everybody. The worst problems were with Landon, and to this day I don't really understand where they came from. There was this climactic scene with Michael that Cobb insisted on writing himself, then admitted he wasn't satisfied with that, either, then said okay to a rewrite that I did, then finally did my version but made sure to throw in some lines of his own. You could feel a real tension beyond that of the characters in that scene with Michael. It was almost like some kind of competition, and I'd bet that Michael wasn't even aware he was in it. Lee simply had a thing about him. Sometimes I've wondered if it had something to do with how Landon's career had developed exactly the opposite way Lee's had—he was still playing teenagers when he was in his mid-twenties while Lee had been playing old men since he'd been a kid. I'm not even sure what that would explain, but I do know that Lee threw a party after the show and Landon was the only one not invited.

Cobb was so taken with the character of Lawrence Doner that he asked Mandel to expand *Project Immortality* for the theater. "I said no, and he got very angry with me. When we did another thing together a few years later, we didn't say a word to one another. As it turned out, I did expand the teleplay for the stage, but with Dana Elcar at the Arena in Washington. It had been better as a teleplay."

Cobb's performance won him an Emmy nomination as Best Actor, but his luck where awards were concerned held—he lost, this time to Laurence Olivier for a new version of *The Moon and Sixpence* in the same Paul Gauguin role Cobb had played a few years earlier. According to some critics, it could have been a double defeat since the actor should have also earned a nomination for a second performance in 1959—the title role in Dale Wasserman's *I, Don Quixote*. Presented by CBS's DuPont Show of the Month on November 9, 1959, and based on the Miguel Cervantes epic, *Quixote* had Cobb in the double role of the novelist and the fabled knight, with Eli Wallach as Sancho Panza and Colleen Dewhurst as Dulcinea. Fred Danzig of United Press International called Cobb's performance "touching and beautiful," reserving special praise for his scenes with the luminous Dewhurst, a last-minute substitution after the originally cast Viveca Lindfors was deemed wrong for the part.

As had become all but obligatory, Cobb's relations with the off-camera powers, especially with Wasserman and director Karl Genus, were rocky during rehearsal. "He had a lot of ideas," Wallach recalled.

> Some of them were good, some of them weren't so good. Sure, that's going to irritate the director and the writer sometimes. But acting isn't being a robot. You're the one up there who has to say the lines. The guy who comes in and just says yes, yes, yes—you can be pretty sure you're not going to get a great performance from him. Lee wasn't that kind of guy. He had that Group background where you asked why you were being told to do something. That wasn't the way you did things in Hollywood or on television, so you end up annoying some people. He didn't really care. He wanted to believe in what he was doing. Maybe some of it had to do with—and this is just my feeling—how he never forgave himself for leaving the stage for Hollywood. But he was going to have his say.[24]

One point on which the actor had his say was in his insistence that the production keep Quixote's "impossible dream" speech—a monologue Wasserman had been about to cut out to accommodate DuPont's ninety-minute running time. The impossible dream remained in the straight TV play and became the most noted moment of the musical *Man of La Mancha* adapted from the piece six years later.

## NOTES

1. *New York Times*, April 13, 1956.
2. *New York Times*, April 15, 1957.
3. Interview with author, March 24, 2013.

4. McGilligan and Buhle, *Tender Comrades*, pp. 299–300.

5. Interview with author, March 2, 2009. Subsequent quotes from Robert Loggia are taken from this interview.

6. Peter Bogdanovich, *Who the Devil Made It* (New York: Alfred A. Knopf, 1997), p. 788.

7. *New York Herald Tribune*, May 18, 1957.

8. *New York Times*, September 27, 1957.

9. *New York Times*, February 21, 1958.

10. Interview with author, August 2, 2012.

11. Interview with author, November 7, 2011. Subsequent quotes from William Shatner are taken from this interview.

12. *New York Times*, February 21, 1958.

13. *Variety*, December 31, 1957.

14. Because Cobb was ten years younger than his "nephew" Cooper, he wore a white hairpiece.

15. *New York Times*, October 2, 1958.

16. *Variety*, October 5, 1958.

17. *New York Times*, October 29, 1958.

18. Interview with author, January 13, 2013.

19. Fereydoun Hoveyda, *Cahiers du Cinema*, no. 127 (January 1962).

20. Andrew Sarris "The Director's Game," *Film Culture*, Spring 1961.

21. United Press International, June 12, 1959.

22. Interview with author, March 16, 2009.

23. Interview with author, November 18, 2012. Subsequent quotes from Loring Mandel are taken from this interview.

24. Interview with author, March 16, 2009. Subsequent quotes from Eli Wallach are taken from this interview.

# Chapter 20

―――――○―――――

# The Actor: Tele-Emoting

IF ACTING WERE A TEAM SPORT, theater performing would be baseball, film performing basketball, and television performing football. For the stage actor it is only the action that determines the span of each phase of a performance; for the film actor the continuity of the performance depends on the tactical sequence; for the television actor the performance is not only circumscribed by commercial breaks but sometimes addresses them directly as the fourth wall; for example, the quizzical expression that fades slowly to black until, after a few minutes of reminders from Geico and Burger King, it fades slowly back in to explain its quizzicalness. For the television actor far more often than for the motion picture actor staying in the moment requires more than a moment.

It hasn't always been that way. As a medium for acting, television had to grow from barely embedded roots. In the post–World War II years, dread of cameras revealing cardboard sets as mere cardboard sets prompted enough bare stage performances to make Samuel Beckett a plagiarist. Timing was another problem, with broadcasters having to adhere to half-hour and hour signoffs. When there was doubt about how long a drama would run, recourse was made to the convenience of the so-called search scene near the end of a story in which an actor entered a room looking for something. If the timing was right, he would go right to a desk or some other place to find the object he was seeking; if the show had been moving too fast, he would scour the rest of the room to kill time before landing on the object.

Outdoors, with municipal shooting permits more of a bureaucratic suggestion than an observance, live improvisation could mean having an actor run down a block pursued by fictional policemen and suddenly crumple in front of a door after being shot. It was the task of the cameraman to make sure all attention was on the fallen fugitive rather than on the unwarned and alarmed resident who opened the door to see who was dying on his stoop. Other actors performing live outdoors in the early years had to cope with winds, rains, and temperamental horses. None were more tested than the cast of *Action in the Afternoon*, a daily network series originating from WCAU-TV in Philadelphia that eschewed even transitional stock film while using its back lot as a western (Montana) town and surrounding countryside; it was completely up to the actors to mount, dismount, chase, shoot, and brawl before viewers while hoping they wouldn't break their necks following the script. (To blanket the noises from planes on their way to the real Montana and trucks rumbling past the studio building, singing cowboys were pressed into service.)

Indoors or outdoors, there was little doubt from the start that character details were subject to the demands and strictures of advertisers and their agencies. A show sponsored by a cigarette company made sure actors didn't cough, while villains in general weren't to be associated with tobacco (unless it was some foreign brand that made them doubly criminal). The astonishment sparked years later over a Playhouse 90 decision not to incorporate mention of gas ovens in *Judgment at Nuremberg* because one of the sponsors was a gas company was in fact business as usual.

What is commonly referred to as television's Golden Age ran roughly from the late 1940s to the 1956-1957 season, encompassing weekly (mostly) live dramatic series on CBS, NBC, and ABC and featuring emergent writers, directors, and actors ready to ignore the wires over their heads and the cables at their feet for a new expression of stagecraft. The most prominent writers included Paddy Chayefsky, Rod Serling, Horton Foote, Reginald Rose, Gore Vidal, and Tad Mosel; the directors John Frankenheimer, Arthur Penn, Sidney Lumet, George Schaefer, George Roy Hill, and more than one named Mann; the actors the cream of New York acting schools with the gradual infiltration of Hollywood veterans forced to seek new pastures with the demise of the big studios.

One early defense against television's technical impositions on dramatic action was the monologue—its minimal required movement the forte, most conspicuously, of Chayefsky. Long before his lengthy speeches were providing mesmerizing turns for established players in motion pictures (George C. Scott, Diana Rigg, and Barnard Hughes in *Hospital*, or William Holden, Peter Finch, and Ned Beatty in *Network*), they were making the country aware of a Don Murray in *The Bachelor Party* and a Rod Steiger in *Marty*. (Ensconced within their monologues actors could become *too* unaware of their surroundings, such as on February 19, 1956, when while delivering a rousing speech on the Alcoa Hour's *Tragedy in a Temporary Town*, Lloyd Bridges let loose with a few *goddamn this* and *goddamn that* emphases that woke up the NBC switchboard.) Also useful for the dramatics of the new medium was a fixed venue synonymous with speech-making or extended duologues, none more obvious than a courtroom or its extensions. *12 Angry Men* and *Judgment at Nuremberg* were only two of many dramas that had their natural births on television.

By the late 1950s the Golden Age was over, exception made for another season or two of Playhouse 90 in Los Angeles. In its final stages it resorted more and more frequently to videotape—more a convenience for scheduling than an influence on content and performance. But what really ended the era was a combination of sponsors and film. No matter how much prestige car companies and toothpaste manufacturers had gained from underwriting the dramatic series, their association with stories offering human complexity clashed with their commercial boasts of providing *the* remedy for this lack or that insufficiency; who needed mixed messages from the Roses and the Serlings with so many millions on the line? And once film took over as television's main technical medium—a process under way since Desilu had begun filming *I Love Lucy* in the mid-1950s—there was little reason to center production in New York rather than in the film capital of Los Angeles.

After a flurry of cop dramas and international intrigue tales that allowed for some setup footage of the Pantheon and the Parthenon, the genre that captured the national fancy was the western. But they weren't the kind of westerns that could be confused with what John Ford, Howard Hawks, or Anthony Mann had been doing in the movies. Lacking the panorama potential of the motion picture screen and wary of betraying that several series were sharing the same desert Arizona and California sets, the shows were heavy on dialogue exchanged in close-up only when it wasn't in extreme close-up. It was a formula that provided more than one impetus to what, when transferred to motion pictures, became known as the "psychological western," psychology in this instance reduced to meaning a lot of gab and intense reactions as a substitute for shooting down the Sioux hordes charging across the plains. While a minority of the shows (*Rawhide* and *Wagon Train* for CBS, *Cheyenne* and *Maverick* produced for ABC by Warner Brothers) were an hour long, far more were a half hour in length and starred performers (Steve McQueen, Robert Culp, Richard Boone, James Arness, Brian Keith) Hollywood wasn't quite ready to let shoulder anything of CinemaScope size. Except for Arness's Marshal Matt Dillon in *Gunsmoke*, they were usually centered on hired gunmen or bounty hunters who, as the personifications of cool, never came across a line of dialogue they couldn't skip. At the beginning of the fad, more established actors avoided such series, not only because of the pervasive perception that it would have marked a comedown in their careers but in some cases for very specific artistic reasons. What eroded some of these arguments were residuals. Thus Henry Fonda could justify his decision to go after the long-term money because he appeared only briefly in the weekly half-hour western *The Deputy*, telling a reporter, "I don't think I need to feel any conscience pangs [of just going for the money]. . . . I still have a career and, frankly, I wouldn't want to jeopardize it by identifying myself with one part week in and week out. That's risky business, I think."[1]

Unlike Fonda, some actors were eager to exploit the popularity of their week-in and week-out characters to wield power behind the camera as well. As long as they kept their ratings high, they were seldom opposed by producers or the networks when they wanted to direct or write episodes, or even have the final say on casting. On occasion, more than versatility was on display. One series star, for example, won praise for mixing the usual James Coburns and Martin Balsams as guest villains with prominent roles for actors who until then had rarely played more than bartenders or stagecoach drivers. Only those on location witnessed the megalomaniacal star-as-director repeatedly interrupting scenes to lash into the lesser known actor in front of the crew with pronouncements on "why you've only ever been good for playing walk-on parts," then proceeding to give him a lesson in Acting

101. Other series leads were known either to write for themselves every meaningful piece of dialogue in an episode or, if they had become bored actually acting for their checks, writing themselves nearly out of an installment altogether. In more instances than not, the actor donning a second hat meant that the western series was heading for its final showdown.

With one exception, film remained the preferred medium for the dramatic genres that followed the half-hour western as a viewing fad—the hour-long (*Bonanza, The Big Valley, High Chaparral*) and even longer[2] (*The Virginian*) westerns set on a ranch that rotated regular cast members as the weekly protagonist; medical dramas that, thanks to the long halls and various examination rooms of a hospital, did the same; and cop and lawyer shows with their squad rooms and paralegals, respectively, as relief for the top-billed player. While the business calculation was that the more variety in a fixed cast, the more patience at home for tuning in the program every week, there was also artistic fallout for the actor—that of having to adhere a little more rigidly to the contours of his character so as to distinguish it swiftly from those of fellow cast members. Nobody wanted—or had time to see—Ben Cartwright indulging a years-long fantasy to burn down the Ponderosa on *Bonanza*.

The biggest exception to the filmed series was the taped sitcom—usually but not always in front of a live audience. What actors also mostly had to play before were timing calculations for the laugh tracks that would be added after the performance. In itself this mechanical intrusion was hardly fatal to a performance; anybody who had ever done comedy on the stage had had experience with taking extra beats so as not to trample over expected laugh lines. But what not even Henry Fonda's wariness of entering living rooms every week as the same character had foreseen was that some sitcom roles would push an actor well beyond even typecasting into a career persona surviving through second and third series. Rather than the actor's discoveries from exploring, the ideal for this kind of tele-emoting was always being welcomed back into the home, never becoming a stranger.

Not all actors have allowed television to dictate progressively smaller creative horizons. While cable's weekly cop and lawyer and doctor series are indistinguishable from what can be found on CBS or NBC give or take a few four-letter words, cable channel movies and miniseries, if at a production level resembling small-budget motion pictures more than traditional network dramas, have repeatedly provided dramatic material more stimulating than that to be found in a movie house or a theater, with corresponding energies in performance.

And then there is the view of TV acting held by Shelley Winters. Asked once by Johnny Carson how she was able to project one kind of character in her tell-all memoirs, not to mention the scores of others she had in her pictures, while offering a totally different persona on the talk show's couch, Winters replied, "Simple. I'm now playing a guest on the Johnny Carson Show."

## Notes

1. *New York Herald Tribune*, June 11, 1959.

2. "The program's chief method of filling an hour and a half when 60 minutes would have been ample is to have the actors talk more slowly and the horses run longer." *New York Times*, September 20, 1962.

The announcement of Cobb's marriage with Mary Bako in his father's paper, *The Forward* (1957).

געהייראַט ניט לאַנג צוריק. — דער באַואוסטער שוי־
שפּילער פֿון דער בינע און פֿילם, לי דזשעי קאַב,
(אידישער פֿאַמיליען־נאָמען דזשעיקאב) 45 יאר אַלט,
און מערי הירש, 27 יאָר אַלט, וועלכע האָבען געהייראַט
מיט איינינע חדשים צוריק אין קאַליפֿאַרניע. ביידע
צום צווייטען מאָל. די נייע מרס. קאָב איז ביז איצט
געווען אַ לערערין.

NEWLYWEDS: MR. & MRS. LEE
J. COBB. — Actor of the stage and
screen Lee J. Cobb, 45, and the former Mary Hirsh, 27, who were married in California a few months ago.
It is the second marriage for each.
The bride is a school teacher, who
will give up teaching "to make a
career of marriage".        (I. N. P.)

As an ambiguous manufacturer trying to explain himself to son Kerwin Mathews in *The Garment Jungle* (1957).

Cobb as Juror Number Three in *12 Angry Men* (1957) accepting Henry Fonda's dare on wielding a switchblade. Looking on are (standing) John Fiedler, Edwards Binns, Ed Begley, and George Voskevic; (seated) E. G. Marshall, Jack Klugman, Jack Warden, and Martin Balsam. *Photo provided by Photofest*

Karamazov *père* reminding his sons (Yul Brynner and Richard Basehart) how he has them over a barrel (1958).

The demented Doc Tobin in *Man of the West* (1958).

Exacting vengeance on a betrayer in *Party Girl* (1958) while John Ireland looks on.

Second wife Mary, more of a homebody than Cobb's first wife, working in her garden (1958).

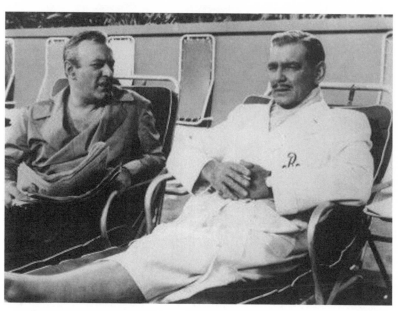

Relaxing between takes of *But Not for Me* (1959) with Clark Gable.

With David Opatoshu (center) and Israelis during the shooting of *Exodus* (1960).

Cobb and Paul Newman shared a loathing of director Otto Preminger during the shooting of *Exodus* (1960).

Cobb as Judge Garth with James Drury as *The Virginian* (1962).

With Frank Sinatra, Molly Picon, and Tony Bill in *Come Blow Your Horn* (1963).

With Mary aboard the *Delia* (early 1960s).

King Lear and his daughters played by Barbette Tweed, Patricia Elliott, and Marilyn Lightstone (1967).

In drag for his adventures with Derek Flint (*In Like Flint*, 1967).

With Clint Eastwood in *Coogan's Bluff* (1968).

Cobb and Nehemiah Persoff as two Sicilian Mafiosi in *Il giorno della civetta* (*The Day of the Owl*, aka *Mafia*, 1968).

A TV parody of *The Three Faces of Eve* with Anne Bancroft (*Annie, the Women in the Life of a Man*, 1970).

With Vincent (1970).

With Jason Miller in *The Exorcist* (1973).

With Julie during their shooting of a *Gunsmoke* episode (1974).

He was not a good mix with Shelley Winters in his last English-speaking film, *That Lucky Touch* (1975).

Half-brothers Tim (left) and Tony (right) celebrating Jerry's wedding. Tim is a pediatrician, Jerry a media consultant, and Tony a musician and composer (1997).

# Chapter 21

───────────○───────────

# Jewish and Other Kinds of Westerns

BETWEEN HIS GAMBLING DEBTS and his new family Cobb couldn't afford taking many days off between projects, and at the turn of the 1960s that meant television as much as motion pictures. For the home screen he not only made himself available for drama specials such as the DuPont Show of the Month's *Men in White* (CBS, September 30, 1960) and Westinghouse's *Footnote to Fame* (CBS, February 3, 1962), but for episodes in the weekly half-hour G.E. Theater series (CBS, January 17, 1960, and again on May 6, 1962) and even for the fluff-ball *June Allyson Show* (January 30, 1961). His oddest television project came in May 1960, when he earned his only official directorial credit for a goof called *Tennessee Ernie Ford Meets King Arthur*, an episode of the Startime weekly series based on Mark Twain's *A Connecticut Yankee in King Arthur's Court*. Adapted and produced by Cobb's friend Roland Kibbee, it had the comedian/hillbilly singer Ford sent back to Camelot in a time machine and dealing with the likes of Arthur (Alan Mowbray), Merlin (magician Carl Ballantine), and slinky Sir Bars (Vincent Price) in his desperate attempts to get back to the twentieth century.

The best to be said about the motion pictures he did in the period was that they were A productions with some big names, not to be confused with the bad old days of *Day of Triumph*, but neither did they send audiences home exalted by their exposure to cinematic art. Cobb himself hardly diverted attention from the mediocrity of his surroundings. With the odd exception, the actor projected an unprecedented detachment in his work, all but commenting on the character as he

227

was playing it. "I can only say it in retrospect because I was barely around in those days," said Tony Cobb, "but I think he was really focused on family in a way he hadn't been before. Maybe for the first time his life wasn't *all* about acting. Then again he always told us that the scripts he rejected were twice as bad as the ones he did, especially around that time before the big take-off when the studios didn't seem to know what they wanted or what they were doing."

Whatever the cause, it was appropriate that his character of a gangster on the lam in *The Trap* (1959) spent most of his scenes sitting in the back of a car, lending a general turgidness to his underworld snarling. The dramatic focus throughout is on Richard Widmark as a corrupted lawyer helping the gangster get out of the country through his family home in the Southern California desert near Barstow where his iron-rod father (Carl Benton Reid) is the sheriff and his resentful brother (Earl Holliman) a deputy. Bad things happen to one and all. "I got in it because Arthur Kennedy said no," according to Holliman.

> Maybe he saw what was coming, maybe he had other commitments, I don't remember. But the whole thing was Dick's show. I even heard him tell Norman Panama, officially listed as the director, not to get it in his head that he would be doing a lot of directing. I know Lee had a reputation like that, but so did Dick. Lee was just a big bear for the whole shoot. That I saw he never got into it with Dick or Norman about anything. He was just along for the ride—in more than one way—like everybody else.[1]

The lush vegetation of Venezuela and Colombia for his next picture, *Green Mansions*, didn't work to Cobb's advantage any more than the desert shrubs of Southern California. Based on a novel by William Hudson, *Green Mansions* was a mishmash of fable, jungle adventure, and morality tale set in the nineteenth century in which a fugitive (Anthony Perkins) stumbles through a lot of greenery bent on finding enough gold to hire gunmen for avenging his father's death, gets captured by a primitive tribe terrified of a presence known as Rima the Bird Girl because she communicates with animals, and falls in love with the girl (Audrey Hepburn). She probably dies in the end, maybe he does too, or maybe we've imagined the whole thing through him: the critics who cared weren't all that sure. The least of the picture's problems was that the twenty-nine-year-old Hepburn was about twice as old as the girl in the novel: the film was something of a vanity project

for director Mel Ferrer, Hepburn's husband, who envisioned it launch-
ing a series of projects for the couple.[2] What it mainly launched was a
critical fusillade against Cobb in what the *New York Times* called his
"shaggy and tattered" role of Rima's enigmatic guardian, as well as darts
against Sessue Hayakawa, Henry Silva, and everybody else in the cast.[3]
*Green Mansions* registered mostly for lost opportunities: Hepburn's in
choosing to make it instead of *The Diary of Anne Frank* and that of the
producers in rejecting a musical score by Heitor Villa-Lobos (that he
later turned into an independent composition).

In *But Not for Me* Cobb had one of his drollest roles as a playwright who would rather do anything but write plays. For the most part
his character sits around mocking the libido of a more-than-middle-
aged producer (Clark Gable) fencing with the advances of his much
younger secretary (Carroll Baker). Although a minor comedy in itself,
*But Not for Me* prompted some discussion at a time when Gable, Cary
Grant, James Stewart, and other long-in-the-tooth actors were still being cast as romantic leads opposite women frequently half their age.
Along with Lilli Palmer as the producer's ex-wife, Cobb received most
of the favorable notices. He also had the picture's best line when, seeing a candle-lit cake being brought in for the producer's birthday, he
roared, "That looks like the Chicago Fire!"

*Exodus* was a crapshoot from the start. On the one hand, Cobb
had never disguised his support for the birth of Israel or his contempt
for anti-Semitism. As recounted by Bessie, his phrasing in angrily
refusing a role in the anti-Soviet propaganda picture *The Iron Curtain*
was to compare playing in it to assuming the character of an anti-Semite. On May 15, 1946, in a letter to his parents, he also disclosed that
he had been doing extensive research on the historical period around
the writing of *The Merchant of Venice* after director Benno Schneider
had proposed they team up for a production of the play with Cobb as
Shylock. His conclusion was that Shakespeare had profited from the
anti-Semitism of his time, basing the character of the usurer on a publicly vilified Portuguese Jew named Lopez: "True, Shakespeare, great
genius that he was, didn't simply draw two-dimensional characters.
Even his villains had human sides to them, he gave even the Devil his
due. . . . But what a negative, dubious triumph for an actor—for me—a
Jewish actor—to bend over backwards—to distort and contort myself,
trying to read into, to 'interpret' in a 'sympathetic' light a character in a
plot and a play which are essentially designed to do the opposite! No,

that is simply not good enough!" But all that said, he then went on to tell his father and mother that he thought he and Schneider had found a way to do the play "truthfully." He didn't provide particulars, though, and the project was never realized.

Even with his intense interest in Jewish subjects, though, Cobb was aware of the underside of *Exodus*. Its story of the wresting of Palestine from British colonial hands and the subsequent conflict between Jewish and Arab residents was based on a wildly popular but artless novel by Leon Uris; in both its sales and writing, it was the model mass paperback. Despite knowing both Uris and the adapter of the novel, Dalton Trumbo, he acknowledged he was not enthusiastic about being part of the screen version. Moreover, the picture was being produced and directed by Otto Preminger whose reputation as a tyrannical filmmaker had few equals. So why did Cobb end up in the picture anyway? First, because Preminger mapped out a very compressed shooting schedule for him, allowing him plenty of time to travel around and satisfy his curiosity about the new nation. Second, and hardly insignificant, he was offered an unprecedented salary (for him) of ninety-five thousand dollars to play a conservative Israeli pioneer.[4]

At first, Preminger put on the charm. Eva Marie Saint recalled being surprised at how easily he relented before her demands for taking the role of the Gentile nurse who falls for the protagonist (Paul Newman). "I told him I wasn't going to the Middle East for so many months unless I could bring my husband, two kids, parents, and mother-in-law," Saint told the author. "He started sputtering, 'You want your own exodus!' But he agreed. When we were over there and I told him I wanted to watch an operation at a hospital to have more of a grasp of my role as a nurse, he encouraged me to go ahead. I think he thought it was unnecessary, more of that Method stuff he didn't like, but he said he understood." As she went along in the picture, though, Saint became increasingly unhappy because of Preminger's open contempt for that "Method stuff," especially from her and Newman. "Some stories said that I cried myself to sleep every night. That's a bit of an exaggeration. I don't like saying anything bad about anybody, but let's just say he did a lot of yelling and I knew a lot of directors before and after him who were able to get their points across in more effective ways."[5] As for Newman, Foster Hirsch quoted actress Jill Haworth as recalling that he simply refused to take direction from Preminger after a while. "They had an arrangement: If Otto had something to say, he was to say it to Paul privately, away from the rest of us."[6]

But the iciness that prevailed between Newman and Preminger dropped to a footnote to the public explosion between Cobb and the director; indeed, the scene couldn't have been any more public since it was played out before an estimated forty thousand residents in the Russian Compound plaza of Jerusalem. The crowd had been attracted not merely by the prospect of being extras in a big Hollywood movie but as the fruit of a calculation by Preminger for reducing production costs. Under the scheme he had his assistants buy up twenty thousand Israeli lotto tickets at the equivalent of two dollars apiece, then offer them at half that price to whoever showed up for the shooting at the Russian Compound. A further incentive was that six winners would be flown to New York for the premiere of the film. The outlay ended up at about thirty thousand dollars—about one-third of what it would have cost with a straightforward payment for extras.

The scene prompting all the lottery-ticket buying revolved around Cobb on a balcony reporting to the crowd the progress of the United Nations vote for acknowledging Israel as a sovereign state. At a considerable distance across the plaza was Preminger, perched on the camera crane and indulging his well-known penchant for long shots at key dramatic moments. Because of the oppressive heat the director had called for shooting to begin at five in the afternoon, then put that off for a couple of more hours, all the while telling local officials who were also getting their moments in as Hollywood extras that he would need only five or ten minutes to wrap up everything. Those five or ten minutes grew to twelve hours when the director insisted on take after take. Whose fault that was depended on whether you listened to Preminger and his coterie or to Cobb and a good part of the *Exodus* crew.

The Preminger camp's story was that the endless retakes were necessary because Cobb, with a mere fourteen lines in the scene, kept forgetting them; variations were that he didn't deliver them the way the director wanted and even barked across the square at one point for Preminger to stop worrying and fix up things in the editing room. Then and there the two men kept shouting at one another over forty thousand heads, with Cobb also pointing out that the director's obsessiveness was causing physical hardship to the Israeli extras. In a piece on Preminger for *McCall's* magazine some years later, Helen

Lawrenson had to pull teeth to get Cobb to talk about the incident. "It seems criminally inconsequential to be discussing Otto Preminger," he told her in his best florid manner. "I feel squeamish talking about him. [But his] story is a complete fabrication." According to Cobb, he hadn't wanted to do the picture from the beginning, having been impressed by neither the book nor the script. But "[Preminger] was so flattering and generous in his terms. . . . During my time in Israel I was really embarrassed by the flattery and attention he paid me."[7]

At least until the evening of the big scene. "To pinprick this idiocy, it wasn't a question of any 14 lines. I *knew* those lines, for god's sake! Otto Preminger forced thousands of extras to stand in the square—these were local people, some quite elderly—and it got to be 3 A.M. I suggested something should be done. Unpredictably, like a madman, Preminger flared up. So I gave him a piece of my mind."[8]

Preminger's fury didn't end when the scene was finally concluded. With Cobb's role in the picture over, he immediately canceled the actor's room at the King David Hotel. "Everyone thought his behavior to Cobb was unforgivable," Hirsch quoted Michael Wager, another member of the cast. And a member of the crew who requested anonymity even years after the incident told Hirsch, "Before Cobb left Israel every member of the company shook his hand and thanked him for having the guts to do what nobody else had."[9]

Whenever Cobb was asked about *Exodus*, he dismissed it as a "Jewish western," "Cowboys and Indians in Palestine," or something that "could have been shot in Arizona as easily as in Israel." Most reviewers preferred to be solemn about the subject rather than the cast-of-thousands opus made out of it. The word *stirring* was thrown around a lot, such as by reviewers for the *New York Herald Tribune*[10] and the *Daily News*,[11] but almost only indirectly in reference to the picture. The best reviews went to Sal Mineo as a recruit for guerrilla violence and for a scene between Cobb and his fellow Bronxite David Opatoshu in the role of a revolutionary leader.[12] Opatoshu apparently agreed. "Dad and Lee had a lot in common," his son Danny observed.

> They were both from the Bronx. Just like Lee took off for California as a teenager, Dad was fifteen when he set off for Hollywood determined to find Mae West and get a job in one of her movies. He only got as far as Chicago before relatives got him back to New York, but

like with Lee he had more successful tries later on. Like Lee, he was also blacklisted for a few years and had to have one of those closed-door sessions with HUAC investigators. All told, the two of them did four pictures together—*Exodus, Karamazov, Party Girl,* and *Thieves' Highway,* but he was always pretty clear that his scene with Lee in *Exodus* was a highlight of his career.[13]

For a few years after *Exodus* Cobb's film appearances were squeezed into his time off from his first regular television series—*The Virginian.* At eighteen thousand dollars a week, there was little mystery about the show's appeal to him. And even though the series managed to wind up a ninety-minute (seventy-five minutes without commercials) episode every six days, Cobb, top billed though he was, was just one of several regular cast members, allowing him reasonable time off. "He wasn't even the Virginian," James Drury laughed, "I was. But he was making eighteen grand a week and I was making only one. Did I bitch about it? I bitched about a lot of things in those days, and sometimes I was even sober doing it."[14]

According to Roberta Shore, another cast member, Drury's drinking was hardly a secret on the show, but Cobb said nothing at all until one day when he was due to do a scene with the younger actor.

> You have to remember I was only nineteen, and really thought of Lee, the Judge Garth character, as the "old man." I knew something, but not a lot, about his New York background. He was always totally professional and disciplined, and that was something that seemed common to all the New York actors who came out to do a guest episode on the show. That wasn't always true of the younger actors without that kind of training. Then one day we were supposed to be doing a scene with Jim, and he didn't show up. Lee and I had lunch, and even forty-five minutes later Jim wasn't there. When he finally did show up, he made all sorts of excuses about where he had been, none of them believable. I think some people were waiting for Lee to explode. But he didn't. After listening to Jim come up with one more unconvincing story, he simply flicked at the smelly cigar that was always in his hand and said in that very authoritative way he had, "We have been waiting here for you." He said it so calmly that it was a lot more effective than if he had ranted. Was that Method acting? I don't know, but Jim got the message, at least where his scenes with Lee were concerned.[15]

Cobb never disguised his sense of having fallen low to be doing a TV series. As his son Vincent put it, "By the time he was doing *The Virginian* he was often pretty disgusted by both what he was doing and the general direction of the industry." Drury got the same message: "He really thought the show was beneath his dignity. I remember him telling one interviewer that he wished he had enough money to buy up all the shows and turn them into banjo picks." If nothing else, though, he had overcome the passivity of his time on *The Trap* and reverted to being the "difficult" actor. Drury: "He was always arguing with the producers and the writers about making things better, but for the most part it was too late to do much changing because of the schedule pressures. I tried working with him in remaking scenes, but you could only do so much when you were already committed to sets and delivery dates and all that." Shore: "We pretty much knew going in to any episode with Lee that there would be changes from the scripts we started out with. Was he satisfied with the rewrites he insisted on? I suppose not really because if he'd had a choice, he wouldn't have been doing the show at all. One time I asked him straight out why he was doing it, was it just the money, and he didn't hesitate to say yes. It was security for his family, he said, and since he'd had heart problems in the past, he couldn't afford to leave them unprotected."

Another series regular, Gary Clarke, admitted to having the same "intimidation" problem that had worried Henry Fonda about Jack Klugman in *12 Angry Men*:

> At the start I was in as much awe of him as some others. But after two or three months I thought I needed more, some words of wisdom. So I tell Jim [Drury] and Doug [McClure] that I intend talking to him. We all drive out to the location where we're shooting, and when we get there, Jim and Doug tell the chauffeur to get out with them so I can be alone in the back with Cobb. He pulls out a cigar while I go on about how tongue-tied I've been with him. He says nothing, just blows smoke while I'm saying he must've had that kind of a reaction before. Nothing. And not only isn't he saying anything and just blowing smoke, he's not even looking at me! We go on like that for a good five minutes—me stumbling over words and him blowing smoke. Finally I have enough. I tell him: "Well, excuse me! Stick that cigar where the sun don't shine!" I jump out of the limo and hurry over to where Jim and Doug are looking at me. Jim nods and says sarcastically, "Yeah, I figured that would go well."

Well, I'm in a rage. The rest of the day my scenes happened to involve Cobb, and I go tearing into every one of them. During one pause the director comes up to me and says, "That's great, Gary. What's gotten into you? Whatever it is, keep doing it." Finally we get to the last scene and this time I'm really going to give it to Cobb. And then I see him sitting in his director's chair and smoking another of those goddamn cigars. And I see this little twinkle in his eye and then he's laughing and wrapping me in a bear hug. He had done exactly what I had needed. He had actually been directing me from the back of the limo. From that point on we were friends. He and his wife came to my wedding. Friendship had replaced awe.[16]

For Drury, Cobb was a "tough read."

As a person I found him enormously compassionate, with a tremendous sense of humor. I was close to Barry Goldwater in those days and one time I came on the set in my wife's Buick with a Goldwater sticker on it. As we're going over lines, he just sneaks in "I think vandals have been at your car," then goes right back to the lines. But that was the guy—one-on-one. Then you had Lee J. Cobb the actor who really didn't want to be where he was and didn't go out of his way to hide that fact. Granted we didn't have Shakespeare writing *The Virginian*, but they were damn good writers and Lee never had the patience to see that. Riding was another thing. There might have been forty guys on the set who knew how to ride and ride well and who would have taught him to sit more easily in a saddle just for the asking. But he never wanted to know. He just wouldn't take the time for it. I never really understood that. If you're going to play a trombone player, every little bit you know about playing a trombone is going to make you easier in the role. Maybe at bottom he just didn't want to think about having to play it for too long into the future.

As it turned out, Cobb did *The Virginian* for four years, and got paid even beyond that under the terms of his contract while the producers were trying to replace his "old guy" character first with John Dehner, then with Charles Bickford and John McIntire. How much money he saved from the series remained in doubt. Drury: "From things he said, he was dropping a good four or five thousand a week at the card table. And some of that wasn't just because he didn't play well."

Cobb was in fact one of the victims of the Beverly Hills Friars Club cheating operation started by Maury Friedman, taken over by the connected Johnny Roselli, and brought to light in the 1960s. Roselli discovered it shortly after winning membership in the club upon the sponsorship of Frank Sinatra. Friedman's scheme, which he had previously worked with success in Las Vegas, depended on the mounting of an optical lens in a ceiling peephole; by installing a soundman in the crawlspace for revealing the cards of players, a significant portion of the estimated thirty thousand dollars exchanging hands every day in the club's main game room went to Friedman and his cohorts. Aside from Cobb, the biggest losers were thought to be comedian Phil Silvers, singer Tony Martin, the unfunny Marx brother Zeppo, and, especially, Harry Karl, the millionaire husband of actress Debbie Reynolds. One thing was sure: Cobb lost enough to have to keep working, and then work some more.

## NOTES

1. Interview with author, January 5, 2009.
2. It turned out to be the only film in which Ferrer directed Hepburn, though he was the producer some years later of her suspense hit *Wait until Dark*.
3. *New York Times*, March 20, 1959.
4. Foster Hirsch, *Otto Preminger: The Man Who Would Be King* (New York: Alfred A. Knopf, 2007), p. 335.
5. Interview with author, November 9, 2011.
6. Hirsch, *Otto Preminger*, p. 332.
7. Helen Lawrenson, "Is It True What They Say about Otto?" *McCall's* 92, no. 6 (March 1965).
8. Ibid.
9. Hirsch, *Otto Preminger*, pp. 335–336.
10. *New York Herald Tribune*, December 16, 1960.
11. *New York Daily News*, December 16, 1960.
12. *New York Times*, December 16, 1960.
13. Interview with author, November 3, 2012. Subsequent quotes from Danny Opatoshu are taken from this interview.
14. Interview with author, December 17, 2012. Subsequent quotes from James Drury are taken from this interview.
15. Interview with author, November 29, 2012. Subsequent quotes from Roberta Shore are taken from this interview.
16. Interview with author, December 4, 2012.

# Chapter 22

# Comedy Is Hard

Lee J. Cobb and comedy were rarely part of the same sentence. As far back as the Theatre Union, with its priorities of politically militant theater, and the Group Theatre, where wit chronically contained the word *fascist* somewhere, humorlessness seemed like a subpoena waiting to be served on the actor. Robert Walden recalled a publicist once telling him that "when Lee J. Cobb is your comic relief, you're in trouble." George Segal settled on the word *gravitas* to articulate his overall impression of the man who played his father in a 1966 television adaptation of *Death of a Salesman*: "What was it you didn't see—maybe that little glint in his eye hinting at light, funny things?" But James Drury wasn't the only one who saw that glint.

"I know he intimidated a lot of people, but he also did a lot of crazy things around the house," daughter Julie recalled. "Sometimes he would get down on his haunches like a monkey and then lift his entire body up with a jump into a chair. We were too busy laughing to realize just how hard that was to do from a physical point of view." Son Tony remembered the morning he had asked his father to stay inside the house when his school bus came because he was "in his pajamas and slippers and looked like some crazy person." Then the bus arrived. "He sneaked out the door anyway as I was getting into the van and proceeded to do a whole wild rant in front of the kids like some Doc Tobin *Man of the West* dude, pajamas flailing, unshaven, and wild wispy hair. After hurling an invisible rock at us and putting on a crazed face he stumbled back inside. He got me good and of course I was now a permanent weirdo to all the other school kids."

Son Vincent recalled the time he accompanied his father back from a commissary to a western town set. Like all such sets, it was necessary to negotiate the endless piles of horse manure, to which Cobb muttered: "Scripts, scripts everywhere!"

Producer Dean Hargrove was one of several who called Cobb "one of the wittiest, funniest people I ever met. It wasn't just some sarcasm, some line, it was the whole persona with the mind and the vocabulary and the sense of timing behind it. He threw away remarks others struggled to come up with."[1] But the comic Cobb wasn't always the man in charge; sometimes he involuntarily played a slapstick character at the wrong end of the action. Danny Opatoshu recalled one July 4 visit with his mother to the Cobb house:

> It was going to be the usual holiday barbecue, hamburgers and hot dogs. But Lee being Lee, he wasn't going to leave it at that. He had set up a giant fireworks show. Then when the time came he lit the fuses—and one after another they all fizzled! He got more and more furious, running from one deck of fireworks to the other. Everybody was laughing, or at least trying not to laugh too loud because that infuriated him even more. Back and forth, back and forth, but not a single one of them went off. For years afterward whenever Lee's name came up, my mother and I would laugh all over again over that debacle.

Could he take a joke? "One time Julie came by the house with Richard Dreyfuss, and Dreyfuss insisted on doing his impression of Dad," youngest son Jerry Cobb related. "On and on he went, and we're all torn between laughing because it was a great impression and noticing how quietly Dad was sitting and taking it all in. It was like those scenes where you wait for the big boss to laugh before you dare to. Finally, he roared out his approval, and we were free to laugh."[2]

Professionally, though, Cobb had seldom come to mind when producers and directors were casting comedies. In the odd instance such as *The Luck of the Irish*, he had done the specifically noncomic role. About the only movie exception entering the 1960s (there had been his widely praised Turkish bath scene in *The Gentle People* on the stage) had been *But Not for Me* in which he had come close to Hargrove's description of the sardonic wit. But with the new decade he hadn't been striking much of a dramatic figure on the screen, either. With his commitment to *The Virginian*, his motion picture roles had to be squeezed into the calendar, and as often as not were either cameos or performances that could be shot in a few days, making for good money and attractive working schedules but not always for the wisest additions to his filmography. His worst misadventure was Vincent Minnelli's *The Four Horsemen of the Apocalypse* in which he played the Argentinian patriarch of a family (Glenn Ford, Charles Boyer, Paul Lukas, Karl Boehm) that was about as persuasive as a family as a Laundromat's display of left-behind socks. Based on the Spanish novel by Vicente Blasco Ibanez but updated from World War I to World War II, Cobb came and went practically before the credits were over. Even that was too long for Crowther, who seemed to have gone to a screening directly from the dentist: "The less said of . . . Lee J. Cobb as the Argentine grandfather whose anti-Hitler sentiments in 1938 are as fiery as those of a Jewish character in *Exodus*, the better for all concerned. Indeed, the less attention paid to this picture, the better for the simple dignity of the human race."[3] Crowther got his wish: attention wasn't paid.

In *How the West Was Won* Cobb was one of dozens of Hollywood names recruited for telling the story of the settling of the West in Cinerama. In a cast that counted (among others) John Wayne, James Stewart, Gregory Peck, Henry Fonda, Debbie Reynolds, and Richard Widmark in interrelated segments narrated by Spencer Tracy, he was featured in the climactic episode of a train robbery with George Peppard and Eli Wallach. "We did a lot of standing around for that thing because of all the technical problems they had with Cinerama," Wallach related.

> Just for a change of pace, one night Lee and I decide to go off to the fights that were being held not too far from where we were shooting. What happens? One of the boxers gets killed in the ring. I was appalled. My insides were a mess. Lee's face was as white as a sheet. I don't think we said a single word to one another going back to the hotel. We were both glad to get that shoot over with. That dead boxer is still what I think of every time I hear somebody talking about that picture, and I have a feeling Lee had a similar reaction.

A frequent footnote to the story of Frank Sinatra's intervention after Cobb's heart attack was that the actor-singer asked him to appear with him in the screen version of Neil Simon's *Come Blow Your Horn*.

"That's not true at all," said producer Norman Lear. "It was my partner Bud Yorkin and I who approached Lee with it. I knew him pretty well, originally through the screenwriter Roland Kibbee. The Lears, the Cobbs, and the Kibbees went to Sunday dinner regularly in those days. The story that it was Sinatra kind of coming around to Lee and playing on his gratitude is pure Hollywood."

According to Lear, in fact, it was Sinatra who had to be pressured into doing the picture. "We were after him for a good year because we were convinced only he could play the part. We sent him chickens because the piece was originally entitled *Cock-a-Doodler-Do*, flew planes over his house, even sent him a truck with a living room inside and the kind of smoking jacket and pipe he would need for the part. When he saw me at a taping with Judy Garland, he had me thrown out. But we wore him down."

To nobody's particular benefit. Based on the first of Simon's many long-running Broadway plays, *Come Blow Your Horn* tells of a young man's (Tony Bill) inept attempts to emulate the skirt-chasing habits of his older brother (Sinatra) even as the latter is having second thoughts about his lifestyle. Whatever Simon or the screen adapter Lear had in mind, Sinatra turned it into an extension of his ring-a-ling-ding Rat Pack follies, to the point of having Dean Martin do a cameo as a wino. Allowance made for the Jewish identity of his parents (Cobb and Molly Picon), what came out was a goulash from two earlier Sinatra audience pleasers, *The Tender Trap* and *A Hole in the Head*, but without the breeziness of the former or astute sentimentality of the latter. Credibility hadn't been guaranteed in any case with the older brother Sinatra being twenty-five years older than Bill and only four years younger than his father Cobb.

As for Cobb, he went at his role as though Papa Bonaparte had come through an ethnic transplant and was finally free to say what had been on his mind for decades. What he mostly said to the Sinatra character was "You're a bum." When his wife scolded him for throwing a newspaper on the dining table, he assured her he had boiled it first. For these and similar mots, some reviewers complimented him for stealing the picture, while a majority said there was nothing to steal. Although Crowther was no more of a fan of the actor's work in *Come Blow Your Horn* than he had been for *The Four Horsemen of the Apocalypse*, he saved his best shots for Sinatra and Bill: "Mr. Sinatra appears so indifferent and coolly self-satisfied that he moves and talks in the manner of a well-greased mechanical man. Tony Bill . . . is so callow and inexperienced that he is a windmill of arms and legs that squeaks from want of greasing."[4]

Lear's opinion? "It wasn't my favorite picture, but I thought Lee was great. Anyone who says he doesn't have comic timing doesn't know what he's talking about. I think he just disappointed some people's expectations. When he wasn't Willy Loman or Johnny Friendly, they were lost. It certainly wasn't Lee who was lost."

*Come Blow Your Horn* was Cobb's last theatrical feature for three years. But he at least took away from it a new pastime. "Lee was really my orientation on that picture," Tony Bill said. "Cobb and Sinatra and Molly Picon and Lear and Yorkin—I'm the Catholic kid from Notre Dame and suddenly I'm being thrown into the middle of all this show business history. And then just to keep me on edge a little more, Frank was impatient whenever Yorkin wanted to do another take, so he started getting a little approximate about his lines, started Sinatra-izing them. Lee saw what was going on and got me talking about a thousand things to relax me. When I mentioned I had a boat in San Diego, that became *the* topic."[5]

According to his sons, Cobb had in fact been hungry for a new pastime since his heart troubles had put an end to his flying. "He couldn't pass the physical," Vincent said, "and it really depressed him. He was an active man. He always had to be doing things. And his cars satisfied him just so far." Bill hadn't been prepared for the extent of Cobb's questions when he brought him aboard his boat for the first time. "He wanted to know everything there was to know. It was almost like a Coast Guard inspection. What was this for? What was that for? Was this working as well as it should have? But you could see when we went out how much he enjoyed it I knew before we went back in that I'd made another sailor." "He had," Tony Cobb confirmed. "Dad eventually got his own boat and moored it at San Pedro. It was a thirty-eight-foot yacht that he called the Delia after Cordelia in *King Lear.* Whenever we could, we'd go out with the family and friends, usually in and around Catalina. And guess who the captain was?"

Tony Cobb also related that, newly passionate sailor or not, his father had not let go of flying so easily. "One time we took a vacation in the Bahamas and got into this sleepy little island-hopper. I dozed off for a few minutes, and when I woke up there was Dad in the pilot's cabin. He must have talked or charmed his way into taking the controls for a little while. Wore the headset and everything. It was hilarious. He was a kid again for hours after we landed."

For three years after *Come Blow Your Horn* Cobb's only paid job outside *The Virginian* was for the television drama special *It's Mental Work*, presented within NBC's Bob Hope Chrysler Theater on December 20, 1963. Adapted by Rod Serling from a story by John O'Hara, the piece might have seemed closer to home than normal for its study of a weary saloon keeper who is hospitalized with a heart attack. It certainly seemed that way to Vincent Cobb, who acknowledged wincing at the heart seizure scene. "I really don't remember much else about it except the way he had the attack. That has stayed with me all these years." Otherwise, he recalled no comment from his father about the role. While Cobb came in for critical praise for his performance, he was again left watching as only Serling from the show was awarded an Emmy.

Mid-decade in the 1960s there were few more popular movie attractions than Sean Connery as James Bond. Among the runners-up—not just as theatrical features but also as television series, not just in what was turned out by Hollywood but also as staples of some European film industries—were take-offs on Agent 007 and his license to kill. Cobb's contribution to the lampoon genre came with the back-to-back *Our Man Flint* and *In Like Flint* as the M figure overseeing James Coburn's title role. The character was seldom this side of buffoonery: When he wasn't shouting into a red telephone about the latest threat to the world, he was prancing around in drag or warning Flint to stop indulging the high-living vices Flint had no intention of stopping. It was the actor as worker, with few pretensions of being anything else.

For some time, however, Cobb had been building up to having the last laugh—and it didn't involve anyone laughing.

## NOTES

1. Interview with author, June 6, 2013.

2. Conversation with author. Subsequent quotes from Jerry Cobb are taken from conversations with the author over the course of several years.

3. *New York Times*, March 10, 1962.

4. *New York Times*, June 7, 1963.

5. Interview with author. Subsequent quotes from Tony Bill are taken from this interview.

# Chapter 23

———————◯———————

# Between the Dragon
# and His Wrath

TWO OF SHAKESPEARE'S UNINTENDED legacies to actors have been in the superstition about never pronouncing the title of *Macbeth* (it's always and only "the Scottish play") and in the assumption that only those who have played King Lear can claim sovereign professional standing. Although there have been scattered actors who haven't keeled over as soon as they referred to *Macbeth* as *Macbeth*, far fewer have won acceptance as classical luminaries without putting up with five acts of three contrary daughters and the Fool in *King Lear*. And a perilous undertaking it has always been for the actor—in the words of British director Peter Brook, "a mountain whose summit has never been reached, the way up strewn with the shattered bodies of earlier visitors."[1] But ever since Richard Burbage became the first to start up the mountain at the dawn of the seventeenth century, actors with the talent and the ambition have seldom ignored the challenge. Among the more noted Lears in the twentieth century were John Gielgud, Donald Wolfit, and Paul Scofield. Laurence Olivier made it the last Shakespearian role he did before a camera, and Charles Laughton died while doing the play. According to Julie Cobb, it was also Laughton who, thunderstruck by her father's performance as Willy Loman, went backstage after a performance of *Death of a Salesman* and planted the deepest seed that he had to do Lear.

"[Laughton] voiced what a lot of people had been saying: 'You must play King Lear! You must!' From that point on, that was Dad's dream. During the next twenty years there were often plans for productions of *King Lear* submitted to my father—plans that he would deem unsatisfactory or proposed productions that never quite panned out. He became so obsessed with the role that finally he *had* to play the part. I think he realized he had to tackle it before he was too old."[2]

Anyone who ran into Cobb more than once in the late 1950s and 1960s knew that was his goal. For many years he worked up to the part by punctuating Hollywood dinner parties with Lear's monologues. His ambition became so well known (he hadn't named his boat Desdemona) that an apocryphal story had him crying out in despair on the gurney taking him to the hospital after his heart attack that he wouldn't be able to do the part. At one point he was said to have approached Olivier to direct him in the play, but Olivier begged off because of his frail health. Michael Cacoyannis, whom Cobb admired for his direction of *Electra* and *Zorba the Greek*, said no because of scheduling problems. He didn't have much more luck trying to put together a cast for attracting a producer. When he asked Melvyn Douglas to commit to playing Gloucester, Douglas bristled before the idea of not playing Lear himself and having Cobb do Gloucester. None of the rejections deterred him, however. At least in retrospect, he also told several interviewers that taking on Shakespeare's monarch had been part of his calculation in first building up a small nest egg for his family by doing *The Virginian* for four seasons. In his November 1968 interview with Patricia Bosworth for the *New York Times*, for example, he declared, "It's always the uncreative people who wonder why I played Judge Garth on television for so long. I played it partly so my epitaph won't read: 'Cobb died wanting to play Lear.'"

After leaving *The Virginian*, though, there was at least one project that meant as much to him as making *King Lear* affordable down the road—a television production of *Death of a Salesman*, adapted for the medium by Arthur Miller himself and directed by Alex Segal for CBS on May 8, 1966. In addition to Cobb, seventeen years older than he had been on Broadway and much closer in age to Miller's original conception of Willy Loman, Mildred Dunnock returned to her role as Linda Loman. As Willy's brother there was Albert Dekker, a Group Theatre member who had also succeeded Cobb in the leading role for a brief spell in 1949 and who had played it over the years for numerous theater companies. But the David Susskind production was no mere reunion of some of the principals from the agonizing good old days. In the opinion of many critics, the TV version was even superior to what had been seen on Broadway in 1949, thanks in part to Miller cuts that made the drama leaner and more direct. Nobody was more enthusiastic than Jack Gould of the *New York Times* who called the presentation "exalted theater," throwing in the notion that if television's Golden Age had been more advanced in 1949, *Salesman* would have been the perfect play for the home screen even then. He cited Cobb's performance as a "towering accomplishment." "By now," Gould asserted, "Mr. Cobb *is* Willy Loman."[3] Other reviewers were equally lavish in their praise. For United Press International, it was "the most unforgettable production in the history of the video medium";[4] for the Associated Press, Cobb was "overwhelming."[5]

Aside from Cobb, Dunnock, and Dekker, the cast included George Segal and James Farentino as the sons and Gene Wilder as Bernard. Both Segal and Wilder had seen the original Broadway production and called their participation in the TV adaptation a "closing of a circle." "That play really dropped an anchor on me twice, first as a kid seeing it with my family and then as an actor being in it," said Segal. "It was life changing." His worries going in?

They weren't really worries. I was an actor, I had been considered good enough to play Biff so I just had to be good enough to play Biff, end of story. Hey, I was even younger than Arthur Kennedy and Lee was much older, so we didn't have to dance around that problem they had back then. But, sure, at the same time in the back of your head you don't want to be the one responsible for lousing up this American classic. Especially when you're the outsider, the new face, and Cobb and Dunnock have already become part of theater history because of the play. But almost as soon as our first rehearsals started I was fine. No question that Cobb was the top of the pyramid. He dominated everything. The guy was really a bear. But lovely Milly, she made sure there was no feeling of separation between the people who had done it before and the new arrivals. She loved me! I was her boy! Linda and Biff, Milly and George! I didn't know whether to be disappointed or not when I found out later she'd had the same relationship with Kennedy. And he was older than me, don't forget. What does that say about her discrimination?

According to Segal, the biggest obstacle to the production was the CBS censors. "They were always at us, and like all television censors did, turned what hadn't been a problem into one. For instance, they wanted the camera above for a scene where Cobb slaps Dunnock on the ass. But by being so high, you couldn't tell if he slapped her on the ass or somewhere else. The usual Standards and Practices stupidity."

Wilder admitted being anxious about whether or not to tell Cobb about how, after seeing the Broadway production, he had managed to play practically every role in the play through his school days.

> I mean, this was all pretty surreal. There I am as nerdy Bernard fifteen years after all these years of fantasy. And there's a real Lee J. Cobb standing in front of me. I didn't say a word through rehearsals. I don't know, maybe I thought he would take me less seriously. But then he invited the whole cast to his home, and I blurted it out. He thought it was hilarious. In fact, whatever you saw up on the TV screen, he was pretty happy to be doing the play again. The only thing I remember him getting annoyed about—and actually we all were—was Susskind refusing to pay for the rights for the haunting music by Alex North that was part of the Broadway play. But outside of that I didn't get any of that gloom thing associated with him.

Although Miller, Alex Segal, and Susskind carted off Emmy prizes for their work, and later on even a Peabody Award, Cobb (along with Dunnock) had to be satisfied yet again with a nomination. The Best Actor trophy went to Peter Ustinov.

The nest egg Cobb was putting together to be able to focus on *King Lear* without too many money worries came not just from *The Virginian* but from four pictures he squeezed into the months leading up to rehearsals for the play. The least taxing was *MacKenna's Gold* in which he, Edward G. Robinson, Raymond Massey, Burgess Meredith, Anthony Quayle, and Eli Wallach played ostensibly honest citizens who tried to cut themselves into a gold hunt by Gregory Peck and Omar Sharif. After one long ensemble scene, they were all shot dead. The most curious thing about the wide-screen pyrite called *MacKenna's Gold* was that it was written and produced by Carl Foreman and directed by J. Lee Thompson, who had previously collaborated on the box-office blockbuster *The Guns of Navarone*. By contrast, *MacKenna's Gold*, despite its big billboard names, was so ramshackle even at a technical level that it stayed on the shelf for long months before being released. "I haven't been so unimpressed by a climactic earthquake," Vincent Canby of the *New York Times* remarked in a typical comment, "since the gods became angry when Dorothy Lamour refused to be dropped into Paramount's backlot volcano in . . . *Aloma of the South Seas.*"[6]

Cobb's next role was one of his best and also one of his most enterprising. Once Clint Eastwood and Charles Bronson had established beachheads there, American actors were increasingly drawn to European film industries, especially those of Italy and France. But unlike some who went abroad at the beginning just to beef up the cast of a war picture or western with a couple of scenes, Cobb said yes to a highly dramatic Mafia story based on a book by one of Italy's most respected writers, Leonardo Sciascia. *Il giorno della civetta* (*The Day of the Owl*[7]) cast the actor as the Mafia don of a Sicilian village who has been targeted by a rigidly upstanding policeman (Franco Nero) after a murder. The don's subtleties have little in common with Johnny Friendly or the mobster in *Party Girl* except for their black cynicism; they are also far less vulnerable to justice-will-prevail Hollywood comeuppances. But those were hardly the only differences in the production directed by Damiano Damiani in the Sicilian town of Parteneco. Nehemiah Persoff, who played one of the don's henchmen, remembered that both he and Cobb had some initial problems with the Italian way of shooting:

> They don't do live sound. The recorders are working, but everything is put together in a dubbing studio after the shooting is over. So when you have a scene, say, with American actors and Italian actors and French actors, everybody is speaking his own language, knowing it's all going to be cleaned up in the dubbing. The first time it really hit home was when I was distracted by this Italian actor who kept looking at his watch while I was doing my dialogue. The reason was that he had timed my dialogue in English down to the second so that he would know when exactly to jump in with his Italian because he didn't speak a word of English. That was very disorienting. Maybe a little bit more for me than for Lee because he was doing a good part of his scenes in English either with me or Franco Nero, who did speak English.

Nero confirmed there were minimal language problems in his scenes with Cobb, but said the older actor had arrived in Sicily with both his penchant for doing things his own way and his insecurity about his hairline in place.

He was always very sweet with me, but he definitely had his own ideas. There was a scene in particular where he has this monologue about men and half-men, and Damiani was trying to get him to speed it up. But Lee took his own sweet time, drawing out everything with the help of this cigar he always had in his hand. And as far as his baldness was concerned, he was completely obsessed with it. One day in makeup we were going over lines and he kept interrupting to make sure the people working on him got his toupee right. When I reminded him about the lines, he just said "I know the lines, I know the lines, don't worry about them," then went back to what was bothering him about the toupee.[8]

Both Nero and Persoff painted the picture of somebody not at all at ease with his first foreign film. Nero: "I'd heard all the stories about card games and the like, but I didn't see any of that. He went to bed early every night. He was very introverted." Persoff:

I'd known Lee and worked with him before, of course. He was always a little defensive, but in Italy much more so. I'd say he was almost stiff once the day's work was done. Damiani saw this and invited the two of us out to dinner to loosen him up a bit. It really didn't work. Lee was cordial and polite, but he was very uncomfortable the whole dinner. Finally, I said something to him about it and he looked at me as though I should have known better. "We're not tourists," he said. "We're here to do a picture." That was enough of an explanation for him.

But there was one chink in the defensiveness. "Cars," Persoff said. "He met these people from Maserati and bought himself this sleek car. Suddenly, all the hows and wheres of shipping it over to America were the most important thing on his mind. And about that Maserati he was ready to talk for hours, tourist or no tourist."

*Il giorno della civetta* barely appeared on the critical radar in the United States where, five years before the release of *The Godfather*, Sicilian Mafia tales were generally regarded as nothing more than Sicilian Mafia tales best served by co-feature B programmers. But the picture's portrait of an almost fatalistic submission to political gangster power had a far more serious reception in Europe, where Sciascia's name alone had a cachet it did not have across the Atlantic. In Italy both Nero and Claudia Cardinale as the widow of a murder witness won David di Donatello awards, the equivalent of Oscars. Cobb's prize was the praise of his director. "Damiano Damiani made dozens of films," said Nero, "but he always told me that the smartest casting choice he ever made was Cobb for our picture. The man might not have been born Sicilian, Damiani said, but he *was* Sicilian."

What *Il giorno della civetta* didn't do at the box office in America, *Coogan's Bluff* did multiple times over, establishing that Clint Eastwood didn't always have to be the Man with No Name from spaghetti westerns and pushing him into the anteroom of his Dirty Harry fame. The forerunner of the popular TV series *McCloud, Coogan's Bluff* stars Eastwood as an Arizona sheriff come to New York to escort a wanted man back home. When he loses the suspect, he spends the rest of the picture smashing his way through Manhattan to recapture him. Cobb plays a perennially harassed detective who can't stand the sheriff's Stetson, his carelessness, or anything else about him; the role wasn't all that far from the exasperated M-type director in the Flint movies.

*Coogan's Bluff* raised some eyebrows for its violence and some noses for Eastwood's performance. According to Canby, the star "doesn't act in motion pictures, he is framed by them." As for Cobb, Susan Clark, and the rest of the cast, they were said to turn in "the kind of good stock performances that one day may be filmed in advance and stored in the movie equivalent of a food freezer."[9]

Nobody could say even that much about *They Came to Rob Las Vegas*, a coproduction with Spain that established its American authenticity with a lot of stock footage of Nevada casinos, then went back to Europe for most of its tinny interiors. In the words of Howard Thompson of the *Times*, the heist tale "may not be the worst picture of the year, but it will do." As for Cobb in the role of the shifty operator of an armored car service, "let's just pretend that such a fine actor isn't in it."[10] *Vegas* took even longer to be released in the United States than did *MacKenna's Gold*.

The linchpin for finally getting *King Lear* on its feet was Jules Irving, the director of the Repertory Company at Lincoln Center's Vivian Beaumont Theater in New York. It was no small commitment by Irving. Despite success with individual productions, the company had come under regular attack for not consistently offering plays equal to its institutional setting and *Lear* especially had a notorious history in America of very brief runs, whether because of general critical brickbats, reverse snobbism that only a Briton should undertake the leading role, or simple exhaustion by the star player. In the specific case of

Cobb, there was also the actor's past heart problems to be considered. But Cobb persuaded Irving he was more than ready to take on the role, also assenting to the hiring of Gerald Freedman as the director. The choice of Freedman would feed impressions that the actor had no intention of working under a director with stronger views on *Lear* than his own. Although he would later have a distinguished Broadway and Public Theater career, Freedman's most conspicuous credits up to that point had been as assistant director on revivals of *West Side Story* and *Gypsy* and as the director of episodes in minor television series. The casting, at least for the male roles, was completed fairly quickly, with Philip Bosco (Kent), Stacy Keach (Edmund), Rene Auberjonois (the Fool), Stephen Elliott (Gloucester), and Robert Stattel (Edgar) among those signed. Partly because of hopes by both Freedman and Cobb that Anne Bancroft would join the cast, the women's roles were left for last. "That was a very odd situation," assistant director Amy Saltz recalled. "Bancroft said no, but then she showed up for practically every rehearsal and would just sit there taking it all in. I thought she might have been working herself up to change her mind, but no, that wasn't it at all. She just seemed to like taking in the rehearsals."[11]

When the women were finally cast, it was Patricia Elliott as Regan, Marilyn Lightstone as Goneril, and Barbette Tweed as Cordelia. Elliott's biggest credit otherwise would be as a regular on the soap opera *One Life to Live*, Lightstone's as Miss Stacy on the Canadian miniseries *Anne of Green Gables*, and Tweed's as Helen Hunt's aunt. From a distance of fifty years Freedman acknowledged that, prodded by Cobb and Irving, he had sought more star power in the women's roles. "These were all professional actors, so it wasn't like Amateur Night," the director said. "But they didn't have the ring of somebody like a Bancroft, either, that extra dimension that might have rippled through the stage and affected everybody up there. We just had to get on with it."[12]

Getting on with it created different impressions among different members of the cast. For Stattel, Cobb's Lear was more influenced by his film roles than by his performances as Willy Loman or other stage characters. "He was an enormously giving actor; he always had time to rehearse with anybody who asked. But I had also worked with James Earl Jones and others and I couldn't help noticing a big difference. An actor like Jones constructed his character from start to finish. Lee always struck me as being more attuned to scenes than to the whole play as such, the way you might be if you'd been working in the movies for a long time. He was absolutely brilliant in the scenes, but sometimes there really wasn't a connection between one scene and the next."[13]

Keach seconded Stattel's evaluation of Cobb as a fellow actor, but also thought he grew in the part as the performances went along.

> I thought he was a wonderful, supportive man and have never understood stories that have said the opposite. The company adored him. He was very funny, starting with the red socks he always wore. But I don't think there was any question he was intimidated at first because he didn't have much Shakespeare in his background. And then he also had a problem of being Lee Cobb with this great emotional power, and sometimes the vocal and technical demands simply weren't up to that power. Was he better in some scenes than in others? Sure. But I've done the Lear role since and I've stolen for my own some of the personal and untricky things he did in the part, especially in the later scenes.[14]

Cobb's worst critic, at least before the professional critical fraternity chimed in, was Auberjonois. "It was my first experience in New York, and I was as intimidated by meeting him as by working in the city." According to the actor, the pair got off on the wrong foot immediately when Cobb said he could see doing a version of the play without the character of the Fool altogether.

> It didn't come to that, but maybe I should have wondered why it didn't. I should have seen the writing on the wall right there. He had his own ideas and even the ones he sounded like he was throwing off lightly, like getting rid of the Fool, he had clearly thought a great deal about. He was really in charge of things, and there was absolutely no connection between him and Freedman. Whenever he disagreed with Freedman about something, he stopped rehearsing with him. I shouldn't have been surprised after what he had said about the character of the Fool, but I did a lot of my rehearsing with one of Freedman's assistants.[15]

Auberjonois said he was so dispirited by his lack of rapport with Cobb that he handed in his notice the day after the play opened in New York.

I could see where we were heading, and it just wasn't a fulfilling experience. But then a curious thing happened. When he heard I had
handed in my notice, he refused to say a word to me offstage but at
the same time our performance together became more interesting.
I found some nerve of my own. For instance, one of the very first
things he told me was that the Fool was never to touch Lear—not because of some phobia, but just because that was the way he saw their
relationship. Well, once we got into this cold war of sorts, I began
threatening to touch him, and it felt like it raised the temperature on
the stage. My own feeling is that betrayal was a big theme in his life
and I had tapped into it without realizing it. Now he suddenly knew
who I was—the one who had put in his notice—so now he knew me
for the traitor I was and could deal with me. When I mentioned this
to his daughter Julie, she just nodded. She seemed to recognize it as
a familiar syndrome in his career.

Vincent Cobb was also aware of the tensions with Auberjonois. "I
never did know what went down there, but there was definitely a problem. A mutual friend of mine and Rene's told me at the time that Dad
was absolutely cruel to Rene. I was really astounded by that because
my impression of Dad was one of very professional behavior during the
work. But it must have been true. I know that he hated Rene . . . and
it certainly couldn't have been just because of Rene's performance.
There was something about him that simply violated Dad."

When the paid critics descended on *Lear*, they did with a thud.
Although some reviewers were captivated just by the idea of Willy Loman, Johnny Friendly, and Judge Garth branching out into Lear and
applauded him simply for that, their number did not include the two
heaviest weights on the aisle—John Simon and Walter Kerr. Writing
for the weekly magazine *New York*, the chronically nasty Simon said
Cobb's performance was that of "a slow, rusty steam engine rolling over
a magnificent part and painstakingly flattening it out." And "his Lear
is one long, weary shuffle. From the start he seems tired, defeated."
And again, more familiarly from other critiques the actor had received
from as far back as Lee Strasberg, "[his] laggardly pacing is exacerbated
by a prodigality of pauses popping up all over, as if he were reading
from very fine print in darkness." And before Auberjonois or anyone
else could say I-told-you-so, Simon added, "The rest of the cast is bad.
Not undistinguished, spotty, or weak. Bad." This one was found to be
"squeaky," that one "empty," a third "insipid." And as for Freedman's
overall direction, what he had produced was "a great stage of fools."[16]

By comparison, Kerr's antipathy was benevolent. After giving the production as a whole the back of his hand as being "acceptable," he trained his focus on Cobb the actor versus Lear the character. Under a commentary entitled "No Madness in His Method," the *New York Times* critic declared in part, "Mr. Cobb's mind is so set on dominating the material before him that it cannot be breached, cannot come unstuck, cannot convey to us a sense of emptiness. . . . It is an intelligent actor's defense against the role, the result of his determination not to get lost in it."[17]

Kerr's observation did not come as much of a surprise to Saltz or Freedman. "I was always terribly sorry the audience never got to see the dress rehearsal when he wasn't holding back," the assistant director said. "You couldn't look away from the stage he was so powerful. Once the show started running, though, I think he started becoming afraid of another heart attack with all the effort he had to put into it."

Freedman admitted a similar impression.

> I went into it with Lee J. Cobb as Lear. I wanted Lee J. Cobb, the actor we knew from *Death of a Salesman* and so many movies. And that was the Lear we had in the last rehearsals and in out-of-town tryouts. This was a Lear to be feared! But then as soon as we got to Lincoln Center for the opening, he cut back. Suddenly he was this classical actor with a capital C, doing John Gielgud instead of himself. All that danger he'd been showing up to then disappeared. Was it because of worries about his health? Yes, I think that had a great deal to do with it. He was working out at the Y or someplace fairly regularly during the run, so he had to have been in pretty good shape overall. But he had some voice problems, and went to a doctor for them. And one time I had to go to his hotel room after he called and said he was sick. He missed a performance or two, but that seemed like a blessing compared to the fear I saw in his eyes when I walked in that room. He also tore a calf muscle in one performance carrying Cordelia. Between that and the heavy costume he was wearing, he started slowing down as we went along, but even much younger actors in perfect condition probably would have, too.

Vincent Cobb added that his father had been suffering for years from a benign tumor on one of his heels, necessitating periodic radiation treatments. Because of the limited effectiveness of the treatments, Vincent said, the heel pain gradually affected Cobb's back, so much so that he was actually given a harness under his costume in *Lear* to help him carry Cordelia.

Freedman's evaluation of Cobb's performance overall? "There were times when he was wonderful. In the end I thought he was okay, but he could have been great."

According to Keach, Cobb acted unfazed by the reviews, but then again he had long since adopted the posture that critics might have been a necessary evil if they had been necessary. Plus, he had opinions more reassuring closer to home. "[Lear] makes savage emotional demands on the actor and requires huge reserves of strength and stamina," daughter Julie noted. "Dad thrived on it! I don't remember ever seeing him so happy. The thing that struck me most about his Lear was his humanity. It was real. I remember being in the opening night audience and hearing sobs at the end of the play. I was almost unconscious with excitement and pride."[18]

Cobb himself was also eager to dispel any notion that the physical requirements of the play affected either his performance or his health to any appreciable degree. In his November 1968 interview with Patricia Bosworth of the *Times*, he admitted only that he was "absolutely exhausted when the curtain comes down. I have to drag myself back to the dressing room." But then added, "And yet as soon as I take off my makeup I start filling up with a kind of buoyant, pounding energy and by the time I leave the theater I'm mysteriously more alive than when I began the performance."

Bad reviews or good reviews, torn calf muscle and voice problems or not, the play gave seventy-two performances, the longest run up to then by *King Lear* in America, before closing on February 12, 1969.

## NOTES

1. "What Playing King Lear Does to an Actor," *Financial Times*, February 26, 2010.
2. Peary, *Close-Ups*, p. 347.
3. *New York Times*, May 9, 1966.
4. United Press International, May 9, 1966.
5. Associated Press, May 8, 1966.
6. *New York Times*, June 19, 1968.
7. The Italian title is something of a double entendre since *civetta* means *flirt* as well as *owl*.
8. Interview with author, December 19, 2012. Subsequent quotes from Franco Nero are taken from this interview.

9. *New York Times*, October 3, 1968.

10. *New York Times*, February 6, 1969.

11. Interview with author, May 6, 2013. Subsequent quotes from Amy Saltz are taken from this interview.

12. Interview with author, May 13, 2013. Subsequent quotes from Gerald Freedman are taken from this interview.

13. Interview with author, February 26, 2011.

14. Interview with author.

15. Interview with author, April 7, 2011. Subsequent quotes from Rene Auberjonois are taken from this interview.

16. *New York*, November 25, 1968.

17. *New York Times*, November 17, 1968.

18. Peary, *Close-Ups*, p. 347.

# Chapter 24

Bullies and Connivers

Just as he had after *Death of a Salesman*, Cobb took time off after *King Lear* to retune his energies. But that didn't mean sitting around the house all day doing nothing. From their earliest ages he drove sons Tony and Jerry to piano lessons, engaging in long conversations with their teachers on their progress. "He was profoundly musical," Jerry said. "Even when we were kids he would drag us off to concerts. He and my mother were season subscribers. In my case it just didn't take, but in Tony's it did." According to musician Tony, the fact that he was able to retain thousands of songs in his head for his regular gigs as a hotel pianist owed to his father's technique for memorizing lines. "He explained to me once how he broke dialogue down into little units, like the cars of a train. With each unit he would rehearse aloud in his studio. He did all the parts in the script because that made it real, an object *out there*. Then after getting down his first unit he would move on to connect it to the next one and start all over again until he had the whole train down. I didn't realize it for some time but that has been more or less how I've memorized so many songs, too."

Another incident touching on Tony's education proved memorable in a different way.

If there was one thing Dad couldn't stand, it was bullying. One night at dinner he asked me the usual about how school was going and instead of giving him the usual answer that things were fine, I told him that this kid who had the locker next to mine had been bullying me. Well, there was this deathly silence at the table, and he turned absolutely red. He stopped chewing his food right in the middle. Tell you the truth, he looked briefly insane. Then he composed himself, told me not to worry about it and go do my homework, oh and by the way, what was my locker number? The next morning I go to school, and the principal calls me in to his office. Very early that morning Dad had barged into the school—imagine that happening today with all the security guards around!—and he takes up a position at my locker. This kid comes along, and suddenly Johnny Friendly is close to throttling him with a warning about what's going to happen if the kid ever bullies me again. And that's all very nice, except it was the wrong kid!

And his father's reaction when he found out? "He had gone to locker 646 instead of 746, and great shame came over him. He felt so bad that I was the one who ended up doing the comforting. But I was also so mad that the real bully had escaped Johnny Friendly's wrath that the next day I went to school and stood up to the kid. He never bothered me again. I knew my Dad had my back."

When the boys went away to summer camp, Cobb kept in touch with them with regular letters. One letter sent to Tony on July 13, 1974 said,

Dear Son,
    A warm, quiet Saturday morning. On my way down to breakfast, I glance at the piano; particles of very fine dust dancing in the sun's rays over its smooth, beautiful surface. The sight arrests me. It seems to be looking back at me—accusingly! "Where's my dear friend?" it seems to be saying to me. "The young man with the understanding touch—a touch now firm, now caressing?"
    Oh, sweet Yammy (in the family we never refer to him as Yamaha—it's too stiff and formal), dear Yammy, you need to be happy for Tony. He's away, having a good time for the summer. But he'll be back before long. And then what a reunion! What joy!
    Love,
    Dad

When he wasn't overseeing the musical and schoolroom corridor education of his sons, Cobb was working on one of his numerous pastimes—his cars, photography, carpentry, woodworking, or simply reading the novels, manuals, and magazines that filled his home. "He was really into photography," the professional photographer Vincent said. "He didn't just snap away, either. He had been doing all his own developing and printing since he had been a kid. He said that if you didn't do that, you couldn't consider yourself a real photographer. I'm sure I must have gotten the bug from him. His best things are his family pictures, and I don't just mean because we were in them. He put a great deal of care into them. Many of them are really artistic in the best sense."

Meredith Kibbee, daughter of the screenwriter Roland Kibbee, said some people in their Laurel Canyon neighborhood also came to think of Cobb as a general handyman on perpetual call. "Whenever something went wrong in the kitchen or bathroom, the first reaction was always 'Call Lee.' And Lee would come over with his tool kit and get under the sink or open the toilet tank, whatever it was, and go to work. I think he loved it as much as we needed it."[1]

On at least one occasion, according to Kibbee, the actor also provided fashion support.

> I must have been sixteen and I had this new dress and I wanted to show it to Mary to see what she thought of it. So I called over to the Cobbs and Lee answered and said Mary wasn't home, could he help? When I told him what I'd called for, he said to come over. I walked into their driveway, and he was standing up on this balcony he had outside his studio. He motioned for me to whirl around in the dress, I did, he gave me the OK sign, then went back into his studio to return to work. That kind of thing sounds silly in retrospect, but it was very important to me that day. As a child, when you first met him, he could be very intimidating. There was something in his eyes that said I-know-what-you've-been-up-to-even-if-your-parents-don't. So when you got approval from him, it was like getting it from your parents plus one.

Meredith's brother Jeff had an identical impression.

> I guess a lot of people have called him intimidating. And he was. But in a very peculiar aristocratic way. He had this incredibly dry sense of humor, this air of brilliance that he really didn't want to have to demonstrate if he didn't have to. Sometimes he'd be around the table with my father, Norman Lear, Burt Lancaster, and other friends, and he always seemed a bit removed from them or like where he was seated was the center of the conversation even when he was quiet.

Somebody like Lancaster, for instance, a fine actor, a producer, somebody of very strong opinions and intelligence, compared to Lee he could sound like a teenager at times. There was something cultural about him with a capital C. He hadn't just accumulated the things he knew and could talk about, he *breathed* them in some way.[2]

Another part of that breathing culture, though, remained his perennial gambling. And sometimes he couldn't win for losing. "One time he went to Las Vegas in that Citroen with the Maserati engine he was so proud of," Tony Cobb recalled, "and he hit it big at a casino. When he came out, he put all his winnings behind the car radio, and just in time because one of the bookmakers he owed money to came up and asked him how he had done. 'Broke even,' he says, and the guy went away. Dad gets in the car and starts back to Los Angeles. Suddenly he smells smoke and sees it coming out of the radio. The radio burned up all his winnings!"

Another time he simply lost, leading to an intervention, yet again by Frank Sinatra. As Norman Lear told it, "One night Mary telephoned me saying she had just heard from Lee in Las Vegas and that he was in trouble. I called Sinatra. Frank had his own plane at the Van Nuys Airport. He flew to Vegas, and pulled Lee back to Los Angeles, practically leaving all his stuff in his hotel room."

While Tony Cobb had been too young to know of that specific incident, he said the particulars supplied by Lear fit his picture of his parents. "Dad always called her when he knew he had crossed some line and she never went halfway in calling him an addicted gambler, then tried to help him out of whatever mess he was in." But both Tony and Jerry Cobb also voiced skepticism about some of the stories that circulated because of their father's gambling. "There was no doubt he was into bookmakers and loan sharks for most of his life," Jerry said.

He couldn't play enough. Sometimes we'd come home from school and see he'd spent a good part of the day playing gin with his agent Peter Witt. Peter was as obsessed as Dad was. And yes, he seemed to have lost a lot. But that didn't mean we were on Poverty Row because of his gambling. We weren't rich, but we were comfortable. Tony and I went to private high schools. I ended up going to Brown, which was never cheap. And I know my father did some of the heavy lifting for putting my half-brother, Tim, through medical school. His high-end cars, the boat for a while, vacation trips to places like the

Bahamas and Mexico—I mean, just how bad could it have been with
the loan sharks?

For some of the same reasons, Tony has tended to discount a story
his father reputedly told Dustin Hoffman about loan sharks.

> Hoffman played Bernard on the album they made of *Death of a
> Salesman*. During a break one day, he said, he and Dad were talk-
> ing about doing the play back in 1949 and Dad told him there had
> been evenings when he would come out of the theater completely
> high because of the performance he had given and then he would
> see one of these loan sharks hanging around Shubert Alley and he
> would become immediately depressed. There's something about that
> story that has never really convinced me. I don't know if it was Dad
> just saying things or Dustin maybe misinterpreting, but to me it rings
> false. When Dad had a good performance, nothing could have taken
> him down. He was king of the world. When he had a bad perfor-
> mance for whatever reason (not feeling comfortable about a delivery,
> not convinced of his own interpretation, wrong rhythm, whatever)
> nothing, but nothing, on earth could console him. He would slump
> into a heap of melancholy so deep it practically strangled him until
> it passed over. Gamblers or loan sharks waiting for him after a show?
> I'd be surprised if he'd even notice them. And what kind of loan
> sharks hang around like that and just keeping walking away without
> their money, anyway? It's not like they wouldn't know where to find
> him. They really wouldn't have registered with him if he was so in-
> side himself the way that story has it.

When Cobb returned to work, it was with top billing as an eleventh-hour replacement for Henry Fonda in what would turn out to be
William Wyler's last picture. It would also be the long-time director's
most disputable film in a career of them, with some reviewers going so
far as to counsel readers to stay away from it. For those comforted by
the image of race relations in America presented by such Hollywood
hits as *Guess Who's Coming to Dinner* and *In the Heat of the Night*, *The
Liberation of L.B. Jones*, based on a novel by Jesse Hill Ford, flared up
like a bad toothache.

The plot of *Liberation* has the black undertaker (Roscoe Lee
Browne) of a Tennessee town asking the county's most influential
lawyer (Cobb) to handle divorce proceedings against his wife (Lola
Falana) because she has been carrying on with a white cop (Anthony

Zerbe). The lawyer's attempts to keep the racially explosive details out of a public courtroom sow tragedy. In violent order, the cop beats up the wife for looking forward to the divorce proceedings, the cop and his partner (Arch Johnson) kill the undertaker, the partner mutilates the body so it will look like a black-against-black homicide, the cop takes his guilty conscience to the lawyer and asks to be arrested, the lawyer and the town mayor tell him his guilt is enough and to go home while they sweep everything under the rug, and a friend of the undertaker (Yaphet Kotto) exacts vengeance by killing and mutilating the partner before leaving town.

What became clear from the mainstream press reaction to the picture was that, however violent some of the earlier moments in the story, what particularly offended the media citizenry was the Kotto character's dancing off unpunished at the end. A mere two years after the assassination of Martin Luther King, in some eyes this not only capped a completely false picture of contemporary race relations in the South but represented an apology for black-against-white violence. "It's a shame," the *Saturday Review* asserted, "that a director of Wyler's stature has seen fit to perpetuate these outdated images of the South."[3] For the weekly *Variety*, the picture was nothing more than "an interracial sexploitation film."[4]

Kotto, for one, had seen that kind of reaction coming.

> *Liberation* was messing with a lot of sacred cows. The image of the black man had suddenly gone from the Do-Good-Nice-Guy Negro like *In the Heat of the Night* to the cold-blooded ruthless killer in *Liberation*. If anything surprised me about the reaction, it was attacks from blacks on me for doing the picture. Many in the black community in Hollywood started accusing me of having an "in" with producers because I have some Jewish blood. I didn't realize there was so much anti-Semitism in certain black circles in Hollywood. One well-known black actor who saw the picture warned his daughters that my name was never to be mentioned again in his house. I found that criminal.[5]

Kotto also said that he had talked Wyler out of a less brutal approach to the scene where he kills the character played by Arch Johnson. "Willie said to me, 'After you push him into the machine, I'd like to see a little tear, like you're almost sorry for what you've done.' I said to him, 'Willie, every movie where there's a black and white . . . the

black guy cries or is the first killed. Can't we do something different?'"
When Kotto showed him what he had in mind, the startled Wyler was
said to have replied, "Gee, Kid, if I let you do it like that, we're going to
make history. There's going to be a storm. . . . But do it your way. Push
him into the machine. No tears. No emotion. Nothing. Just a cold,
unmoving face." Said Kotto, "The black guy killing the white guy in a
big studio picture—it was Hollywood history, and Wyler had made it.
He called me at home after the production and thanked me."

The racial tensions on view in *Liberation* might have been more
grotesque, but they blossomed in the same social climate enveloping
two weeks of exteriors in Humboldt, Tennessee. When the company
arrived at the location, it was greeted with accommodations that put
up Cobb, Zerbe, and the other whites in a Holiday Inn outside town
and Kotto, Falana, Browne, and the other blacks in boarding rooms
in the black community. The transportation back and forth for the
African-American actors was a jalopy of a cab. "I'll never forget the look
on Cobb's face when he saw this happening," Kotto recalled. "I knew
he resented the racism, but he was powerless to do anything about it.
That look on his face told me all I needed to know about his character.
At least that's what I thought at first. But then Willie told me that Lee
had raised hell with Columbia and demanded we be moved to where
the rest of the cast lived. Whatever he said to Hollywood worked, and
we were moved to the Holiday Inn."

To blunt trouble over the picture itself, Wyler had talked Columbia into giving him two crews so that one could be shooting indepen-
dently of the other, neither in a position to blurt out the plot as a whole
to locals. "That had no effect on me as an actor," Kotto said. "Staying
loose and playing it safe in Humboldt, a place filled with race hatred,
was enough for me to worry about."

Not all reviewers were as hysterical as the one for the *Saturday Review*. In the *Los Angeles Times* Charles Champlin observed that "there
are no punishments, no deathbed repentances, nothing to suggest that
anything has changed or will change tomorrow. . . . The argument of
the movie is that we can only be served by the truth, unpalatable as
it may be."[6] Even more enthusiastic was Andrew Sarris, who called
it "the most provocative brief for Black Power ever to come out of a
Hollywood studio . . . the first American movie, either black or white,
to dramatize the matter-of-fact exploitation of black women by white
supremacists. Certainly it is the first American movie to countenance

and even condone bloody revenge by the black against his white oppressor."[7]

According to Wyler's biographer, Jan Herman, the director never stopped believing in the picture, antagonistic reviews and dismal box office notwithstanding. "If I had been a black director," Wyler was quoted as saying a couple of years later, "it would have made a big difference. It was one of the first black pictures. It came just before the wave of black films, and black people went to see it. But it was made for white people. The whites stayed away because it made them uncomfortable. It embarrassed them. I saw it recently, and I'm highly prejudiced in its favor."[8]

As for Cobb, he indicated more than once that he had harbored high hopes for the picture at the start but had ultimately been let down. He declined to go into specifics, at least publicly. In his November 1977 interview with Pickard for *Films in Review*, for instance, he said only, "That was a big disappointment to me. I'd rather not comment further." But he did share his views with his son Vincent:

> He was disappointed in it on several levels. It was supposed to be a prestige product from a highly regarded author and novel, plus Wyler and all that implied, and he was the nominal star. But it turned out to be quite a formulaic and static piece in his opinion. It would have meant a lot to him at that stage of his career for it to have been better. Instead, he felt Wyler wasn't equal to the task, even physically. According to Dad, he couldn't even hear without being plugged into the shooting sound system. And then to make matters still worse, Columbia released the picture within spitting distance of both *Easy Rider* and *Five Easy Pieces*—pictures that were looking toward the future while *Liberation* was looking toward the past.

Biographer Herman backed up Cobb's assessment of Wyler's frail physical state, to the point that an assistant shot much of the Tennessee location footage. Kotto said he didn't see too much sign of that. "He was still Hundred-Take Willie where I was concerned. For one scene I had to eat fifteen pieces of cake until he was satisfied with the way I was eating it. That's the Wyler everybody knew. But maybe things were different with the scenes he directed with Lee."

What Kotto had no doubts about was the relationship he forged with Cobb on the set.

The first thing he told me was that I would go far but that I also had to keep an eye out for a superstar then in Hollywood who didn't like black actors cutting into his territory. That was why he said he admired my ideas about the killing scene. I had nerve, he said, and he liked that, but I was also going to need it with some of the jealousies around Hollywood. . . . Overall, I got the feeling that he felt Hollywood had passed him by and he was sort of warning me that my enemies would do the same to me if I wasn't careful. . . . I believe that Lee J. Cobb passed on with a broken heart, but because of him I learned how to fight. I thank God for his presence. Outside of all the things that happened while shooting our picture, it was because of him that I received a lesson in business politics that helped me have my career.

Three of Cobb's next four pictures—his last full burst of work in Hollywood for the big screen—were westerns. The first one, *Macho Callahan*, was a ludicrously violent tale of the title character (David Janssen) falling for a con man's (Cobb) pitch to join the Union Army, getting instantly thrown into a hellhole of a Confederate prison, then breaking out bent on getting even with the con man. That was the comedy part. Callahan then proceeds to kill a crippled Rebel officer (David Carradine), his widow (Jean Seberg) sends gunmen after him, he rapes her, she falls in love with him, he catches up to the con man and hangs him from a windmill, then he gets his. Some reviews called the picture an attempt to emulate spaghetti westerns, but despite that Italy didn't break off diplomatic relations with the United States.

Almost inevitably after *Death of a Salesman*, Cobb's meetings with the press precipitated questions about how he could wind up in a picture such as *Macho Callahan*. His reply was more or less the one he gave Patricia Bosworth for the *New York Times* in November 1968 when looking at his career as a whole:

It was never my intention to die pure because suffering for your art can be pretty degrading. Now I just want to keep on living to fight another day. . . . Sure I was greedy for similar opportunities [doing Willy Loman], for more peaks. But they didn't come right away, and that shattered me. I had to cope with realities like paying the rent, etcetera. . . . I'm flattered when people say I've wasted my talents, but it isn't so. I've been working all the time developing my craft. I know this even if nobody else does. . . . What people don't know is that I've turned down double the crap I did. With very few exceptions I'm not doing the things I want to do. I've had to compromise. I wish it weren't necessary to compromise, but it is. I've hoped I could do something I could take pride in, not simply something I'm successful in.

*Lawman*, the second western, was a gray-haired, slow-motion relative of the panoramic action pictures (*Gunfight at the O.K. Corral, Last Train from Gun Hill*, etc.) that had reaped profits for Hollywood in the 1950s. Its chief cachet was a startling cast—Burt Lancaster, Cobb, Robert Ryan, Joseph Wiseman, Robert Duvall, Sheree North, Richard Jordan, J. D. Cannon, Albert Salmi—that couldn't be mistaken for a community theater roster. Somewhere within its plot of a marshal (Lancaster) intent on arresting a land baron (Cobb) and his hands for the killing of an old man back in his district was a message about the immorality of violence, even the legal kind at times: Not only was the killing of the old man accidental, but the marshal is the first to acknowledge that the land baron will just buy off the judge even if arrested. This, of course, only underlines the futility of all the bloodshed that ensues, but also led some reviewers to find "baffling" many of the plot's mechanics.[9] Most accolades went to Ryan as a jaded marshal under the land baron's influence and to North as the woman of one of the men Lancaster has come to arrest. What was noticeable in riding scenes was how Cobb sat uncomfortably on a horse, and that didn't do much for his characterization of a rancher. Aside from the disinterest he had shown during *The Virginian* in riding more expertly, he continued to suffer from the calf muscle he had torn during *Lear* and by way of compensation sought to shift more weight to his back, and the stiffness showed.

He had the same riding problem in the third western, *The Man Who Loved Cat Dancing*. While of the action-packed pursuit genre, it wasn't nearly as tumultuous as events surrounding its shooting in Gila Bend, Arizona. The man of the title is a bandit (Burt Reynolds) who has been on the wrong side of the law since he killed the rapist and murderer of his Indian wife. While fleeing with his gang from a robbery, he kidnaps the abused wife (Sarah Miles) of a cattleman (George Hamilton), who sets off after the band with a bounty hunter (Cobb) in tow. Much of the action before the final reckoning has the outlaw falling in love with the abducted wife while having to keep his sleaziest henchmen (Jack Warden and Bo Hopkins) away from her. A lot of people get kicked or shot in the groin, and *The Man Who Loved Cat Dancing* didn't remind many of *High Noon*. For the *New York Times* the primary culprit was director Richard Sarafian: "It's a festival of incompetence. Each shot is held slightly too long or too short, and is somehow off-center. Each performance is uncertain, like something seen in an early rehearsal. Even the Indians look fake, including good old Jay Silverheels, who is real."[10]

But by the time *Cat Dancing* hit theaters bad reviews were the least of its problems. For those involved in the film it became synonymous with Richard Whiting.

Whiting had the title of leading lady Miles's business manager. According to tabloid stories (subsequently denied by all the interested parties), he doubled as a spy on her for the actress's husband, playwright Robert Bolt, back in England. Whether spy or just business manager, Miles would tell police, the decidedly creepy Whiting went beyond both roles early on the morning of Sunday, February 11, 1973, and shortly afterward was found dead on the floor of her bathroom in the Travelodge motel where the film company was staying. A police report quoted the actress as telling the first officer on the scene, "Yes, he was my business manager. He was my business manager, but all he wanted to do was fuck me all the time and I wasn't going to be fucked by him."[11] An autopsy would rule death by suicide from an overdose of "methaqualium and other depressant drugs," but that was Act XX.

As put together by the police, the trouble started on Saturday evening, February 10, when the cast and crew held a birthday party for Reynolds at the Pink Palomino cafe thirty-five miles away from the Travelodge motel. Although she went there with Reynolds, Miles returned to Gila Bend with Cobb because she wanted to ride in the Citroen with the Maserati racing engine he had been boasting about. After saying goodnight to Cobb, she went into the motel bar for a drink, then started back toward her room. Along the way, she said, she decided to drop in on Reynolds to apologize to him for not driving back with him and found him getting a massage from a Japanese masseuse employed by the motel. The two spoke until 3 a.m., she said, then she returned to her room, where Whiting suddenly jumped out at her and demanded to know where she had been. When she told him it was none of his business, he slapped her, she screamed, and Jane Evans, the nanny taking care of the actress's five-year-old son, ran in to see what was going on. As soon as Whiting heard Miles tell Evans to get Reynolds, he fled. Reynolds arrived, and took Miles to his room, where the two remained until between eight and ten o'clock in the morning. It was only then, in the brightness of the new day, that she returned to her room and found Whiting sprawled out dead.

What followed for weeks was a circus of lawyers, contradictory statements on the record by some principals, more lawyers, MGM's decision to move the exteriors for the picture from Gila Bend to Nogales, more lawyers, and, not least, a woman who, claiming to be Whiting's mother but with her own questionable background, arrived to accuse everyone from the movie studio to Arizona officials of colluding in a cover-up over the exact circumstances of the business manager's death. The suicide verdict of the inquest had to negotiate such glaring contradictions as the masseuse's testimony that she had found Miles already in Reynolds's room when she had gone there; Miles denying that she had ever told the police that Whiting had wanted to fuck her; Miles telling police in another statement that Whiting hadn't just "slapped" her but had given her "the nastiest beating of my life"; Miles saying that it had been closer to 11:30, not between 8 and 10 a.m., when she had returned to her room to find Whiting's body; blood found all over Whiting's motel room and a gash on the back of his head. Had Reynolds run into Whiting after being summoned by the nanny? He didn't think so, but he had seen "somebody" on his way over to Miles's room. Had Reynolds wanted to go after Whiting and beat him up? Yes, according to the masseuse: "Mr. Reynolds wanted to go down and fight him, Mr. Whiting, but Sarah, she stopped him. She told Mr. Reynolds it would cause more trouble."

Glen Birchfield, then the owner of a bus stop cafe and now the editor of the weekly *Gila Bend Sun*, said,

> Everybody in town assumed a cover-up was going on, but you had different opinions about who was being protected and no real evidence. There really wasn't all that much interaction between the movie people and the locals, small as the town was, so it's not like somebody had special insights. But the cover-up feeling was definitely in the air. The only one who came into the cafe that I recall was Cobb. He'd drive up in that great-looking car of his and come in for steak and fries, something like that. He was always alone. He was polite, but obviously wanted to be by himself. Just coming into the cafe said that much because there were plenty of better restaurants in town. But I guess if he went to them, he'd run into some other movie people.

Julie Cobb said her father declined to talk about the events at the Travelodge. "I know he had very concrete ideas about what had happened, but he preferred not to say what they were." Whatever Cobb's ideas were, they couldn't have been more concrete than those of Miles. The actress, who had been among the most in demand in the world before *Cat Dancing*, made only two films over the next fourteen years, attributing that to being blacklisted. In a 1992 interview with Lynn Barber of Britain's daily *Independent*, she replied evasively but suggestively about the events at the Travelodge: "Q: Would she agree that the inquest verdict was unsatisfactory? A: Yes, it was. Seven years later I found out the truth about which I cannot speak. Q: Was it murder? A: I cannot speak."[12]

Between *Lawman* and *The Man Who Loved Cat Dancing* Cobb appeared in the most popular movie of his career—or at least the only one to sell the most tickets in a given year and to rank for some time among Hollywood's highest-grossing pictures. Indeed, *The Exorcist* became an international phenomenon for its tale of the demonic possession of the preteen daughter (Linda Blair) of a Hollywood movie star (Ellen Burstyn) and the two priests (Max Von Sydow and Jason Miller) who seek to drive the evil out of the girl. Although the story had created a stir with William Peter Blatty's original best-selling novel, the graphic depiction of such moments as Blair's head spinning 360 degrees and her vomiting a river of pea soup at the priests, all accompanied by the satanically dubbed voice of Mercedes McCambridge, invited both lavish praise as elements in the scariest horror film ever made in Hollywood and snickering for its Technicolor excesses. One way or another, *The Exorcist* became a *must see*, and it generated sequels, spoofs, and simple knowing references in global culture.

Among those championing the film was the weekly *Variety*, which lauded it as "an expert telling of a supernatural horror story. . . . The climactic sequences assault the senses and the intellect with pure cinematic terror."[13] Of the opposite view was Canby of the *New York Times*, who called it "a chunk of elegant occultist claptrap . . . a practically impossible film to sit through. . . . It establishes a new low for grotesque special effects."[14]

Cobb's scenes were the least hysterical in the picture, the actor playing a homicide detective investigating the death of one of Satan's victims. The relative banality of his character's objective within the esoteric surroundings of the plot made his cop the most human figure in the story, especially for a scene in which he puts aside his police cunning to ask for an autograph from the actress. That may have also partly explained Cobb's admitted disappointment with a story that had certainly not disguised its shock aims as either a novel or as a screenplay. "They decided to go with the sensational," he grumbled to Pickard in *Films in Review*. "Cut me down a great deal."

Like many of the other principals, Cobb's involvement in the picture was an afterthought on the part of director William Friedkin, who had gone to a Los Angeles theater to see an actor he wanted for the cop role, spotted Cobb in the audience, and decided that was a better idea. Similarly, Burstyn was brought in after Jane Fonda and Audrey Hepburn had said no, Miller after Jack Nicholson had declined (and Stacy Keach had already been signed and had to be paid off), and Von Sydow after a debate about making Marlon Brando the exorcist. As Vincent Cobb told it, his father was amused by the picture's financial success but mainly recalled the production for the exteriors in Washington, DC, that gave him the opportunity to visit Ethel Kennedy in Hickory Hill and see other sights in the capital.

*The Exorcist* was the first horror film to be nominated for an Academy Award, one of ten nominations it received, including for Burstyn (Best Actress), Blair (Best Supporting Actress), Miller (Best Supporting Actor), and Friedkin (Best Director). The only two it won were for Blatty's screenplay and sound mixing. The writer took home another trophy at the Golden Globes, as did Blair and Friedkin and the picture as a whole for Best Drama. Except for *The Man Who Loved Cat Dancing*, it was the last major American theatrical film in which Cobb took part.

## NOTES

1. Interview with author, May 1, 2013. Subsequent quotes from Meredith Kibbee are taken from this interview.

2. Interview with author, May 1, 2013.

3. *Saturday Review*, March 28, 1970.

4. *Variety*, December 31, 1969.

5. Interview with author, February 5, 2013. Subsequent quotes from Yaphet Kotto are taken from this interview.

6. *Los Angeles Times*, March 15, 1970.

7. *Show Magazine*, March 1970.

8. Jan Herman, *A Talent for Trouble: The Life of Hollywood's Most Acclaimed Director, William Wyler* (New York: G.P. Putnam's Sons, New York, 1995), p. 453.

9. *New York Times*, August 5, 1971.

10. *New York Times*, June 29, 1973.

11. The case was reconstructed in meticulous detail by Ron Rosenbaum in "The Corpse as Big as the Ritz" for *Esquire* magazine, August 1973, and it is to him that many of these particulars are owed.

12. *Independent* (Britain), July 12, 1992.

13. *Variety*, January 1, 1974.

14. *New York Times*, December 27, 1973.

# Chapter 25

─────────○─────────

# The Actor:
# The Journeyman

IF CHARACTER ACTOR MEANS less than it purports to mean, then *journey-man actor*, like *journeyman writer* and *journeyman ballplayer*, conveys the mildly drudgerous, suggesting someone reliable over the years but also interchangeable with a multitude of others, range made syn-onymous with the acceptably predictable. The journeyman actor, goes the insinuation, will acquit credibly any character craft, physical ap-propriateness, and a financial reasonableness permit, sometimes with a striking élan but more often without it. His selectivity is less than gold standard; he works because the work is there. The producer or casting director calls his agent at the end of the day, making it sound as if he had wanted to make the call in the morning. On the other hand, the actor who waits for "peaks" to come along, as Cobb put it to Patricia Bosworth in the *Times*, may not be a journeyman actor in the most humdrum sense of the term, but he also risks being more diva than actor in his inactivity. Instead of honing his craft, he is mainly unemployed and without the advantages of Greta Garbo's money and enigmatic reclusiveness.

Cobb was not a diva. By the 1970s, more than forty years af-ter his professional debut at the Pasadena Playhouse, in walk-ons, featured roles, and leads, in every medium open to an actor, on both sides of the Atlantic, the subject of wild praise and object of untempered scorn, he remained unlike Willy Loman in one critical respect: while it was never spelled out what Arthur Miller's salesman actually sold, Cobb sold acting. It was something he knew

271

was durable and that everybody else was better off for being exposed
to. To be who he was he had to be *on*—on the stage, on the screen, on
television. When traditional Hollywood features dried up, there were
foreign productions for the movie house and American telefilms for the
living room. Was it always by choice? Hardly. As he noted more than
once, the things he did were merely a fraction of worse (or even occasionally better) stuff he had rejected. If he had missed out on anything,
it was in the subtleties of equivocation—the kind that permitted some
actors (Paul Newman and Woody Allen, for example) to be above
doing TV ads in the United States but to do them abroad and others
(Robert Mitchum and Gene Hackman, for two) to eschew even that
lavishly paid compromise in favor of voice-overs. But in the end, commercial journeymen all, with the negatives falling where they might.

And some journeys were more encompassing than others. As Cobb
had progressed from the Pasadena Playhouse to the Theatre Union to
the Group Theatre, then from New York to big-screen Hollywood and
small-screen Hollywood, American acting itself had loped along with
him. No, he wasn't its sole personification, but he had embodied more
of its twentieth-century history—psychological explorations and psychiatric excesses, social militancy and ethnic stereotypes, the height
of the American theater and the mass entertainment assembly line of
good, bad, and indifferent pictures, the terror politics of who could
work and who couldn't—than most. It was impossible to miss him.
He represented *size* for more than Arthur Miller. And above or below
the title he was not only invariably there, but he underlined acting's
pretensions in being there. He might have relished being a plumber
in his off-hours, might have thrilled to flying, but he had never bowed
before the hierarchical argument of acting as mere interpretative art,
as subordinate to the higher calling attributed to writers and directors.
Neither his Theatre Union nor his Group Theatre experience had promoted so much humility; on the contrary, they were *actor* collectives at
a time when everybody knew something was seriously wrong and didn't
need lectures about it, but were grateful for human representations of
personal crises. And no matter how readily he acknowledged film was a
director's medium, that didn't mean he was going to accept robotically
whatever a director told him. The actor was an artist, full stop, and
he was an actor. Let others work out where the creativity supposedly
broke off into primary and secondary inspiration.

As Sidney Lumet observed, Cobb didn't tiptoe around such views. He had invested his life in acting, and resorted to directing, the common option for performers at his level, only anonymously and when it threatened his priority, and he expected everyone to respect that. No surprise, his attitude often translated as arrogance. Laurence Olivier wasn't the only one who, behind a slap at Method acting with his jeweler comparison, mocked the notion of nonprofessionals intruding in his business. Cobb was of the same implacable view. Asked during a 1975 television show on photography in which he appeared with his son Vincent how he responded to critiques of his screen and stage work, he replied, "I have no problem with people saying they liked it or they didn't like it. That's their right, more than their right. But what I can't tolerate is people saying 'Oh, he overacted' or something. That's presumptuous. How do *they* know what overacting is? They're not professionals."[1]

The generous reading of that declaration would be that it fit snugly into his oft-stated impatience with classroom exercises for acting; that is, there was no substitute for actual performing, and anybody who wasn't performing had nothing valuable to say about the endeavors of somebody who was. If that was true of fellow actors and acting teachers, it was doubly true of laymen—a category that by Cobb's definition included professional critics. Aside from redounding to someone who, even taking into account the blacklist years, had had more opportunity than most for practicing his craft, it was a viewpoint that made actors seem priestly in their distance. One did not go through the rigors of acting's novitiates and seminaries as he did to have anyone at all who hadn't claim equal expertise. What had *they* ever learned about plumbing one's experience, finding in it what was relevant to a role, and then applying mastered techniques for expressing it? Superiority complexes left more room for discussion.

But the irony is that Cobb's attitude has been one shared, if with more tiptoeing, by the audience told to keep its craft analyses to itself. There is no more common refrain heard after an incoherent play or film than "but the acting was good." Even when this is merely a stab at sounding like ruminated opinion on the bafflingly opaque or relentlessly soporific, it exonerates the actor from his surroundings. It wasn't the actor's fault that he dropped into the mess as accidentally as the viewer did; whether squandering established talent or good money, both had had the best of intentions. The human connection represented by the actor in his dramatic or comedic world is surrendered only very reluctantly. The actor is guide and reassurance, and all the more so when playing a role that doesn't fit into the viewer's world.

Portrayals of bus drivers, mailmen, and supermarket checkout clerks, the safe and all but invisible people in one's daily life, are amusing in their normally faint condescension toward the role models: who can take the love life of a bagger for anything but comedy? Sharing the viewer's attitude as he might, the actor must nevertheless remain sober at his task, careful not to be accused of overacting, underacting, or sideways acting. Playing gladiators and cowboys? The foreignness there is so fundamental that any kind of performance at all seems plausible. But then there are the contemporary roles the viewer would prefer to keep out of his daily life, to deal with only vicariously in a theater. Mobsters, obviously, but also cops, lawyers, and doctors. Too much insight into their portrayal means either somebody in the family with a lot of degrees on the wall or too many anxious office visits of one kind or another. Otherwise, the viewer's main point of reference here is previous portrayals of cops, lawyers, and doctors—that school of experience that everybody from Stanislavsky to Michael Caine had warned against attending. But what is the viewer to do? Left to his own devices, he welcomes as comfort anything between dirty cops and Serpico, between Perry Mason and an ambulance chaser, and between Doctor Kildare and Gregory House as reality. He has little else to draw upon. Given his own happily limited experience in such areas, the viewer is more than ready for the actor to romanticize—as hero, crook, or maniac—the figure up on the stage or screen. Not merely a nonprofessional, but glad to be one. Just keep it what they call "realistic." If not, vicarious betrayal.

Presumptuous? Journeymen viewers have their training to consider, too.

## NOTE

1. The program, *Talk about Pictures*, was originally shown on KNBC in Los Angeles and subsequently picked up as a series by PBS.

# Chapter 26

———————○———————

# Finishing Touches

By the time he reached his sixties Cobb had eased off from some of the fixations that had preoccupied him through much of his career. The quest for being viewed as a romantic leading man had evaporated not only before his advancing years but before the careful-what-you-wish-for endeavors such as *The Man Who Cheated Himself*. The desire to play any leading man at all, romantic or not, had taken on sand with such pictures as *The Garment Jungle* and *The Liberation of L.B. Jones* in which top billing had been undercut by the far more colorful characters around his. Plus, of course, he had the satisfaction of having played Willy Loman and King Lear, probably the most exacting tandem of protagonists ever undertaken on the stage by any American actor.

His more relaxed attitude was also apparent when it came to his obsession about his hairline. Although his bald-headed appearance in *The Brothers Karamazov* had not impinged on the best movie reviews of his career, he had still devoted inordinate attention to his toupees for another decade, as evidenced by the Franco Nero story during the shooting of *Il giorno della civetta*. But only a few years later that concern too had lost its urgency, and he went before the cameras several times (for example, in *Lawman*) without the help of a wig maker. Moreover, he was suddenly given to relating somewhat surreal tales involving his hairpieces. In 1975, for instance, he told the Los Angeles *Times*: "One time I went for an audition wearing a wig, and the director takes one look at me and says, 'Sorry, we need a bald guy.' So I whip off the wig and the director sits there in silence for a long minute, then finally says, 'Sorry, but I can't visualize you as a bald guy.'"[1]

Some of his professional appearances in the 1970s also contradicted George Segal's evaluation of a man of gravitas. On one variety TV show produced by Mel Brooks he teamed with Anne Bancroft in a parody of the psychiatrist-patient relationship from *The Three Faces of Eve*. On another he did a soft shoe with Buddy Ebsen, Dean Martin, and others, and also showed up on Martin's Roast hours to exchange one-liners with the likes of Milton Berle, Don Rickles, and Jonathan Winters. For those awaiting even more incontrovertible acts of "selling out," he provided them by doing voice-overs for an airline company and going on camera to hawk the life insurance policies he had once told his father weren't necessary.

Then there was the work. Despite his condescending remarks about *The Virginian* and with no more *King Lear* on the horizon as a self-justification, he took on a second weekly series and a third that was stillborn, while being unable to accept a fourth that would have made the others even more forgettable than they proved to be. The series that lasted one season (from September 1970 to May 1971 on ABC) was *The Young Lawyers*, sold off an earlier pilot in which he did not appear. The premise for *The Young Lawyers* had him as the paternal presence in a legal clinic for the poor and needy, with the attorneys of the title (mostly Zalman King and Judy Pace) on the front line. The weekly plots reminded some critics of the relatively progressive George C. Scott series *East Side/West Side* and the arcane legalities and ethical dilemmas of E. G. Marshall's *The Defenders*, and more than a decade since those shows had been off the air, neither comparison worked to the benefit of *The Young Lawyers*.

A second projected series in early 1974 on CBS, *Dr. Max*, never got beyond a telefilm aspiring to be a pilot. It was loosely inspired by Gerald Green's novel *The Last Angry Man*, about a Baltimore doctor whose commitment to treating the poor rather than going after the big medical bucks causes frictions within his family. The Green story, set in Brooklyn, had been filmed in 1959 with Paul Muni making his last screen appearance and had also been adapted separately for a telefilm with Pat Hingle that was broadcast within weeks of *Dr. Max*. That scheduling plus gobs of sentimentality doomed the enterprise despite Cobb's own rich role. The best of the series offers, from friend Roland Kibbee and the Levinson-Link production company, would have cast him as the down-at-the-heels homicide detective Columbo, but he had already committed to films abroad and couldn't immediately work it into his schedule. (Only after Cobb and Bing Crosby proved unavailable did the producers go to Peter Falk for the long-running series.)

Among his telefilms in the period (October 13, 1973, ABC) was a lame remake of *Double Indemnity*. Although he received passing marks for his insurance company investigator (more avuncular than the snapping turtle Edward G. Robinson had played in the Billy Wilder picture), the substitution of Richard Crenna and Samantha Eggar for Fred MacMurray and Barbara Stanwyck was not received as charitably. One DVD packager thought so little of it that it was bundled with the Wilder film for educational purposes. It also figures conspicuously on a website called Cinema de Merde.

There was a more benevolent reception for *The Great Ice Rip-Off* (November 6, 1974, ABC), with Cobb playing a retired detective taking a bus trip from Seattle to San Francisco with his wife (Grayson Hall) and noticing how some passengers boarding along the way are coming from the scenes of big jewel robberies. Robert Walden, who played one of the robbery gang, said he had heard ahead of time about Cobb's obsession with gin rummy but was still surprised to see it. "He was incredibly competitive in everything, and if he wasn't an actor, the first thing he would have been was a professional gin rummy player. You went out before he did, he looked offended."

According to Walden, Cobb's willingness to improvise made the production go faster, as opposed to the wariness of Gig Young, in the role of the gang leader:

> The director Dan Curtis loved the way Geoffrey Lewis and I kept pushing things, and insisted we do more. Young wasn't used to that, and he once asked me to write him some extra lines so it would look like he was improvising. Frankly, the guy was usually frazzled. He insisted he wasn't drunk, that it was sleeping pills that kept him edgy all the time, but you wondered. Lee was always game, but you could also tell that he thought improvisation was useful only up to a certain point. When he came back at you with nothing more than an unscripted grunt, you knew it was time to get back to the lines. It wasn't Robert Walden who was the star.

Another time-filler was *Trapped beneath the Sea* (October 22, 1974, ABC) in which Cobb and Martin Balsam played the rescuers of four seamen trapped in a minisub in Florida; the drama got some notice because it reached the air little more than a year after the real incident upon which the story was based. The actor also made the rounds as a "special guest star" in such popular weekly series as *The Naked City* and *McCloud*. Son Vincent had bits on both *The Virginian* and *The Young Lawyers* (as well as in the *Our Man Flint* feature). But the most substantial thing Cobb did with one of his children was in an episode of *Gunsmoke* on December 16, 1974, the only time he worked with his daughter, Julie. "It was an absolutely thrilling experience," she said. "Okay, he was my father, but he was also the greatest actor I had ever worked with. He made me feel so safe even as everything seemed to be elevated. I found it so easy to open up with him."

Daniel J. Travanti, who costarred with the Cobbs in the episode entitled "The Colonel," about a town deadbeat who helps Marshal Matt Dillon (James Arness) foil baddies at the cost of his life, said he was struck by the chemistry between the father and daughter. "When I first heard Lee was going to be in it," Travanti said, "I thought to myself, 'Lee Cobb in a *Gunsmoke*! Why?' For an actor where I was at that point, you did a *Gunsmoke* or they'd tell you your career was in trouble. But Willy Loman and Johnny Friendly??!! But he and Julie were really good together. And believe me, I consider myself a misanthrope, so if there was anything off about any of it, I would've been only too happy to see it."[2]

Cobb's second trip to Italy for work didn't have an assignment like *Il giorno della civetta* waiting for him. For Italian producers he appeared in five films between 1973 and 1975 that were mainly distinguishable by which wasn't a *poliziesco* (cops and robbers) and which was the worst of the batch. The winner in both categories was *Il venditore dei palloncini* (*The Balloon Seller* or *The Last Circus Show*), a tear-gusher about a young boy who loses his mother to prostitution, has to support an alcoholic father, then discovers he has leukemia; his last wish is to go to the circus. The picture didn't have to leave Italy to be ripped apart by critics, who also chided Cobb, James Whitmore, and Cyril Cusack for allowing themselves to be imported for being part of it. But Cobb also had another problem during the shooting, one going back twenty years.

The actor was accompanied to Rome by agent Jimmy Cota. As Cota remembered,

We're barely in Europe when I get a call from LA saying there's been an agreement with the producers that would make Jim Whitmore play the part Cobb had been signed for and Lee would play that character's father. It was up to me to break the news to Lee. His first reaction was dismay. He'd studied the part, he said, he had developed a real taste for it. That was the word he used—*taste*. But then he just shrugged and said okay, he'd do Whitmore's father. I really never figured out whether he needed the money that badly and didn't want to get into a brawl with the producers, or what. It certainly wasn't because the part of the father was better than that of the son.[3]

And, according to Cota, Cobb could have had more ideal actors to be parachuted in for the role of his son.

Everybody considered Whitmore a class actor, so from that point of view there shouldn't have been any difficulty. But one day I go out to where they're shooting, and the two of them are at makeup tables that couldn't have been more separated if they'd been at first base and third base in some baseball stadium. Later that evening I go shopping with Whitmore for some wine because he and his wife have invited me to their apartment for dinner, and I ask him how things are going with Lee. Oh, fine, he says, I do the scenes and then I'm out of there. The way he said it made me look at him twice. I'm certainly not going to socialize with Cobb, he says to me. He named names before the House Un-American Activities Committee. Why would I want to socialize with somebody who did that?

Cota said he didn't know what to reply, but assumed that was the explanation for the widely separated makeup tables. As for whether Cobb was aware of his fellow-actor's attitude: "Lee never said anything to me about it, but you would've had to be pretty dense not to pick up something."

The *poliziesco* that took itself most seriously was *La polizia sta a guardare* (*The Great Kidnapping*), one of several melodramas of the time that sought to mix the odors of cordite and high-level corrupt characters from the screen with the sitting Christian Democratic government's pieties about being against "violence from the opposite extremes." In the picture, Enrico Maria Salerno plays an ardent official assigned to a northern industrial town to stop a plague of murders and kidnappings. To put the brakes on him, the villains kidnap his son, and nothing good happens after that. Cobb's role is of a retired police administrator whose ostensible attempts to aid the visiting policeman aren't nearly ambiguous enough. The film received limited distribution in America, while in Italy it was viewed (according to the political lights of the daily newspaper involved) as pro-government propaganda,[4] as not strong enough propaganda,[5] or as a so-so feature promoting the gunplay and kidnappings it had allegedly set out to denounce.[6]

The other pictures, all of a decidedly B level, didn't prompt even that much discussion. In *Mark il poliziotto* (*Blood, Sweat and Fear*) he was an underworld drug czar, in *La legge violenta della squadra anticrimine* (*Cross Shot*) a mobster trying to catch up to a cop killer before the police do to get his hands on an incriminating document in the fugitive's possession, and in *Ultimatum alla citta* (*Ultimatum*) an official trying to stop a madman from blowing up a city (exteriors shot in Quebec). He also appeared in some of the earlier scenes of an Italian-produced pseudo-historical telefilm variously called *The Legend of the Black Hand* and *The Origins of the Mafia*.

While shuttling between the Italian productions and the Hollywood telefilms, Cobb squeezed in what turned out to be his final English-language feature. Although formally designated as a British film, *That Lucky Touch* was one of those international projects that had more insurance and production companies sharing the financial weight than it had cast members and with a sound track that had been left out in the rain too long. Set entirely in Belgium, it strove to be comic about an arms dealer (Roger Moore) selling weapons to Saudi Arabia and a journalist (Susannah York) trying to get the goods on him before both of them decide that being in love with one another is more important than their respective professions. Cobb played a lampoon of an army general within a United Nations gallery of performers (Shelley Winters, Jean-Pierre Cassel, Raf Vallone). For director Christopher Miles (brother of Sarah), the actor was a source of reassurance during a tight eight-week shooting schedule in Brussels, Bruges, and other Belgian locales. "I knew about his heart problems, so I tried to pace him as slowly as I could, but he was always up for things," said Miles, who also echoed Norman Lear in praising Cobb's "enormous sense of comedy timing."[7]

Both Miles and star Roger Moore agreed that the most contentious relationship on the picture was between Cobb and Winters, but gave different reasons for it. Miles: "He didn't get along with Shelley because she was always inventing stuff, sometimes on what seemed only a dare, and he would immediately invent something opposite. She was really a little too exuberant for him, and while he always remained professional, there was no disguising that she irritated him. The good thing, though, was that this was also the relationship between the characters in the film, so there was an extra layer of authenticity to their scenes together." For Moore, though, the real bone of contention was yet again over Cobb's favorite pastime—gin rummy. "I never played cards so much in my life as I did with Lee during that picture. And then sometimes Shelley would sit in, and she would have this pose as the innocent who knew nothing about the game while Lee sat there as the experienced professional. Well, guess who did most of the winning? That annoyed Lee no end."[8]

In what would turn out to be his last published remarks on the pictures he made, Cobb told Pickard in *Films in Review*, "At the risk of sounding falsely modest, I don't think the film industry would be affected one way or another if I should disappear."[9]

## NOTES

1. *Los Angeles Times*, February 12, 1975.
2. Interview with author, August 12, 2011.
3. Interview with author, November 12, 2012. Subsequent quotes from Jimmy Cota are taken from this interview.
4. *L'Unita*, November 24, 1973.
5. *Il Tempo*, November 24, 1973.
6. *Il Messaggero*, November 24, 1973.
7. Interview with author, January 8, 2011. Subsequent quotes from Christopher Miles are taken from this interview.
8. Interview with author, March 30, 2011.
9. Pickard, "The Self-Preservation Gene."

# Chapter 27

———————O———————

# The Actor

Lee Cobb died midmorning on February 11, 1976, at the age of sixty-four. He was overcome by a sudden, swiftly fatal heart attack while sitting in his Woodland Hills living room talking with his wife. Although he had not complained of feeling ill before the seizure, both Vincent and Julie Cobb digested the news through thoughts of odd incidents a few days earlier.

"It was simply devastating, particularly because he was as young as he was," Vincent said.

I was working, and received a phone call from Mary, who asked me if I was sitting down and then told me he had died a little earlier. There was a rushing in my ears I've never experienced any other time. The immediate thought that came to mind was that I had just seen him at dinner with others at his home the weekend before. When my wife at the time and I were leaving at the end of the evening, he took her face in his hands and held her, looking deeply into her eyes, as if he knew he wasn't going to see her again. Then we just left.

Julie said,

That day I was filming a TV pilot. I was engaged to be married to Victor French. He grabbed me with a hug and the news. There was an enormous silent NO in my body. . . . We went to the house and sat with everybody. There was a small bud vase on the coffee table. As I half-listened, a single rose bud dropped to the table. I reached for it before anyone else noticed. I have it to this day. I took it as a gift

282

from Dad. He and Mary had been to my house for dinner the Friday before. In what was a very unusual gesture, Dad lay down on the sofa and fell asleep. At the time I thought how nice that he could feel so relaxed in my home. For two months after he died I felt numb. The sound of any classical music, which he had always loved, sent me into a well of sadness. . . . It was as if perfect stillness might take me to where Dad was.

Tony and Jerry were at school when their father passed away and didn't learn about what had happened until they returned home in midafternoon. "There were no arguments or strenuous activities, no nothing," Tony recalled his mother telling them. "He was there one second and then he just was gone."

Every major newspaper in the country ran a lengthy, detailed obituary, with much of the accent on Willy Loman, Johnny Friendly, and, what would have undoubtedly been to Cobb's chagrin, Judge Garth. The House Un-American Activities Committee testimony of a quarter century before was largely disposed of in a couple of sentences. The *New York Times* headlined its piece by describing Cobb as a "veritable landmark."[1]

A memorial service was held at Mount Sinai Memorial Park for what Vincent estimated at about thirty people. "There was a rabbi, but it really wasn't a religious service. He spoke, I spoke, and David Opatoshu, Dad's friend from the Bronx, spoke." One of the mourners was notable for his presence, another for her absence. "Mary organized everything. Uncle Norman showed up after being estranged from Dad most of his adult life. On the other hand, Mary wouldn't hear of my mother being invited. Julie and I had to take her to the cemetery the next day."

Beverley's not being invited turned out to be one of the earliest rounds of strife between Cobb's two families, an iciness that, despite a period of relative rapprochement when Tony and Jerry grew up, continues to the present day. "Nobody shares Dad in this family," Jerry said of the friction.[2]

On the other hand, Norman's attendance at the memorial service led to more frequent contacts between him and the second Cobb family, including treating the boys to lunch every now and then. But, according to Tony,

whenever the subject of Dad was brought up, his patented response was "family stinks!" He had his reasons, I suppose, but he also had a lot of easily conjured up resentment that was part of his makeup. One thing he always said was that he and my Dad didn't have the same parents. By that he meant that my grandparents were fairly well off in the 1920s when my father was around, but then afterward, when Norman was alone with them, it was the gloomy Depression years with worries all the time about money. My dad wasn't totally innocent about everything, but that resentment was a good part of what Norman could never let go of.

For all that, according to Tony, he developed a bond with his uncle, one extended to the present day with his close friendship and occasional collaboration with Norman's son, guitarist and composer Danny Jacob.

For the public at large the most protracted reminder of the actor's passing came from the insurance company for which he had done a television commercial. Weeks after Cobb's death, TV stations continued to run the commercial, either in (unlikely) ignorance at what most of the rest of the country knew or in a sleazy attempt at cleverness aimed at those hesitating about whether to buy policies. It wasn't exactly throwing coins over bedroom furniture, but it came across as another variation on the money game.

## NOTES

1. *New York Times*, February 12, 1976.

2. Helen Beverley died on July 15, 2011, at the age of ninety-four at the Jewish Home for the Aging in Reseda, California. Mary Cobb died on September 11, 1994, at home after a lengthy illness at the age of sixty-four. Among the condolence messages sent to Tony and Jerry Cobb on the passing of their mother was one from Frank Sinatra with a check for five thousand dollars enclosed.

# Filmography

1934   *The Vanishing Shadow* (serial, dir. Louis Friedlander)

1937   *North of the Rio Grande* (dir. Nate Watt); *Rustlers' Valley* (dir. Nate Watt); *Ali Baba Goes to Town* (dir. David Butler)

1938   *Danger in the Air* (dir. Otis Garrett)

1939   *The Phantom Creeps* (serial, dir. Ford Beebe and Saul Goodkind); *Golden Boy* (dir. Rouben Mamoulian)

1941   *This Thing Called Love* (dir. Alexander Hall); *Men of Boys Town* (dir. Norman Taurog); *Paris Calling* (dir. Edwin Marin)

1943   *Tonight We Raid Calais* (dir. John Brahm); *Buckskin Frontier* (dir. Lesley Selander); *The Moon Is Down* (dir. Irving Pichel); *The Song of Bernadette* (dir. Henry King)

1944   *Winged Victory* (dir. George Cukor)

1946   *Anna and the King of Siam* (dir. John Cromwell)

1947   *Boomerang* (dir. Elia Kazan); *Johnny O'Clock* (dir. Robert Rossen); *Captain from Castile* (dir. Henry King)

1948   *Call Northside 777* (dir. Henry Hathaway); *The Miracle of the Bells* (dir. Irving Pichel); *The Luck of the Irish* (dir. Henry Koster)

1949   *The Dark Past* (dir. Rudolph Mate); *Thieves' Highway* (dir. Jules Dassin)

1950   *The Man Who Cheated Himself* (dir. Felix Feist)

1951   *Sirocco* (dir. Curtis Bernhardt); *The Family Secret* (dir. Henry Levin)

1952    *The Fighter* (dir. Herbert Kline)

1953    *The Tall Texan* (dir. Elmo Williams)

1954    *Yankee Pasha* (dir. Joseph Pevney); *Gorilla at Large* (dir. Harmon Jones); *Day of Triumph* (dir. Irving Pichel and John Coyle); *On the Waterfront* (dir. Elia Kazan)

1955    *The Racers* (dir. Henry Hathaway); *The Road to Denver* (dir. Joseph Kane); *The Left Hand of God* (dir. Edward Dmytryk)

1956    *The Man in the Gray Flannel Suit* (dir. Nunnally Johnson); *Miami Expose* (dir. Fred Sears)

1957    *12 Angry Men* (dir. Sidney Lumet); *The Garment Jungle* (dir. Vincent Sherman); *The Three Faces of Eve* (dir. Nunnally Johnson)

1958    *The Brothers Karamazov* (dir. Richard Brooks); *Man of the West* (dir. Anthony Mann); *Party Girl* (dir. Nicholas Ray)

1959    *The Trap* (dir. Norman Panama); *Green Mansions* (dir. Mel Ferrer); *But Not for Me* (dir. Walter Lang)

1960    *Exodus* (dir. Otto Preminger)

1962    *The Four Horsemen of the Apocalypse* (dir. Vincente Minnelli); *How the West Was Won* (dir. Henry Hathaway, John Ford, and George Marshall)

1963    *Come Blow Your Horn* (dir. Bud Yorkin)

1966    *Our Man Flint* (dir. Daniel Mann)

1967    *In Like Flint* (dir. Gordon Douglas)

1968    *MacKenna's Gold* (dir. J. Lee Thompson); *Coogan's Bluff* (dir. Don Siegel); *Il giorno della civetta* (*The Day of the Owl*, dir. Damiano Damiani); *They Came to Rob Las Vegas* (dir. Antonio Isasi)

1970    *The Liberation of L.B. Jones* (dir. William Wyler); *Macho Callahan* (dir. Bernard Kowalski)

1971    *Lawman* (dir. Michael Winner)

1973    *The Exorcist* (dir. William Friedkin); *The Man Who Loved Cat Dancing* (dir. Richard C. Sarafian)

1974    *Il venditore dei palloncini* (*The Last Circus Show*, dir. Mario Gariazzo); *La polizia sta a guardare* (*The Great Kidnapping*, dir. Roberto Infascelli)

1975    *Mark il poliziotto* (*Blood, Sweat and Fear*, dir. Stelvio Massi); *Legge violenta della squadra anticrimine* (*Cross Shot*, dir. Stelvio Massi); *That Lucky Touch* (dir. Christopher Miles); *Le origini della mafia* (*Mafia*, dir. Enzo Musii)

# Stageography

O<small>VER A TWO-YEAR PERIOD</small> between the summers of 1932 and 1934, Cobb took the stage eighteen times at the Pasadena Playhouse. Among his signal roles were as Jacob Engstrand in *Ghosts*, Trampas in *The Virginian*, Horatio in *Hamlet*, Dr. Koutras in *The Moon and Sixpence*, Solveig's father in *Peer Gynt*, Herod in *Salome*, the judge in *Volpone*, Tracy Tupman in *Mr. Pickwick*, and Cromwell in *King Henry VIII*.

For the Theatre Union, he appeared in three plays in 1935: *Crime and Punishment*, *Mother*, and *Bitter Stream*.

For the Group Theatre in New York, he did an off-stage voice for *Waiting for Lefty* (1935), then appeared on stage for the company in *Till the Day I Die* (1935), *Johnny Johnson* (1936), *Golden Boy* (1937), and *The Gentle People and Thunder Rock* (1939). He also did a road company tour with *Golden Boy*.

After the Group Theatre, he appeared on Broadway in *The Fifth Column* (1940), *Clash by Night* (1941), *Jason* (1942), *Winged Victory* (1943), *Death of a Salesman* (1949), a revival of *Golden Boy* (1952), *The Emperor's Clothes* (1953), and *King Lear* (at Lincoln Center, 1968). In addition, he starred in the Actors Lab production of *Noah* in Los Angeles (1945).

# Television Appearances

| | |
|---|---|
| 1951 | *Somerset Maugham Theater*: "The Moon and Sixpence" (NBC); *Tales of Tomorrow*: "Test Flight" (ABC); *Lights Out*: "The Veil" (NBC) |
| 1954 | *Ford Theater*: "The Night Visitor" (NBC) |
| 1955 | *Lux Video Theatre*: "The Life of Emile Zola" (NBC); *Medic*: "Break through the Bars" (NBC); *Producers Showcase*: "Darkness at Noon" (NBC) |
| 1956 | *Alcoa Hour*: "A Patch of Faith" (NBC); *Zane Grey Theater*: "Death Watch" (CBS) |
| 1957 | *Playhouse 90*: "Panic Button" (CBS); *Studio One*: "No Deadly Medicine" (CBS) |
| 1958 | *Zane Grey Theater*: "Legacy of a Legend" (CBS) |
| 1959 | *Desilu Playhouse*: "Trial at Devil's Canyon" (CBS); *Playhouse 90*: "Project Immortality" (CBS); *DuPont Show of the Month*: "I, Don Quixote" (CBS) |
| 1960 | *G.E. Theater*: "Lear vs. the Committeeman" (CBS); *DuPont Show of the Month*: "Men in White" (CBS) |
| 1961 | *June Allyson Show*: "School of the Soldier" (CBS); *Naked City*: "Take Off Your Hat When a Funeral Passes" (ABC); *Vincent Van Gogh: A Self Portrait* [voice] (NBC) |
| 1962 | *Westinghouse Presents*: "Footnote to Fame" (CBS); *G.E. Theater*: "The Unstoppable Gray Fox" (CBS) |

| | |
|---|---|
| 1962–1966 | *The Virginian* [series] (NBC) |
| 1963 | *Bob Hope Chrysler Theater*: "It's Mental Work" (NBC) |
| 1966 | *Death of a Salesman* (CBS) |
| 1970 | *Annie: The Woman in the Life of a Man* (CBS); *Prudential's On Stage*: "To Confuse the Angel" (NBC) |
| 1970–1971 | *The Young Lawyers* [series] (ABC) |
| 1972 | *Heat of Anger* (CBS) |
| 1973 | *McCloud*: "Showdown at the End of the World" (NBC); *Double Indemnity* (ABC) |
| 1974 | *Dr. Max* (CBS); *Trapped beneath the Sea* (ABC), *Gunsmoke*: "The Colonel" (CBS); *Suddenly an Eagle* [narrator] (ABC); *The Great Ice Rip-Off* (ABC) |

# Bibliography

Adler, Larry. *It Ain't Necessarily So: An Autobiography*. New York: Grove Press, 1984.

Barnouw, Erik. *Tube of Plenty: The Evolution of American Television*. New York and Oxford: Oxford University Press, 1990.

Barr, Tony. *Acting for the Camera*. New York: Harper & Row, 1982.

Barzman, Norma. *The Red and the Blacklist: The Intimate Memoir of a Hollywood Expatriate*. New York: Thunder's Mouth Press/Nation Books, 2003.

Bentley, Eric (ed.). *Thirty Years of Treason: Excerpts from Hearings before the House Committee on Un-American Activities, 1938–1968*. New York: Thunder's Mouth Press/Nation Books, 2002.

Bentley, Eric. *What Is Theatre? A Query in Chronicle Form*. Boston: Beacon Press, 1956.

Bessie, Alvah. *Inquisition in Eden*. New York: Macmillan, 1965.

Bigsby, C. W. E. *A Critical Introduction to Twentieth-Century American Drama*. Volume 1. Cambridge and New York: Cambridge University Press, 1982.

Bogdanovich, Peter. *Who the Devil Made It*. New York: Alfred A. Knopf, 1997.

Brando, Marlon (with Robert Lindsey). *Brando: Songs My Mother Taught Me*. New York: Random House, 1994.

Brestoff, Richard. *The Camera Smart Actor*. Lyme, NH: Smith and Kraus, 1994.

Buhle, Paul, and Wagner, Dave. *Blacklisted: The Film Lover's Guide to the Hollywood Blacklist*. New York: Palgrave, 2003.

Caine, Michael. *Acting in Film: An Actor's Take on Movie Making*. New York: Applause Theatre Book Publishers, 1990.

Capote, Truman. "The Duke in His Domain." *New Yorker*, November 9, 1957.

Castle, William. *Step Right Up! I'm Gonna Scare the Pants off America—Memoirs of a B-Movie Mogul*. New York: Pharos Books, 1992.

Chekhov, Michael. *To the Actor*. New York: Harper & Row, 1953.

Chinoy, Helen Krich. "Reunion: A Self-Portrait of the Group Theatre." *Educational Theatre Journal* 28, no. 4 (December 1976).

Christensen, Terry. *Reel Politics*. New York: Basil Blackwell, 1987.

Ciment, Michel. *Conversations with Losey*. London and New York: Methuen, 1985.

Clurman, Harold. *The Fervent Years: The Group Theatre & the 30's*. New York: Harcourt Brace Jovanovich, 1975.

Cole, Toby, and Chinoy, Helen Krich (eds.). *Actors on Acting*. New York: Crown Trade Paperbacks, 1949.

Coquelin, Benoit Constant. "Actors and Acting," *Harper's New Monthly Magazine*, May 1887, pp. 891–909.

Dewey, Donald. *James Stewart: A Biography*. New York and London: Little, Brown, 1996.

Dewey, Donald. *Marcello Mastroianni: His Life and Art*. New York: Birch Lane Press, 1993.

Donner, Frank. *The Un-Americans*. New York: Ballantine Books, 1961.

Eastman, John. *Retakes*. New York: Ballantine Books, 1989.

Fariello, Griffin. *Red Scare: Memories of the American Inquisition*. New York: Avon Books, 1995.

Fisher, James T. *On the Irish Waterfront: The Crusader, the Movie, and the Soul of the Port of New York*. Ithaca, NY: Cornell University Press, 2009.

Flanagan, Hallie. "A Theatre Is Born." *Theatre Arts Monthly* 15, no. 11 (November 1931).

Fonda, Henry. *Fonda: My Life, as Told to Howard Teichmann*. New York and Scarborough, Ontario: New American Library, 1981.

Freedland, Michael (with Barbra Paskin). *Witch-Hunt in Hollywood: McCarthyism's War on Tinseltown*. London: JR Books, 2009.

Friedrich, Otto. *City of Nets*. New York: Harper & Row, 1986.

Garfield, David. *The Actors Studio: A Player's Place*. New York: Collier Books, 1980.

Hagen, Uta (with Haskel Frankel). *Respect for Acting*. New York: Macmillan, 1973.

Harris, Andrew. *Broadway Theatre*. London and New York: Routledge, 1994.

Harris, Marlys J. *The Zanucks of Hollywood*. New York: Crown Publishers, 1989.

Hayden, Sterling. *Wanderer*. New York: Avon Books, 1977.

Heilbut, Anthony. *Exiled in Paradise: German Refugee Artists and Intellectuals in America from the 1930s to the Present*. New York: Viking Press, 1983.

Herman, Jan. *A Talent for Trouble: The Life of Hollywood's Most Acclaimed Director, William Wyler*. New York: G.P. Putnam's Sons, 1995.

Himelstein, Morgan Y. *Drama Was a Weapon: The Left-Wing Theatre in New York 1929–1941*. Westport, CT: Greenwood Press, 1976.

Hirsch, Foster. *Otto Preminger: The Man Who Would Be King*. New York: Alfred A. Knopf, 2007.

Hoberman, J. *An Army of Phantoms: American Movies and the Making of the Cold War*. New York and London: The New Press, 2011.

Hoberman, J. *Bridge of Light: Yiddish Film between Two Worlds*. New York: The Museum of Modern Art/Schocken Books, 1991.

Houghton, Norris. *Moscow Rehearsals: The Golden Age of the Soviet Theatre*. New York: Grove Press, 1936.

Hoveyda, Fereydoun. *Cahiers du Cinema*, no. 127 (January 1962).

Hutchinson, Tom. *Rod Steiger*. New York: Fromm International, 2000.

Kazan, Elia. *Elia Kazan: A Life*. New York: Alfred A. Knopf, 1988.

Kelley, Kitty. *His Way: The Unauthorized Biography of Frank Sinatra*. New York: Bantam Books, 1986.

Knox, George A., and Stahl, Herbert M. *Dos Passos and the Revolting Playwrights*. New York: Lund, 1964.

Langella, Frank. *Dropped Names: Famous Men and Women as I Knew Them*. New York: HarperCollins, 2012.

Langguth, A. J. (ed.). *Norman Corwin's Letters*. New York: Barricade Books, 1994.

Lawrence, Jerome. *Actor: The Life and Times of Paul Muni*. New York: G.P. Putnam's Sons, 1974.

Lewis, Robert. *Slings and Arrows: Theater in My Life*. New York and London: Applause Books, 1984.

Lloyd, Norman. *Stages of Life in Theatre, Film and Television*. New York: Limelight Editions, 1993.

Lobenthal, Joel. *Tallulah: The Life and Times of a Leading Lady*. New York: Harper Entertainment, 2008.

Loggia, Marjorie, and Young, Glenn (eds.). *The Collected Works of Harold Clurman*. New York: Applause Theatre Books, 1994.

Malden, Karl (with Carla Malden). *When Do I Start?* New York: Simon & Schuster, 1997.

Martin, Robert A. (ed.). *The Theater Essays of Arthur Miller*. New York: Viking Press, 1978.

McClelland, Doug. *Forties Film Talk: Oral Histories of Hollywood*. Jefferson, NC, and London: McFarland, 1992.

McGilligan, Patrick. *Nicholas Ray: The Glorious Failure of an American Director*. New York: itbooks, 2011.

McGilligan, Patrick, and Buhle, Paul. *Tender Comrades*. New York: St. Martin's Griffin, 1997.

Miller, Arthur. *Paris Review* 10 (Summer 1966), pp. 71–76.

Miller, Arthur. *Timebends: A Life*. New York: Grove Press, 1987.

Moffitt, Jack. "The Muse Discards Her Mask." *Esquire*, August 1947.

Moldea, Dan E. *Dark Victory: Ronald Reagan, MCA, and the Mob*. New York: Viking Press, 1986.

Navasky, Victor S. *Naming Names*. New York: Hill and Wang, 1980.

Nott, Robert. *He Ran All the Way: The Life of John Garfield*. New York: Limelight Editions, 2003.

Olivier, Laurence. *On Acting*. New York: Simon and Schuster, 1986.

Paris, Barry (ed.). *Stella Adler on America's Master Playwrights—Eugene O'Neill, Clifford Odets, Tennessee Williams, Arthur Miller, Edward Albee, et al.* New York: Alfred A. Knopf, 2012.

Peary, Danny (ed.). *Close-Ups: The Movie Star Book*. New York: Workman Publishing, 1978.

Pickard, Roy. "The Self-Preservation Gene." *Films in Review*, November 1977, pp. 525–528.

Pudovkin, V. I. *Film Techniques and Film Acting*. New York: Grove Press, 1976.

"Riccoboni's Advice to Actors," Pierre Rames (trans.). *Mask Magazine* 3 (April 1911), pp. 175–180.

Rose, Frank. *The Agency: William Morris and the Hidden History of Show Business*. New York: HarperBusiness, 1995.

Rosenbaum, Ron. "The Corpse as Big as the Ritz." *Esquire*, August 1973.

Salvi, Delia Nora. "The History of the Actors Laboratory, Inc. 1941–50." Unpublished PhD dissertation, University of California, Los Angeles, 1969.

Sarris, Andrew. "The Director's Game," *Film Culture*, Spring 1961.

Schickel, Richard. *Elia Kazan*. New York: HarperCollins, 2005.

Silverman, Stephen M. *The Fox That Got Away*. Secaucus, NJ: Lyle Stuart, 1988.

Slide, Anthony. *Actors on Red Alert*. Lanham, MD, and London: Scarecrow Press, 1999.

Smith, Wendy. *Real Life Drama: The Group Theatre and America, 1931–1940*. New York: Alfred A. Knopf, 1990.

Turan, Kenneth, and Papp, Joseph. *Free for All: Joe Papp, the Public, and the Greatest Theater Story Ever Told*. New York: Anchor Books, 2010.

Williams, Jay. *Stage Left*. New York: Charles Scribner's Sons, 1974.

Wilmeth, Don B., and Miller, Tice L. *Cambridge Guide to American Theatre*. Cambridge and New York: Cambridge University Press, 1993.

# Index